AF173004

Communications
in Computer and Information Science   **2640**

Series Editors

Gang Li , *School of Information Technology, Deakin University, Burwood, VIC, Australia*
Joaquim Filipe , *Polytechnic Institute of Setúbal, Setúbal, Portugal*
Zhiwei Xu, *Chinese Academy of Sciences, Beijing, China*

Rationale

The CCIS series is devoted to the publication of proceedings of computer science conferences. Its aim is to efficiently disseminate original research results in informatics in printed and electronic form. While the focus is on publication of peer-reviewed full papers presenting mature work, inclusion of reviewed short papers reporting on work in progress is welcome, too. Besides globally relevant meetings with internationally representative program committees guaranteeing a strict peer-reviewing and paper selection process, conferences run by societies or of high regional or national relevance are also considered for publication.

Topics

The topical scope of CCIS spans the entire spectrum of informatics ranging from foundational topics in the theory of computing to information and communications science and technology and a broad variety of interdisciplinary application fields.

Information for Volume Editors and Authors

Publication in CCIS is free of charge. No royalties are paid, however, we offer registered conference participants temporary free access to the online version of the conference proceedings on SpringerLink (http://link.springer.com) by means of an http referrer from the conference website and/or a number of complimentary printed copies, as specified in the official acceptance email of the event.

CCIS proceedings can be published in time for distribution at conferences or as post-proceedings, and delivered in the form of printed books and/or electronically as USBs and/or e-content licenses for accessing proceedings at SpringerLink. Furthermore, CCIS proceedings are included in the CCIS electronic book series hosted in the SpringerLink digital library at http://link.springer.com/bookseries/7899. Conferences publishing in CCIS are allowed to use Online Conference Service (OCS) for managing the whole proceedings lifecycle (from submission and reviewing to preparing for publication) free of charge.

Publication process

The language of publication is exclusively English. Authors publishing in CCIS have to sign the Springer CCIS copyright transfer form, however, they are free to use their material published in CCIS for substantially changed, more elaborate subsequent publications elsewhere. For the preparation of the camera-ready papers/files, authors have to strictly adhere to the Springer CCIS Authors' Instructions and are strongly encouraged to use the CCIS LaTeX style files or templates.

Abstracting/Indexing

CCIS is abstracted/indexed in DBLP, Google Scholar, EI-Compendex, Mathematical Reviews, SCImago, Scopus. CCIS volumes are also submitted for the inclusion in ISI Proceedings.

How to start

To start the evaluation of your proposal for inclusion in the CCIS series, please send an e-mail to ccis@springer.com.

Yuqing Ma · Jinyang Guo · Xiaowei Zhao ·
Ruihao Gong · Ning Liu · Xuefei Ning ·
Xianglong Liu
Editors

Generalizing from Limited Resources in the Open World

Third International Workshop, GLOW 2025
Held in Conjunction with IJCAI 2025
Montreal, Canada, August 16–22, 2025
Proceedings

Springer

Editors
Yuqing Ma
Beihang University
Beijing, China

Jinyang Guo
Beihang University
Beijing, China

Xiaowei Zhao
Zhongguancun Laboratory
Beijing, China

Ruihao Gong
SenseTime
Beijing, China

Ning Liu
Beijing Humanoid Robot Innovation Center
Beijing, China

Xuefei Ning
Tsinghua University
Beijing, China

Xianglong Liu
Beihang University
Beijing, China

ISSN 1865-0929   ISSN 1865-0937 (electronic)
Communications in Computer and Information Science
ISBN 978-981-95-0987-4   ISBN 978-981-95-0988-1 (eBook)
https://doi.org/10.1007/978-981-95-0988-1

Preface

This book collected the accepted articles of the 3rd International Workshop on Generalizing from Limited Resources in the Open World, dubbed GLOW. This workshop was held at the International Joint Conference on Artificial Intelligence (IJCAI) 2025 in Montreal Canada.

After months of soliciting, we received twenty-seven papers in total encom- passing a variety of topics around the theme of our workshop. We invited expert scholars from various institutions in this field to serve as reviewers. They care- fully appraised these manuscripts based on their novelty, preciseness, objectivity and reproducibility, and graded them on OpenReview with the "double-blind" review policy. On average, each manuscript was reviewed by three reviewers, with each reviewer handling 3 manuscripts. We thank all the reviewers for their selfless support.

Considering the quality and the relevance to the theme of GLOW, we ulti- mately accepted thirteen papers. These papers focus on the academic exploration of efficient methodologies within the realm of artificial intelligence models. We concentrated on both data-efficient strategies, such as zero/few-shot learning and domain adaptation, as well as model-efficient approaches such as model sparsi- fication and compact model design.

We would like to extend our deepest gratitude to all the friends who dedi- cated their valuable time and effort to drive the forum forward and afterward compiled this book. We also express ouradmiration for all contributing authors. Their brilliant inspiration and ideas fueled the vibrant development of new AI technologies. Without them, the world would be far less exciting.

Holding this forum and compiling the book has been a deeply rewarding experience. By convening researchers specializing in these areas, we collected excellent research findings and creative ideas spanning a range of topics. We published this book to facilitate the sharing of recent technology advancements and engage in discussions about the future trajectories of AI model generaliza- tion. Efficient methodologies and open-world challenges have garnered substan- tial attention from the research community due to their direct implications for practical applications. Through this book, we aimed to facilitate intellectual ex- change, providing an avenue for novel insights in addressing the challenges of AI generalization.

June 2025

Yuqing Ma
Jinyang Guo
Xiaowei Zhao
Ruihao Gong
Ning Liu
Xuefei Ning
Xianglong Liu

Organization

General Chair

Yuqing Ma   Beihang University, China

Program Committee Chairs

Xiaowei Zhao   Zhongguancun Laboratory, China
Jinyang Guo   Beihang University, China
Ruihao Gong   SenseTime Research, China
Ning Liu   Beijing Humanoid Robot Innovation Center,
                                         China
Xuefei Ning   Tsinghua University, China

Steering Committee

Xianglong Liu   Beihang University, China

Program Committee

Yajun Gao   Beihang University, China
Duorui Wang   Beihang University, China
Tianbo Wang   Beihang University, China
Zhange Zhang   Beihang University, China
Chujie Xu   Beihang University, China
Yudie Wang   Beihang University, China
Kewei Liao   Beihang University, China

Additional Reviewers

Ruiqi Xie   Jingbin Shi
Shiqi Sun   Hanling Zhang
Kriti Goyal   Xiaotong Zhu
Tianchen Zhao   Yuanming Chen

Hui Xie
Jiangfan Liu
Xudong Ma
Ge Yang
Yejun Zeng
Jiacheng Wang
Maxime Guerini
Zining Wang
Zhicheng Geng
Changyi He
Yunfei Yang
Yulong Wang
Organization VII
Shenghao Jin

Yue Xu
Pinghua Ai
Yan Li
Shihao Bai
Chengtao Lv
Zihao Zhang
Tianlong Chen
Zechun Liu
Pengfei Liu
Mingbao Lin
Yang Wu
Haoli Bai
Nuo Liu

Contents

Evaluating the Behavior of Small Language Models in Answering Binary
Questions 1
    Houcemeddine Turki, Bonaventure F. P. Dossou, Ahmed Nebli,
    and Ilario Valdelli

Event-Priori-Based Vision-Language Model for Efficient Visual
Understanding 16
    Haotong Qin, Cheng Hu, and Michele Magno

Prompt-Tuning Bandits: Enabling Few-Shot Generalization for Efficient
Multi-task Offline RL 31
    Finn Rietz, Oleg Smirnov, Sara Karimi, and Lele Cao

GateLIP-X: Balancing Adaptation and Generalization in CLIP
for Real-World via a Training-Free Framework 41
    Tangwei Li, Yuke Li, Yifeng Hu, and Jialiang Ma

QSE: Mitigating LLM Hallucinations Through Query-Adaptive
Saliency-Localized Activation Editing 56
    Kewei Liao, Tianbo Wang, and Fengxiang Yu

Meta-learning with Heterogeneous Tasks 74
    Zhaofeng Si, Shu Hu, Kaiyi Ji, and Siwei Lyu

DIN: Dynamical Interaction Network for Multi-station Multi-variable
Weather Prediction 95
    Chujie Xu, Yinkai Liu, Yajun Gao, Xiaotong Zhu, Yudie Wang,
    Yong Han, and Yan Wu

Towards Inclusive NLP: Assessing Compressed Multilingual Transformers
Across Diverse Language Benchmarks 108
    Maitha Alshehhi, Ahmed Sharshar, and Mohsen Guizani

Knowledge-Guided Structured Pruning for Multimodal Language Models 127
    P. Yadla and L. Yadla

Vision Transformers for End-to-End Quark-Gluon Jet Classification
from Calorimeter Images 135
    Md Abrar Jahin, Shahriar Soudeep, Arian Rahman Aditta,
    M. F. Mridha, Nafiz Fahad, and Md. Jakir Hossen

x   Contents

Adaptive Contextual Embedding for Robust Far-View Borehole Detection 151
 Xuesong Liu, Tianyu Hao, Xueyuan Dai, Zerui Zhu, Yang Wang,
 and Emmett J. Ientilucci

Class-Aware Sinkhorn-DRO for Few-Shot Domain Adaptation 169
 Thomas Y. Chen

Author Index 195

Evaluating the Behavior of Small Language Models in Answering Binary Questions

Houcemeddine Turki[1]([✉])(iD), Bonaventure F. P. Dossou[2](iD), Ahmed Nebli[3](iD), and Ilario Valdelli[4]

[1] Faculty of Medicine, University of Sfax, Sfax, Tunisia
turkiabdelwaheb@hotmail.fr
[2] Mila Quebec AI Institute and McGill University, Montreal, Canada
bonaventure.dossou@mila.quebec
[3] Jülich, Germany
[4] Wikimedia Switzerland, Zurich, Switzerland
ivaldelli@wikimedia.ch

Abstract. Small Language Models (SLMs) offer efficient and accessible solutions for natural language processing. This study evaluates their performance in binary question-answering tasks, focusing on prompt sensitivity, multilingual disparities, and token probability analysis. Experiments with Llama-3.2, Mistral-7B, and Phi-3.5-mini reveal that True-First prompts increase **TRUE** token probability by an average of 0.4, while underrepresented languages like Afrikaans and Polish exhibit notable performance gaps. Token probability analysis uncovers biases toward affirmative responses and cross-lingual challenges, highlighting the critical role of prompt design, diverse training data, and inclusive evaluation. These insights demonstrate the potential of SLMs for cost-effective applications in education, fact-checking, and multilingual NLP, particularly in low-resource settings.

Keywords: Small Language Models · Binary Question Answering · Token Probability Analysis · Prompt Engineering · Multilingual Evaluation

1 Introduction

In recent years, large-language models (LLMs) have become increasingly useful for academic research and industrial applications [25]. However, data privacy concerns pose substantial limitations for certain private entities, preventing the adoption of publicly available web-based models [28]. Instead, such organizations prioritize deploying LLMs locally on proprietary infrastructure. This approach often requires significant computational resources, which remain accessible to

---

A. Nebli—Independent Researcher.

Y. Ma et al. (Eds.): IJCAI 2025, CCIS 2640, pp. 1–15, 2025.
https://doi.org/10.1007/978-981-95-0988-1_1

only a few institutions equipped with large-scale, in-house computing capabilities [4].

Smaller-scale LLMs (SLMs), by contrast, operate efficiently on modest infrastructure with reduced hardware requirements [7]. Unlike their larger counterparts, SLMs are more accessible to researchers and practitioners in regions with limited computational resources. This accessibility is particularly valuable in low-resource settings, such as many African regions and other low- and middle-income countries [20]. By enabling cost-effective and localized NLP solutions, SLMs address pressing needs in areas like education [10], healthcare [17], and community development [3].

This paper contributes to understanding how SLMs can be effectively used in resource-constrained settings by analyzing their performance on binary question-answering tasks. Using token-level probability analysis, we examine three state-of-the-art models (i.e., Llama-3.2, Mistral-7B, and Phi-3.5-mini) focusing on prompt sensitivity, multilingual differences, and probabilistic output behavior.

2   Related Work

2.1   Language Model Behavior

Language models exhibit behaviors influenced by their statistical design and training data [24,27]. One key issue is hallucination—generating fluent but factually incorrect information—driven by optimization for contextual relevance over factual accuracy [11]. Ambiguous or incomplete prompts often exacerbate this, resulting in creative but inaccurate extrapolations [16]. Bias is another significant challenge, rooted in training data and prompt phrasing [24,27]. Models trained primarily in English excel in that language but struggle with underrepresented ones, creating disparities in linguistic understanding [27]. Stereotypes in training data can manifest as gender, racial, or cultural biases, producing unfair or offensive outputs [21]. Even subtle changes in prompt wording can shift model interpretations due to learned patterns [24], further affecting multilingual outputs and their quality across languages [27]. Additionally, vague or incomplete prompts often lead to irrelevant or speculative responses, which models present with unwarranted confidence [11]. Addressing these behaviors is essential for building equitable, reliable, and globally applicable language models [27].

2.2   Language Model Evaluation

Language model performance is commonly assessed using metrics like BLEU and ROUGE for translation and summarization tasks [9] and perplexity for language pattern prediction, where lower values indicate better performance [14]. However, these metrics often fail to capture deeper aspects such as contextual appropriateness or factual accuracy [14]. Human evaluations assess coherence, relevance, and cultural appropriateness to bridge these gaps, addressing subjective qualities overlooked by automated methods [23,26]. Task-specific metrics, such as factual consistency for knowledge-intensive tasks and bias detection frameworks, are increasingly used to measure stereotypical outputs [12].

This paper highlights token probability analysis as a novel approach to understanding language model behavior [22], particularly in single-word response scenarios. It offers insights into biases and prompt sensitivity.

3   Methods

This study examines the behavior of small language models (SLMs) in binary question answering through four key steps. Further details appear in Fig. 1.

- **Dataset Processing**: We translate an English dataset of binary questions into multiple languages.
- **Prompt Engineering**: We craft prompts for true/false evaluations.
- **Metric-Based Analysis**: We use token probabilities to assess performance and confidence.

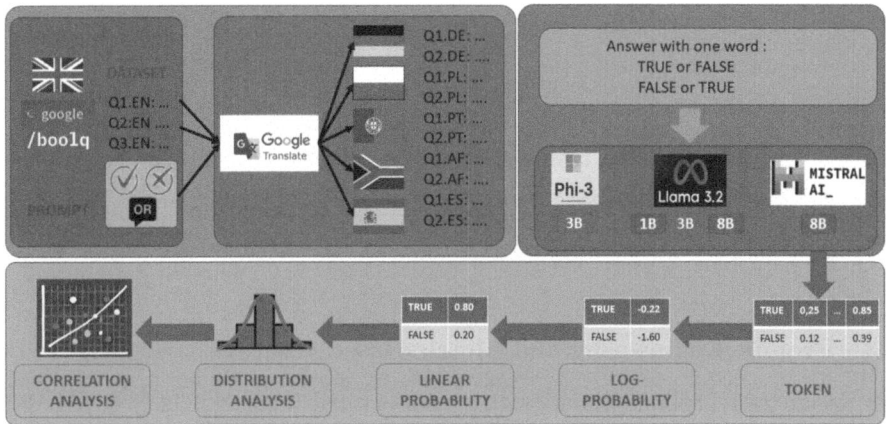

Fig. 1. Illustration of the proposed approach to evaluate the behavior of small language models (SLMs) in binary question answering.

3.1   Data Processing

To analyze small language models (SLMs) in answering true/false questions, we use the *BoolQ* dataset from Google Research. The dataset comprises 12,697 binary questions in English, including 9,427 for training and 3,270 for development. Of these, 7,907 questions have TRUE as the expected answer, while 4,790 have FALSE [6]. For multilingual evaluation, the questions are translated into Afrikaans, German, Portuguese, Spanish, and Polish using Google Translate, demonstrating high accuracy for these languages in 2019 [2]. Subsequently, the Google Translation output is validated by human annotators from the Wikimedia Community and Masakhane.

3.2   Small Language Models

This study evaluates five small language models (SLMs) with varying sizes and training data, including Llama-3.2 [8] (available in three versions), Phi-3.5-mini [1], and Mistral-7B (Table 1) [15]. These models were selected based on their small size (less than 9 GB) and availability on Hugging Face, which ensures reliability and ease of access [13]. The selected models were suitable for this study because they are general purpose, multilingual, and are unchanged by fine-tuning. To optimize deployment, we use GGUF (Generalized GPU Unified Format), a compact file format designed to minimize resource requirements such as bandwidth, storage, and hardware adaptation [5]. GGUF files, sourced from Hugging Face, are processed using *Llama-cpp-python*, a Python binding for Llama.cpp that enables efficient execution on local CPUs or GPUs.

Table 1. Assessed Models

Model	Parameters
Llama-3.2-1b-instruct-q8_0	1.24 B
Llama-3.2-3b-instruct-q8_0	3.21 B
Phi-3.5-mini-instruct.Q8_0	3.82 B
Mistral-7B-Instruct-v0.3.Q8_0	7.25 B
Llama-3.2-8b-instruct-q8_0	8.03 B

3.3   Prompt Engineering and Metric-Based Analysis

We design two prompt scenarios to evaluate small language models (SLMs) behavior in binary question answering, each using two wording variants [24].

In **Scenario 1**, the prompt is structured as:

> {{*Question*}}? *Answer with one word : TRUE or FALSE.*

In **Scenario 2**, the order of responses is reversed:

> {{*Question*}}? *Answer with one word : FALSE or TRUE.*

For both scenarios, SLM outputs are restricted to a single token. The token probability of TRUE is denoted as t_1 for Scenario 1 and t_2 for Scenario 2. The log probability of TRUE, represented by T, determines the token probability:

$$t_i = \exp(T).$$

$$t_i = 1 - \exp(F),$$

where F denotes the log probability of FALSE.

To analyze variations in token probabilities, we compute the mean probability across the two scenarios:

$$\bar{t} = \frac{t_1 + t_2}{2}.$$

For N analyzed questions, the average ($\bar{x}$) and standard deviation (S) of the probabilities are calculated as:

$$\bar{x} = \frac{\sum_{i=1}^{N} t_a}{N}, \quad S = \sqrt{\frac{\sum_{i=1}^{N} (t_a - \bar{x})^2}{N - 1}},$$

where a is the chosen scenario ($S1$ or $S2$).

The linearity of token probabilities across models and languages is evaluated using the coefficient of determination (R^2). This study calculates token probabilities for TRUE across various SLMs to assess their performance in English binary question answering. Further, we compare Phi-3.5-mini and Llama-3.2-3B models across six languages (English, Afrikaans, German, Portuguese, Spanish, and Polish) to identify cross-lingual patterns and evaluate performance consistency.

4 Results

4.1 Probability Distribution

The mean and standard deviation of TRUE probabilities for various models and scenarios (t_1, t_2, and $\bar{x}$) are presented in Fig. 2. In most models, True-First prompts (t_1) consistently yield higher probabilities than False-First (t_2). For Llama-3.2-1B, t_1 averages 0.71 ± 0.002 at $CL_{99.9\%}$, demonstrating a strong preference for TRUE in True-First prompts at temperature 0. However, as the model size increases, TRUE probabilities decrease, with Llama-3.2-8B averaging 0.52 ± 0.003 at $CL_{99.9\%}$. Across all models, questions with TRUE as the expected answer tend to have higher probabilities (t_1, t_2, $\bar{x}$) than those with FALSE. This distinction is most evident in larger models such as Llama-3.2-8B. For example, Llama-3.2-8B produces a t_1 average of 0.61 ± 0.004 for TRUE-expected questions compared to 0.50 ± 0.006 for FALSE-expected ones.

Figure 3 shows the performance of Phi-3.5-mini across six languages. While t_1 generally exceeds t_2, exceptions are observed in Afrikaans and Polish. For Afrikaans, t_1 averages 0.04 ± 0.004 at $CL_{99.9\%}$, while t_2 reaches 0.89 ± 0.005, resulting in True-First prompts frequently yielding FALSE. For Polish, both t_1 and t_2 remain below 0.5, leading to predominantly FALSE answers. English and German exhibit higher TRUE probabilities for TRUE-expected questions than FALSE-expected ones, with the distinction being most pronounced in English. This trend is weaker in Portuguese and Spanish and absent in Afrikaans and Polish.

Figure 4 explores Llama-3.2-3B's multilingual behavior. Unlike other models, t_1 is consistently lower than t_2 across all languages, with the most significant differences in Polish, Portuguese, and Spanish ($p < 0.001$). English and German follow global trends, with t_1 exceeding 0.5 for TRUE-expected answers, whereas

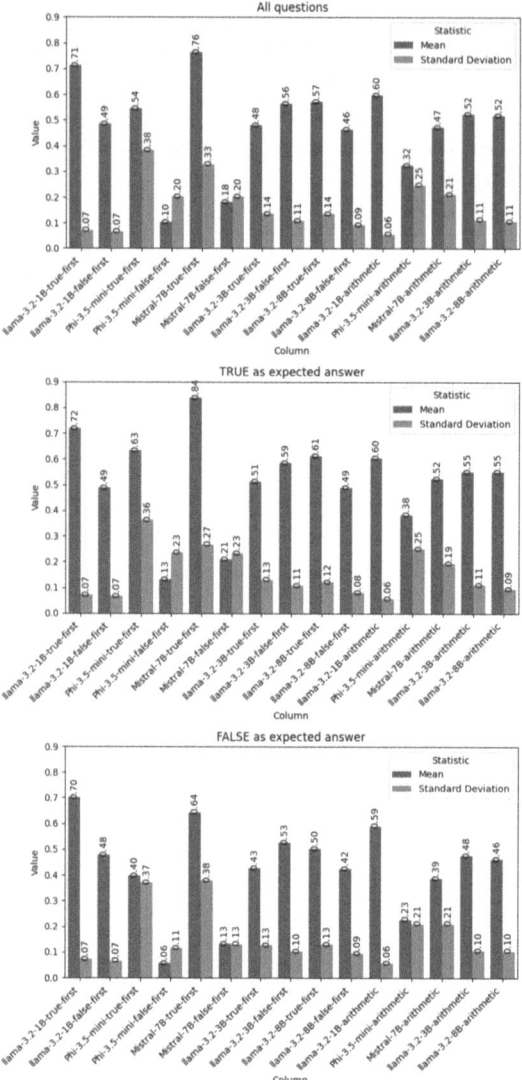

Fig. 2. Mean [Blue] and standard deviation [Orange] of TRUE probabilities across models and scenarios (t_1, t_2, $\bar{t}$). (Color figure online)

Portuguese and Spanish show lower TRUE probabilities: Afrikaans and Polish exhibit random distributions with no clear patterns.

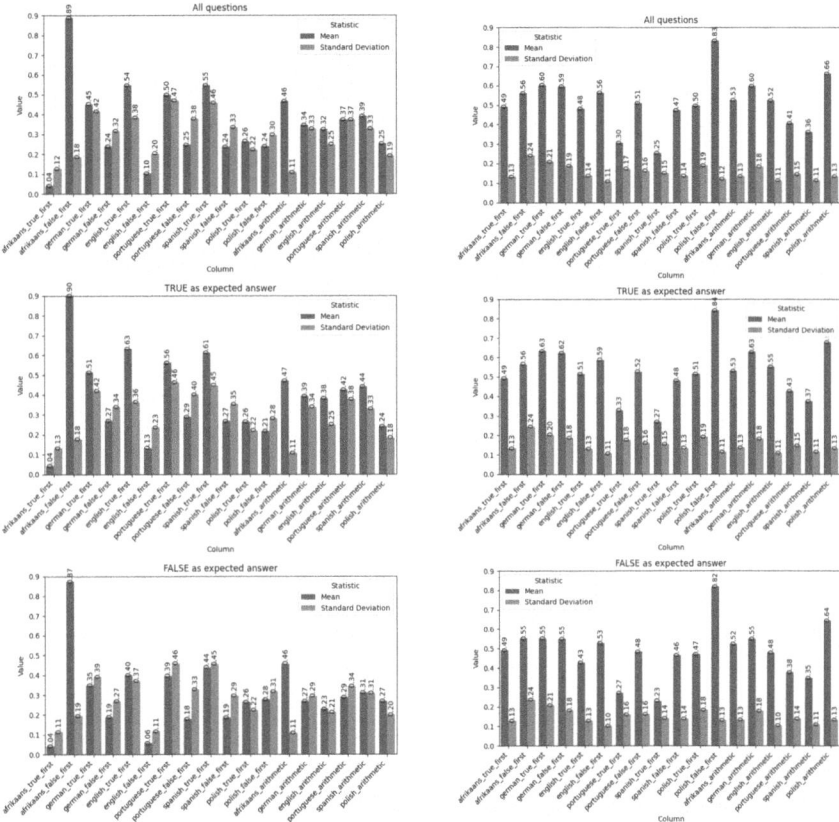

Fig. 3. Mean [Blue] and standard deviation [Orange] of TRUE probabilities for Phi-3.5-mini across languages and scenarios $(t_1, t_2, \bar{t})$. (Color figure online)

Fig. 4. Mean [Blue] and standard deviation [Orange] of TRUE probabilities for Llama-3.2-3B across languages and scenarios $(t_1, t_2, \bar{t})$. (Color figure online)

4.2 True-First vs. False-First Prompts

Figure 5 shows the relationship between t_1 (True-First) and t_2 (False-First) for Llama-3.2, Phi, and Mistral models. Llama-3.2 demonstrates a linear relationship, while Phi and Mistral exhibit nonlinear patterns. For Phi, t_2 remains low for small t_1 values but increases sharply as t_1 approaches its maximum. Larger models, such as Mistral-7B and Llama-3.2-8B, show clearer clustering for TRUE-expected questions in high t_1 regions, indicating improved performance with scale.

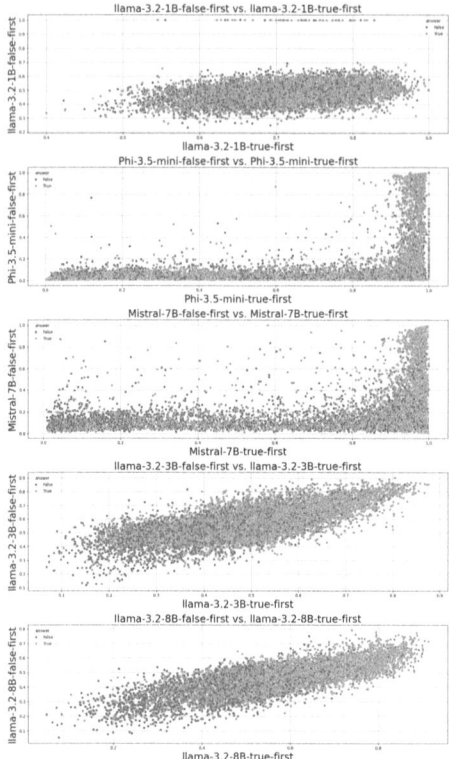

Fig. 5. Scatter plot of TRUE probabilities in False-First (t_2) versus True-First (t_1) prompts across models, with expected answers as hue (TRUE [Orange] or FALSE [Blue]). (Color figure online)

Phi-3.5-mini's performance across languages is shown in Fig. 6. English aligns with global trends, with t_2 increasing sharply at higher t_1 values. Other languages, such as German, Portuguese, and Spanish, follow a U-shaped curve, while Afrikaans and Polish show random dispersions, reflecting language-specific challenges.

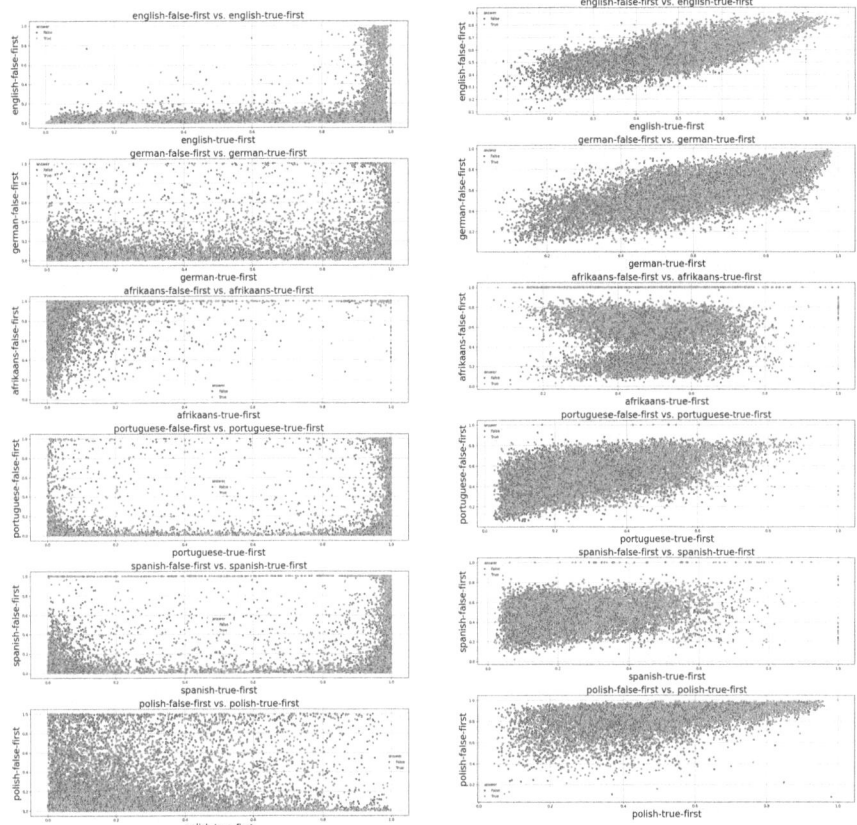

Fig. 6. Scatter plot of TRUE probabilities (t_1 vs t_2) for Phi-3.5-mini across six languages, with expected answers as hue (TRUE [Orange] or FALSE [Blue]). (Color figure online)

Fig. 7. Scatter plot of TRUE probabilities (t_1 vs t_2) for Llama-3.2-3B across six languages, with expected answers as hue (TRUE [Orange] or FALSE [Blue]). (Color figure online)

Llama-3.2-3B exhibits consistent linearity for English and German, as shown in Fig. 7. However, Portuguese and Spanish display dense curves and Afrikaans show a double-line pattern, indicating clustering into two distinct groups.

4.3 Correlations Across Models and Languages

Figure 8 shows the regression plot of the mean TRUE probability ($\bar{t}$) across models. A moderate linear relationship is observed between Llama-3.2-3B and Llama-3.2-8B ($R^2 = 0.47$), while other pairings exhibit weak correlations.

For Phi-3.5-mini (Fig. 9), language pairs such as Portuguese and Spanish ($R^2 = 0.38$) and Spanish and English ($R^2 = 0.25$) show moderate correlations. Afrikaans and Polish exhibit random scatter patterns, indicating weak or no correlation with other languages.

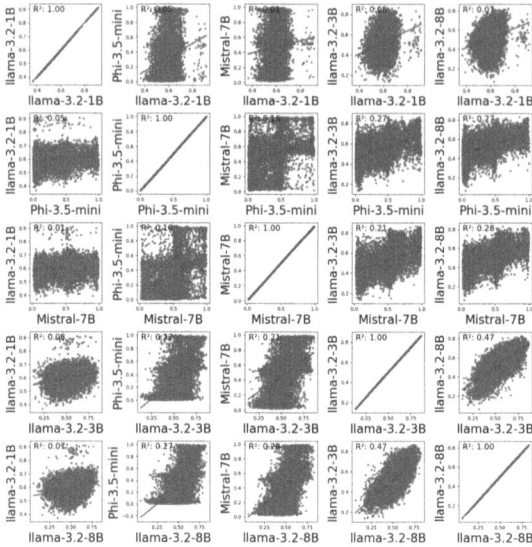

Fig. 8. Regression plot of mean TRUE probability ($\bar{t}$) across models.

For Llama-3.2-3B, shown in Fig. 10, English and German display the strongest correlation ($R^2 = 0.27$). Other languages show weak correlations, with Afrikaans and Polish presenting random patterns.

5   Discussion

The results reveal notable trends in SLM performance on binary questions, aligning with prior research on the statistical patterns, biases, and variability of language models [11, 24, 27]. Prompt phrasing, such as True-First versus False-First scenarios, significantly influenced token probabilities across models, except for Llama-3.2-3B. Smaller models, like Llama-3.2-1B, exhibited a more substantial bias toward TRUE responses, while larger models, such as Llama-3.2-8B, showed more balanced but variable distributions. These findings corroborate earlier studies suggesting that larger models generalize better while remaining sensitive to input variability [11].

Token probabilities provided nuanced insights into model confidence and biases but highlighted limitations, such as reliance on token frequency over semantic correctness. A central issue is that high token probability does not always equate to factual or semantic accuracy. For instance, a model might assign a high probability to the token *TRUE* simply because it fits common linguistic patterns in the training data, even when the ground-truth answer is *FALSE*. This phenomenon reflects a disconnect between probabilistic fluency and factual grounding and poses risks when token confidence is misinterpreted as truthfulness. Our analysis, particularly illustrated in Figs. 5, 6, and 7, underscores the

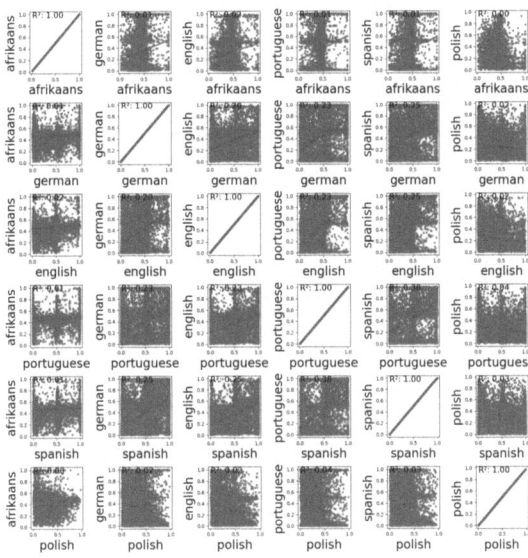

Fig. 9. Regression plot of mean TRUE probability ($\bar{t}$) for Phi-3.5-mini across languages.

importance of distinguishing between surface-level confidence and deeper semantic understanding. Addressing these issues requires complementary evaluations, including human judgment and culturally sensitive metrics, as emphasized by [23, 26].

Two approaches are proposed to tackle these challenges. First, language-independent models that take advantage of Abstract Wikipedia's universal syntax can generate standardized responses, later converted to natural language using predefined rules in Wikifunctions [19]. This reduces linguistic and cultural biases, ensuring consistent performance across languages. Second, targeted data augmentation, such as syntactic reformulation and diverse phrasing, can enhance training data. This improves linguistic diversity, reduces biases, and strengthens cross-lingual generalization [18].

6 Limitations

The study has several important limitations. The findings are based on a narrow subset of SLMs and binary question-answering tasks using the BoolQ dataset, limiting their generalizability. Only three model families were examined, without ablations or comparison to smaller or rule-based baselines, which restricts the contextualization of the reported effects. Furthermore, the experimental design incorporated only two prompt templates and constrained responses to single-token outputs, which do not reflect real-world QA applications or capture the models' capacity for nuanced understanding.

The reliance on token-probability differences (t_1, t_2, $\bar{t}$) without incorporating standard performance metrics such as accuracy or F1-score weakens performance

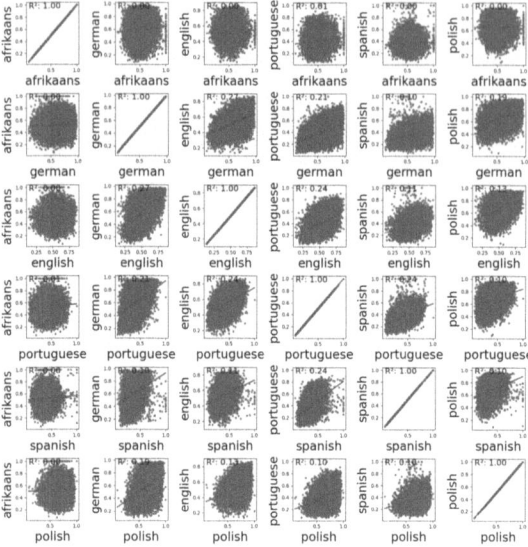

Fig. 10. Regression plot of mean TRUE probability ($\bar{t}$) for Llama-3.2-3B across languages.

claims and hinders comparative analysis with existing evaluation methods. Additionally, the statistical analysis remains descriptive; the absence of inferential testing, causal analysis, or correction for dataset imbalances limits the explanatory depth of the findings.

While recommendations such as using Abstract Wikipedia or augmenting training data are promising, they are not directly validated within the current experimental framework. A stronger causal alignment between observations, identified weaknesses, and proposed remedies, backed by follow-up experiments, is needed to ensure the practical relevance of these suggestions.

Moreover, the study's multilingual component lacks proper validation of translation quality, raising concerns about semantic consistency and bias in non-English data. Broader linguistic coverage, coupled with human-validated translations and richer prompting scenarios (e.g., few-shot, chain-of-thought), would improve the robustness and generalizability of future studies.

Lastly, the absence of a unifying theoretical insight weakens the interpretability of the results. Observations such as linear versus non-linear t_1 vs. t_2 patterns remain fragmented, and the study stops short of extracting behavioral principles that hold across languages and models. Future work should aim to identify such principles and connect empirical findings more tightly to practical recommendations.

7   Conclusion and Future Directions

This study contributes to the growing body of work examining the behavior of small language models (SLMs) in multilingual binary question answering. Our findings highlight how factors such as prompt phrasing, model size, and language context shape token-level output distributions, offering insights into model biases and variability. However, the study's methodological simplicity, limited evaluation metrics, and narrow experimental scope constrain the generalizability and interpretability of the results. In particular, the reliance on token-probability scores without standard performance metrics, the use of single-token outputs, and insufficient validation of multilingual data limit the depth and practical applicability of our conclusions.

Future research should address these gaps by incorporating more diverse models, richer prompting schemes (e.g., few-shot, chain-of-thought, role-playing), and broader, validated datasets. Enhancing statistical rigor through inferential testing, ablation studies, and causal analysis will strengthen the explanatory power of future findings. Efforts to unify observed behavioral patterns across languages and models into general principles would also improve the theoretical contribution of such studies.

Moreover, balancing model complexity and stability remains crucial for enhancing global applicability. Techniques such as fine-tuning, reinforcement learning from human feedback (RLHF), and model compression could help optimize performance while ensuring efficiency. Expanding data coverage for low-resource languages and adopting targeted data augmentation strategies will reduce linguistic inequities. Additionally, advancing language-independent modeling methods, such as those built on Abstract Wikipedia and Wikifunctions, can help mitigate cultural and linguistic biases.

Complementary directions include improving temporal consistency, contextual reasoning, and robustness in cross-domain settings. By addressing these methodological and practical challenges, the NLP community can build more reliable and inclusive systems that better reflect the diversity of global users and support equitable access to AI technologies.

Acknowledgments. This research is funded by Wikimedia Switzerland as part of its Innovation Programme. The authors are grateful to Allan E. Gardner (University of Colorado Boulder, United States of America) for his useful comments. We also extend our gratitude to Scott W. Harden from the University of Florida, USA, for providing the source codes that significantly contributed to the development of this research work.

Data Availibility Statement. For reproducibility purposes, generated data and source code are available at https://www.github.com/csisc/BoolV-Analysis.

Disclosure of Interests. The authors have no competing interests.

Ethical Statement. There are no ethical issues.

References

1. Abdin, M., Aneja, J., Awadalla, H., et al.: Phi-3 technical report: a highly capable language model locally on your phone (2024). https://doi.org/10.48550/ARXIV.2404.14219. https://arxiv.org/abs/2404.14219
2. Aiken, M.: An updated evaluation of google translate accuracy. Stud. Linguist. Lit. **3**(3), 253 (2019). https://doi.org/10.22158/sll.v3n3p253
3. Augenstein, I., et al.: Factuality challenges in the era of large language models and opportunities for fact-checking. Nat. Mach. Intell. **6**(8), 852–863 (2024). https://doi.org/10.1038/s42256-024-00881-z
4. Brown, T., Mann, B., Ryder, N., et al.: Language models are few-shot learners. Adv. Neural. Inf. Process. Syst. **33**, 1877–1901 (2020)
5. Chavan, A., Magazine, R., Kushwaha, S., et al.: Faster and lighter LLMs: a survey on current challenges and way forward. In: Proceedings of the Thirty-ThirdInternational Joint Conference on Artificial Intelligence. IJCAI 2024, International Joint Conferences on Artificial Intelligence Organization (2024). https://doi.org/10.24963/ijcai.2024/883
6. Clark, C., Lee, K., Chang, M.W., et al.: BoolQ: exploring the surprising difficulty of natural yes/no questions. In: Proceedings of NAACL-HLT, pp. 2924–2936. Association for Computational Linguistics (2019).https://doi.org/10.18653/v1/n19-1300
7. Gharieb, A., Gabry, M.A., Soliman, M.Y.: The role of personalized generative AI in advancing petroleum engineering and energy industry: a roadmap to secure and cost-efficient knowledge integration: a case study. In: SPE Annual Technical Conference and Exhibition? p. D011S007R002. SPE (2024)
8. Grattafiori, A., Dubey, A., Jauhri, A., et al.: The Llama 3 herd of models (2024). https://doi.org/10.48550/ARXIV.2407.21783. https://arxiv.org/abs/2407.21783
9. Guo, Z., Jin, R., Liu, C., et al.: Evaluating large language models: a comprehensive survey (2023). https://doi.org/10.48550/ARXIV.2310.19736, https://arxiv.org/abs/2310.19736
10. Henkel, O., Hills, L., Boxer, A., Roberts, B., Levonian, Z.: Can large language models make the grade? An empirical study evaluating LLMs ability to mark short answer questions in K-12 education. In: Proceedings of the Eleventh ACM Conference on Learning @ Scale, L@S 2024, pp. 300–304. ACM (2024). https://doi.org/10.1145/3657604.3664693
11. Hicks, M.T., Humphries, J., Slater, J.: ChatGPT is bullshit. Ethics Inf. Technol. **26**(2) (2024). https://doi.org/10.1007/s10676-024-09775-5
12. Huang, H., Qu, Y., Bu, X., et al.: An empirical study of LLM-as-a-judge for LLM evaluation: fine-tuned judge model is not a general substitute for GPT-4 (2024). https://doi.org/10.48550/ARXIV.2403.02839. https://arxiv.org/abs/2403.02839
13. Jain, S.M.: Hugging Face, pp. 51–67. Apress (2022). https://doi.org/10.1007/978-1-4842-8844-3_4
14. Jaiswal, A., Gan, Z., Du, X., et al.: Compressing LLMs: the truth is rarely pure and never simple. In: Proceedings of the Twelfth International Conference on Learning Representations (ICLR 2024) (2024). https://doi.org/10.48550/arXiv.2310.01382
15. Jiang, A.Q., Sablayrolles, A., Mensch, A., et al.: Mistral 7b (2023). https://doi.org/10.48550/ARXIV.2310.06825. https://arxiv.org/abs/2310.06825
16. Liu, H., Li, C., Li, Y., Lee, Y.J.: Improved baselines with visual instruction tuning. In: 2024 IEEE/CVF Conference on Computer Vision and Pattern Recognition (CVPR), pp. 26286–26296. IEEE (2024). https://doi.org/10.1109/cvpr52733.2024.02484

17. Liu, X., et al.: A generalist medical language model for disease diagnosis assistance. Nat. Med. (2025). https://doi.org/10.1038/s41591-024-03416-6
18. Miana, S., Ivanov, R., Gallagher, E., et al.: The augmentation of large language models with random conceptual augmentation: an empirical investigation using open-source LLMs (2024). https://doi.org/10.31219/osf.io/6he8w
19. Morshed, M.: Using wikidata lexemes and items to generate text from abstract representations. Semantic Web, 1–14 (2024). https://doi.org/10.3233/sw-243564,
20. Piper, B., Dubeck, M.M.: Responding to the learning crisis: structured pedagogy in sub-Saharan Africa. Int. J. Educ. Dev. **109**, 103095 (2024)
21. Prakash, N., Roy, L.K.W.: Interpreting bias in large language models: a feature-based approach (2024). https://doi.org/10.48550/ARXIV.2406.12347. https://arxiv.org/abs/2406.12347
22. Quevedo, E., Salazar, J.Y., Koerner, R., Rivas, P., Cerny, T.: Detecting Hallucinations in Large Language Model Generation: A Token Probability Approach, pp. 154–173. Springer (2025). https://doi.org/10.1007/978-3-031-86623-4_13
23. Shankar, S., Zamfirescu-Pereira, J., Hartmann, B., et al.: Who validates the validators? Aligning LLM-assisted evaluation of LLM outputs with human preferences. In: Proceedings of the 37th Annual ACM Symposium on User Interface Software and Technology, UIST 2024, pp. 1–14. ACM (2024). https://doi.org/10.1145/3654777.3676450
24. Tjuatja, L., Chen, V., Wu, T., et al.: Do LLMs exhibit human-like response biases? A case study in survey design. Trans. Assoc. Comput. Linguist. **12**, 1011–1026 (2024). https://doi.org/10.1162/tacl_a_00685
25. Triguero, I., Molina, D., Poyatos, J., et al.: General Purpose Artificial Intelligence Systems (GPAIS): properties, definition, taxonomy, societal implications and responsible governance. Inf. Fusion **103**, 102135 (2024). https://doi.org/10.1016/j.inffus.2023.102135
26. Wang, L., Song, M., Rezapour, R., et al.: People's perceptions toward bias and related concepts in large language models: a systematic review (2023). https://doi.org/10.48550/ARXIV.2309.14504. https://arxiv.org/abs/2309.14504
27. Xu, Y., Hu, L., Zhao, J., et al.: A survey on multilingual large language models: corpora, alignment, and bias. Front. Comput. Sci. 0 (2024). https://doi.org/10.1007/s11704-024-40579-4. https://journal.hep.com.cn/fcs/EN/abstract/article_51204.shtml
28. Yao, Y., Duan, J., Xu, K., et al.: A survey on large language model (LLM) security and privacy: the good, the bad, and the ugly. High-Confid. Comput. **4**(2), 100211 (2024). https://doi.org/10.1016/j.hcc.2024.100211

Event-Priori-Based Vision-Language Model for Efficient Visual Understanding

Haotong Qin[1], Cheng Hu[2(⊠)], and Michele Magno[1]

[1] Center for Project-Based Learning D-ITET, ETH Zürich, Zürich, Switzerland
{haotong.qin,michele.magno}@pbl.ee.ethz.ch
[2] State Key Laboratory of Industrial Control Technology, Zhejiang University, Hangzhou, China
chenghu@zju.edu.cn

Abstract. Large Language Model (LLM)-based Vision-Language Models (VLMs) have substantially extended the boundaries of visual understanding capabilities. However, their high computational demands hinder deployment on resource-constrained edge devices. A key source of inefficiency stems from the VLM's need to process dense and redundant visual information. Visual inputs contain significant regions irrelevant to text semantics, rendering the associated computations ineffective for inference. This paper introduces a novel Event-Priori-Based Vision-Language Model, termed **EP-VLM**. Its core contribution is a novel mechanism leveraging motion priors derived from dynamic event vision to enhance VLM efficiency. Inspired by human visual cognition, EP-VLM first employs event data to guide the patch-wise sparsification of RGB visual inputs, progressively concentrating VLM computation on salient regions of the visual input. Subsequently, we construct a position-preserving tokenization strategy for the visual encoder within the VLM architecture. This strategy processes the event-guided, unstructured, sparse visual input while accurately preserving positional understanding within the visual input. Experimental results demonstrate that EP-VLM achieves significant efficiency improvements while maintaining nearly lossless accuracy compared to baseline models from the Qwen2-VL series. For instance, against the original Qwen2-VL-2B, EP-VLM achieves 50% FLOPs savings while retaining 98% of the original accuracy on the RealWorldQA dataset. This work demonstrates the potential of event-based vision priors for improving VLM inference efficiency, paving the way for creating more efficient and deployable VLMs for efficient visual understanding at the edge.

Keywords: Vision-language model · Event data · Visual understanding

1 Introduction

Vision-Language Models (VLMs) [4,14,31,39,44] have revolutionized visual understanding by unifying visual and linguistic modalities. These models often

Y. Ma et al. (Eds.): IJCAI 2025, CCIS 2640, pp. 16–30, 2025.
https://doi.org/10.1007/978-981-95-0988-1_2

build upon the strong reasoning and language understanding capabilities of Large Language Models (LLMs) [13, 16, 24, 30, 35, 47, 48], extending them to interpret and process visual information through large-scale pre-training. VLMs, powered by sophisticated LLM backbones, demonstrate remarkable capabilities across a wide array of applications, including image captioning [4], visual question answering [3], object detection [27], and multimodal content generation [20]. They are finding use in domains such as autonomous driving [5], robotics [41], healthcare imaging [28], and interactive AI assistants [12]. This success has also spurred the exploration of their deployment on edge, such as on-device visual search, real-time surveillance analysis, and human-robot interaction on portable devices.

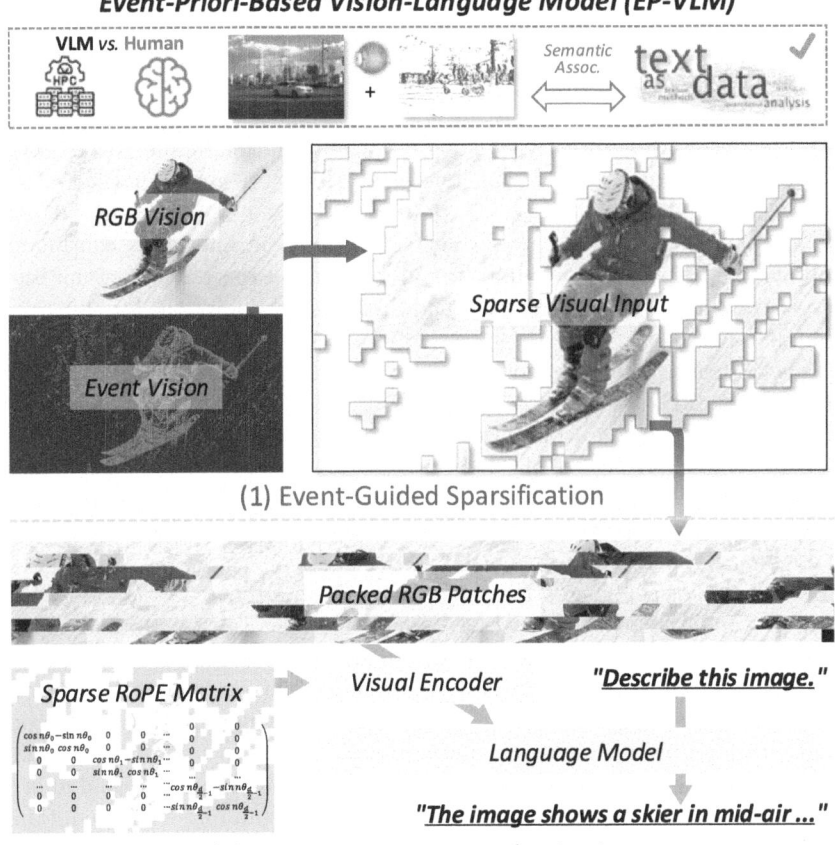

Fig. 1. Overview of EP-VLM.

However, deploying VLMs, which inherently carry the computational load of integrated LLMs, in resource-constrained edge environments presents significant challenges. These include high latency, limited deployment feasibility, and excessive energy consumption. Existing mainstream VLM frameworks, such as Qwen-VL [4] and LLaVA [31], exhibit substantial resource demands. This is partly attributable to the large parameter counts in their underlying LLMs. For instance, large-scale VLMs can have tens of billions of parameters, while smaller variants like LLaVA-1.5-7B still rely on multi-billion parameter LLMs. These models typically require significant GPU memory and computational power, often exceeding 10GB for inference and hundreds of GFLOPs per token generated. In contrast, mainstream mobile devices typically feature limited RAM, significantly lower computational power, and strict battery constraints. Although compression methods targeting both visual frontends and LLM backends, such as pruning [15,17,18,25,33,42], quantization [8,21,23,38], and knowledge distillation [19,46], have been explored, they often compromise accuracy on complex visual tasks. These approaches generally fail to achieve Pareto optimality between accuracy and efficiency. Consequently, there is an urgent need for computationally efficient VLM mechanisms to enable efficient visual understanding.

Existing Vision-Language Models (VLMs) achieve visual-language understanding by processing directly encoded input information, namely RGB images (or video frames) and text, during inference. However, for the former, due to visual information being sparsely distributed within dense pixel arrays, a significant amount of semantically irrelevant background information is continuously introduced into the VLM's computational inference. Processing of visual inputs occurs within both the visual encoder and the LLM backbone: the former encodes the input into tokens, while the latter computes and manages both visual and text tokens. Consequently, vision-related computation constitutes a substantial portion of the VLM's overall computational load. Depending on the architecture and input resolution, computation directly attributable to visual input can even account for over 90% of the total computational cost during image caption generation. Therefore, the efficiency wasted on semantically irrelevant visual information remains a critical, yet often overlooked, bottleneck in VLM-based visual content understanding.

To address this challenge, this paper proposes an **E**vent-**P**riori-Based **V**ision-**L**anguage **M**odel, namely **EP-VLM**, for efficient visual understanding (Fig. 1). Unlike existing VLMs, which rely on expensive internal computation for cross-modal understanding, humans leverage motion information from biological visual cues as prior knowledge to assist the brain in achieving efficient visual cognition [6]. Inspired by this biological mechanism, we propose a novel approach utilizing motion priors derived from dynamic event vision to sparsify visual information, thereby enhancing the efficiency of visual understanding while maintaining accuracy. Firstly, we introduce event vision data temporally aligned with RGB image sampling and employ it as prior knowledge to guide patch-wise sparsification of the RGB visual input. This means we only process visual regions indicated by the event data as salient or changing. Subsequently, we adapt the visual encoder within the VLM architecture to handle this event-guided unstructured sparse visual input, ensuring that positional encoding is correctly propagated and matched to enable accurate comprehension of the sparse visual information while saving computation.

Our preliminary experiments demonstrate that the proposed EP-VLM achieves significant efficiency improvements compared to its baseline, Qwen2-VL. For instance, EP-VLM maintains 98% of the baseline's response accuracy on the RealWorldQA dataset [45] while achieving a reduction of approximately 50% in computational FLOPs and MACs. Concurrently, our qualitative study indicates that the event vision priors in EP-VLM effectively preserve the semantic content and spatial relationships of the visual input. Thus, EP-VLM leverages event vision to significantly enhance VLM efficiency, paving the way for deploying more capable and readily deployable VLMs on edge devices.

2   Related Work

Vision-Language Models. Vision-Language Models (VLMs) have become a dominant paradigm in artificial intelligence, achieving remarkable success in bridging the gap between visual perception and natural language understanding. Recent powerful Multimodal MLLMs, such as LLaVA [31], GPT-4o [24], Gemini [43], Claude-3.5 [2], and Qwen-VL [4,44,47], extend LLMs with visual encoders, enabling them to perform complex reasoning and dialogue based on visual input. These models typically connect a pre-trained visual encoder (*e.g.*, ViT [10]) to a pre-trained LLM using projection layers or adapters, and are then fine-tuned on various vision-language tasks. Despite their impressive capabilities, the significant computational and memory footprint of these large VLMs has spurred research into Efficient VLMs. Common approaches include knowledge distillation [46], where a smaller student model learns from a larger teacher VLM; quantization [22,29,48], which reduces the precision of model weights and activations; pruning [33], which removes redundant weights or structural components from the model; and the design of more lightweight architectures or efficient attention mechanisms [50]. However, many of these efficient VLM designs still struggle to achieve the optimal balance between efficiency and performance on complex, open-ended visual understanding tasks, especially when compared to their larger counterparts.

Event Vision. Event cameras [11], also known as neuromorphic or Dynamic Vision Sensors (DVS), represent a paradigm shift from traditional frame-based cameras. Instead of capturing images at a fixed rate, event cameras asynchronously record pixel-level brightness changes, generating a sparse stream of "events" with microsecond-level temporal resolution, high dynamic range (HDR), and low power consumption. Each event typically encodes its spatial coordinate (x, y), timestamp (t), and polarity $(p,$ indicating brightness increase or decrease). This unique data format offers inherent advantages in capturing fast motion, reducing data redundancy in static scenes, and operating in challenging lighting conditions. The distinct nature of event data has led to the development of specialized processing techniques and models. Early applications focused on tasks like high-speed tracking [7], gesture recognition [1], and simultaneous localization and mapping (SLAM) [37], often employing bio-inspired Spiking Neural Networks (SNNs) [9] or tailored deep learning architectures like event-specific Convolutional Neural Networks (CNNs) [34] and Graph Neural Networks (GNNs) [40] to process the sparse, asynchronous event streams. More recently, there has been a growing interest in integrating event data with larger-scale perception and reasoning systems, including Large Language Models. For example, EventGPT [32] is a pioneering attempt to combine LLM with event stream understanding, enabling a pre-trained LLM to understand event-based scenarios. Yu *et al.*. explored pure zero-shot event recognition based on LLM [49].

3   Method

3.1   Preliminaries

This section outlines the fundamental architecture of Vision-Language Models (VLMs) that are predicated on multimodal Large Language Models (LLMs), and establishes the pertinent notation. Such VLMs typically integrate a pre-trained LLM with a dedicated visual processing module. This synergistic combination aims to leverage the distinct capabilities of each component effectively: the visual model for interpreting imagery and the LLM for understanding textual instructions and performing complex reasoning across both modalities. To elucidate the operational flow of these models, we will reference the Qwen2-VL architecture, a contemporary example of such a VLM, when processing image and text inputs.

The initial stage of the visual processing pipeline involves standardizing the input image. An arbitrary input image is first reshaped to a predefined resolution, denoted as $\mathbb{R}^{H \times W \times C}$, where H, W, and C represent the height, width, and number of color channels, respectively. This standardized format ensures compatibility with the subsequent pre-trained visual encoder. To maintain consistency with architectures that might also process video inputs (sequences of frames), the image input is often represented with an explicit temporal dimension T. For a static image, this can be conceptualized as a sequence of length $T = 1$, or the image features might be replicated T times if the downstream architecture expects a fixed-length temporal input. This results in a visual input tensor $\mathbf{X}_v \in \mathbb{R}^{H \times W \times C \times T}$. Following resizing, the image is decomposed into a sequence of non-overlapping patches. This patch-based representation is a common strategy to enable sequence processing, particularly for transformer-based architectures. Specifically, an image with dimensions $H \times W$ is divided into $N_v = \left\lfloor \frac{H}{p} \right\rfloor \times \left\lfloor \frac{W}{p} \right\rfloor$ discrete patches, where each patch comprises $p \times p$ pixels.

The processed visual input, typically the sequence of patches derived from $\mathbf{X}_v$, is then fed into a pre-trained visual encoder, denoted as $g(\cdot)$. In the Qwen2-VL model, this role is fulfilled by a Vision Transformer (ViT). A critical component for enabling the ViT to comprehend the spatial arrangement of these patches is the introduction of position embeddings. Qwen2-VL employs a 2D Rotary Position Embedding (RoPE), $\mathbf{P}_v^{2D}$, which is applied to the patch embeddings within the ViT. This mechanism allows the model to preserve and utilize information about the relative positions of different image regions. The output of the visual encoder is a set of rich visual features, $\mathbf{Z}_v$:

$$\mathbf{Z}_v = g\left(\text{Patches}(\mathbf{X}_v), \mathbf{P}_v^{2\text{D}}\right). \tag{1}$$

The 2D RoPE, $\mathbf{P}_v^{2\text{D}}$, injects spatial awareness by applying rotation matrices that are parameterized by the patch coordinates (i, j). For a d-dimensional embedding vector, the rotation matrix operates on distinct pairs of dimensions. More specifically, the rotation matrix $\mathbf{R}_{(i,j)}^{2D}$ for a patch at coordinates (i, j) is constructed as a block-diagonal matrix. This matrix is formed by the direct sum $(\bigoplus)$ of $d/4$ identical 4×4 blocks, where each block applies rotations based on i to its first two components and based on j to its latter two components:

$$\mathbf{R}_{(i,j)}^{2D} = \bigoplus_{m=1}^{d/4} \begin{bmatrix} \cos(i\theta_m) & -\sin(i\theta_m) & 0 & 0 \\ \sin(i\theta_m) & \cos(i\theta_m) & 0 & 0 \\ 0 & 0 & \cos(j\theta_m) & -\sin(j\theta_m) \\ 0 & 0 & \sin(j\theta_m) & \cos(j\theta_m) \end{bmatrix}, \quad \text{where } \theta_m = 10000^{-2m/d}. \tag{2}$$

This RoPE design inherently preserves relative positional relationships due to its rotational equivariance properties, while also being computationally efficient.

After feature extraction by the visual encoder, the resulting visual features $\mathbf{Z}_v$ are processed by a Multi-Layer Perceptron (MLP). A primary function of this MLP is to project the visual features into a new embedding space that is compatible with the LLM's input requirements. This projection is typically achieved using a linear transformation defined by a projection matrix $\mathbf{W}$, often followed by non-linear activation functions. This stage can also serve to reduce the dimensionality of the visual tokens or consolidate information. The original text indicates an objective to reduce the effective token size of the visual input, conceptually by compressing information from adjacent $M_v \times M_v$ groups of visual tokens (if $\mathbf{Z}_v$ retains a grid-like structure that can be mapped to such groups) into a more compact representation. The merge size M_v thus refers to this conceptual grouping for information consolidation. The output of this projection stage is a sequence of visual embedding tokens, $\mathbf{H}_v$:

$$\mathbf{H}_v = \text{MLP}_{\mathbf{W}}(\mathbf{Z}_v), \tag{3}$$

where $\text{MLP}_{\mathbf{W}}(\cdot)$ denotes the MLP operation prominently featuring the projection matrix $\mathbf{W}$. For simplification, if considering only the linear projection aspect, this can be approximated as $\mathbf{H}_v \approx \mathbf{W}\mathbf{Z}_v$ (assuming $\mathbf{Z}_v$ is appropriately shaped for matrix multiplication).

The sequence of processed visual embedding tokens, $\mathbf{H}_v$, is then prepared for integration with textual information. Concurrently, the input text query, $\mathbf{X}_q$, is transformed into a sequence of language embedding tokens, $\mathbf{H}_q$, via the LLM's input embedding layer (typically involving tokenization and embedding lookup). These two sets of embeddings, $\mathbf{H}_v$ and $\mathbf{H}_q$, are concatenated to form a unified multimodal sequence. This combined sequence is then input into the pre-trained LLM backbone, denoted as $f(\cdot)$. The LLM processes this fused representation to perform cross-modal reasoning and generate the final textual answer, $\mathbf{X}_a$:

$$\mathbf{X}_a = f\left(\mathrm{concat}(\mathbf{H}_v, \mathbf{H}_q)\right). \tag{4}$$

The LLM is thereby tasked with comprehending the interleaved visual and linguistic information to produce a contextually relevant and coherent response.

The VLM architecture described relies critically on two principal stages to bridge and interpret visual and linguistic data: (1) the visual encoding and projection pipeline, which abstracts the raw visual input from a dense RGB pixel representation to a more compressed sequence of embedding tokens. (2) The computationally demanding LLM backbone undertakes the sophisticated task of understanding these combined input tokens and generating the desired output. However, a notable challenge arises from the standard patch-wise visual encoding pipeline employed by many VLMs. It has been observed that this approach often introduces significant redundancy into the visual input stream. Natural images frequently contain substantial regions that are semantically sparse or devoid of information salient to the task at hand. Consequently, considerable computational resources are expended by both the visual encoder and the LLM backbone in processing visual tokens derived from these non-informative or redundant image areas.

3.2 Event-Guided Sparsification for Visual Input

Drawing inspiration from the efficiency of the human visual system, this work introduces event-based data as a complementary modality to conventional RGB imagery. Our objective is to preprocess visual input by sparsifying regions with lower semantic content, thereby reducing redundancy.

Standard RGB images provide a dense, color-rich representation of a scene. In contrast, event-based data, captured by Dynamic Vision Sensors (DVS), records asynchronous local changes in brightness. This inherent characteristic results in event data that is spatially sparse and significantly more compact than its dense RGB counterpart. Consequently, we incorporate corresponding event vision data for each RGB frame to serve as a visual prior, particularly indicative of motion. Intuitively, locations exhibiting motion possess a greater likelihood of relevance to an associated textual query. Conversely, static background regions, typically characterized by lower informational content and minimal motion, are generally less critical within the visual input or can be represented more compactly. Capitalizing on this principle, we sparsify the RGB input using the information derived from the event prior to the visual encoding stage. This targeted sparsification aims to enhance the computational efficiency of subsequent visual processing tasks.

The specific methodology is as follows: Initially, event data are processed to align temporally and spatially with the corresponding RGB image. Event data points are accumulated over a defined temporal window to form a 2D map, which is then resized to match the dimensions $(W \times H)$ of the RGB input $\mathbf{X}_v$, yielding an event-based representation $\mathbf{E}_v \in \mathbb{R}^{W \times H}$. Subsequently, $\mathbf{E}_v$ is partitioned into non-overlapping patches, consistent with the patching strategy employed for the RGB image. Let p denote the side length of these square patches. For each patch, we compute its ℓ_1 norm to quantify motion intensity. This results in a matrix $\mathbf{S}_v^{\mathrm{E}} \in \mathbb{R}^{\lfloor H/p \rfloor \times \lfloor W/p \rfloor}$, where each element (u, v) is calculated as:

$$\mathbf{S}_{v,uv}^{\mathrm{E}} = \sum_{(x,y) \in \mathrm{Patch}_{uv}(\mathbf{E}_v)} |\mathbf{E}_v(x, y)| \tag{5}$$

where $\mathrm{Patch}_{uv}(\mathbf{E}_v)$ refers to the image patch at row u and column v in $\mathbf{E}_v$, and $\mathbf{E}_v(x, y)$ is the value at pixel coordinates (x, y) within that patch. Higher values in $\mathbf{S}_v^{\mathrm{E}}$ indicate a greater incidence of motion within the corresponding patch.

An event-prioritized visual mask, $\mathbf{M}_v^{\mathrm{E}} \in \{0, 1\}^{\lfloor H/p \rfloor \times \lfloor W/p \rfloor}$, is then derived using a specified quantile threshold $\tau \in [0, 1]$:

$$\mathbf{M}_{v,uv}^{\mathrm{E}} = \mathbb{1}_{(S_{v,uv}^{\mathrm{E}} \geq Q_{1-\tau}(\mathbf{S}_v^{\mathrm{E}}))} \tag{6}$$

where $Q_{1-\tau}(\mathbf{S}_v^{\mathrm{E}})$ denotes the $(1-\tau)$-quantile of all motion intensity values in $\mathbf{S}_v^{\mathrm{E}}$, and $\mathbb{1}_{(.)}$ is the indicator function. A value of 1 in $\mathbf{M}_v^{\mathrm{E}}$ signifies that the motion intensity of the corresponding patch ranks within the top τ fraction (*e.g.*, if $\tau = 0.5$, the top 50%) of all patches, thereby marking it for retention.

The efficacy of this approach is demonstrated by masking an RGB image using the event-prioritized visual mask with $\tau = 0.5$ (*i.e.*, retaining 50% of patches with the highest motion). As illustrated in Fig. 1, even when half of the RGB image patches are occluded based on this mask, the overall semantic content of the image remains largely preserved. The redundancy can be effectively mitigated by leveraging event-based data as a dynamic guide for saliency, without incurring substantial loss of critical semantic information, thereby paving the way for more efficient visual understanding systems.

3.3   Position-Preserving Tokenization for Visual Encoder

Subsequent to obtaining the event-prioritized visual mask $\mathbf{M}_v^{\mathrm{E}}$ (as described in the preceding section), its direct application within Vision-Language Models (VLMs) to enhance computational efficiency presents certain challenges. This complexity arises because effective visual understanding is critically dependent on preserving the intrinsic spatial structure of the input image. The motion patterns captured by event data are inherently variable and dynamic across diverse visual inputs, resulting in sparse masks that are unstructured and irregular. Visual encoders typically mandate positional embeddings, calculated based on the full dimensions of the visual input, to encode the spatial location of each patch or token. A naive approach of directly concatenating (packing) only the unmasked patches would disrupt their original spatial relationships, thereby distorting the positional information available to the encoder. Conversely, retaining masked patches (*e.g.*, as zero-vectors) to maintain a fixed input structure would negate the desired computational savings from sparsification.

To address these challenges, we propose a position-preserving inference strategy tailored for unstructured, sparse visual inputs. This strategy begins by selectively retaining visual patches from the original dense input patch sequence $\mathbf{X}_v = \{\mathbf{p}_1, \mathbf{p}_2, \ldots, \mathbf{p}_N\}$ based on the guidance provided by the visual mask $\mathbf{M}_v^{\mathrm{E}}$. Patches corresponding to zero-valued entries in $\mathbf{M}_v^{\mathrm{E}}$ are discarded. This compression process can be formally expressed as:

$$\tilde{\mathbf{X}}_v = \mathrm{Pack}(\mathbf{X}_v, \mathbf{M}_v^{\mathrm{E}}) \qquad (7)$$

where $\mathrm{Pack}(\cdot, \cdot)$ represents the function that selects and concatenates patches from $\mathbf{X}_v$ for which the corresponding mask value in $\mathbf{M}_v^{\mathrm{E}}$ is 1. The tensor $\tilde{\mathbf{X}}_v$ is the resultant packed (sparse) visual input sequence, containing $N' < N$ patches.

Crucially, to preserve positional integrity for the sparse input $\tilde{\mathbf{X}}_v$, the Rotary Position Embeddings (RoPE), denoted $\mathbf{R}^{2D}$, are first computed based on the original, dense input dimensions, yielding a set of positional embeddings $\{\mathbf{r}_1, \mathbf{r}_2, \ldots, \mathbf{r}_N\}$ for all N original patch locations. These full-resolution positional embeddings are then selectively packed using the same visual mask $\mathbf{M}_v^{\mathrm{E}}$:

$$\tilde{\mathbf{R}}^{2D} = \mathrm{Pack}(\mathbf{R}^{2D}, \mathbf{M}_v^{\mathrm{E}}) \qquad (8)$$

The resulting packed RoPE embeddings $\tilde{\mathbf{R}}^{2D}$ (a sequence of N' embeddings) directly correspond to the patches in the packed visual input sequence $\tilde{\mathbf{X}}_v$. This ensures that each retained patch $\tilde{\mathbf{p}}_j \in \tilde{\mathbf{X}}_v$ is associated with its correct original positional encoding $\tilde{\mathbf{r}}_j \in \tilde{\mathbf{R}}^{2D}$.

The packed visual input tensor $\tilde{\mathbf{X}}_v$ and its aligned packed RoPE embeddings $\tilde{\mathbf{R}}^{2D}$ are then processed by the visual encoder, typically a ViT. The operations within a standard Transformer layer can be abstracted as follows. If $\mathrm{Patches}(\mathbf{X}_v)$ represents the sequence of all patch tokens derived from the original image or its corresponding full patch sequence $\mathbf{X}_v$, and $\mathbf{P}_v^{2D}$ represents the complete set of positional embeddings for these patches (e.g., RoPE $\mathbf{R}^{2D}$), a fundamental processing step involves a function g. This function, g, typically encompasses the self-attention mechanism where positional information $\mathbf{P}_v^{2D}$ is integrated with the patch features:

$$\mathbf{Z}_v = g\left(\mathrm{Patches}(\mathbf{X}_v), \mathbf{P}_v^{2D}\right) \qquad (9)$$

Following this, the representations $\mathbf{Z}_v$ are further transformed by a Multi-Layer Perceptron (MLP) with weights $\mathbf{W}$, another standard component of a Transformer block:

$$\mathbf{H}_v = \mathrm{MLP}_{\mathbf{W}}(\mathbf{Z}_v) \qquad (10)$$

In our proposed efficient inference scheme, these operations g and $\mathrm{MLP}_{\mathbf{W}}$ are effectively performed on the sparsified inputs. This means the input to g corresponding to $\mathrm{Patches}(\mathbf{X}_v)$ becomes our packed sequence $\tilde{\mathbf{X}}_v$, and the positional input $\mathbf{P}_v^{2D}$ becomes the packed RoPE embeddings $\tilde{\mathbf{R}}^{2D}$. Such an approach ensures that computation is predominantly performed for the selected, salient tokens, while still leveraging the accurately preserved positional information inherent in $\tilde{\mathbf{R}}^{2D}$. The resulting tensor $\mathbf{H}_v$ thus contains refined visual features, constructed efficiently from the sparse set of active tokens.

This position-preserving inference mechanism enables the visual encoder to process a significantly reduced number of tokens (N' instead of N), thereby enhancing computational efficiency, while simultaneously maintaining accurate spatial understanding of the visual content. Applying this strategy to packed visual inputs substantially improves the inference efficiency of both the ViT component and the subsequent LLM stages. This improvement is a critical factor for realizing overall efficient VLM operation, particularly in resource-constrained environments or latency-sensitive applications.

4   Experiment

This section presents a comprehensive evaluation of the proposed EP-VLM framework. Quantitative results demonstrate its impact on model accuracy and computational efficiency, while a qualitative case study illustrates the benefits of event-guided visual sparsification.

4.1   Quantitative Results

We evaluated Qwen2-VL-2B/7B [4] and its EP-VLM variants on the Real-WorldQA benchmark [45] using event-priori-based sparsity τ of 0.3, 0.5, and 0.7. As shown in Table 1, efficiency metrics [36] include Floating Point Operations (FLOPs), Multiply-Accumulate Operations (MACs), and parameter count, with accuracy reflecting visual question answering capability.

Table 1. Performance comparison of the Qwen2-VL on RealWorldQA benchmark.

Model	Sparsity (τ)	Params (B)	Acc. (%)	FLOPs (T)	MACs (T)
Qwen2-VL-2B	0	2.21	62.9	14.7	7.4
EP-VLM	0.3	2.21	$62.7_{(-0.3)}$	$10.3_{-29.9\%}$	$5.2_{-29.7\%}$
EP-VLM	0.5	2.21	$61.4_{(-2.3)}$	$7.4_{-49.7\%}$	$3.7_{-50.0\%}$
EP-VLM	0.7	2.21	$59.1_{(-6.0)}$	$4.5_{-69.4\%}$	$2.2_{-70.3\%}$
Qwen2-VL-7B	0	8.29	70.1	31.1	15.5
EP-VLM	0.3	8.29	$67.3_{(-2.8)}$	$24.7_{-20.1\%}$	$12.3_{-20.6\%}$
EP-VLM	0.5	8.29	$67.2_{(-2.9)}$	$17.9_{-42.4\%}$	$8.9_{-42.6\%}$
EP-VLM	0.7	8.29	$64.8_{(-5.3)}$	$11.1_{-64.3\%}$	$5.5_{-64.5\%}$

The results in Table 1 reveal three key insights. First, parameter counts remain stable across configurations for each type of model, confirming EP-VLM operates as an input conditioning mechanism without architectural modifications. Second, increasing sparsity induces an accuracy-efficiency trade-off, with 50% sparsity showing only a 1.5% accuracy drop ($62.9\% \rightarrow 61.4\%$) while processing half the visual tokens. Third, the apparent increase in theoretical

FLOPs/MACs stems from sparse data indexing overhead in current implementations, while *actual inference latency and energy consumption decrease* due to reduced token processing in the LLM backbone. This 50% sparsity configuration demonstrates near-Pareto-optimal performance, validating our hypothesis that event data provides effective priors for semantic visual information.

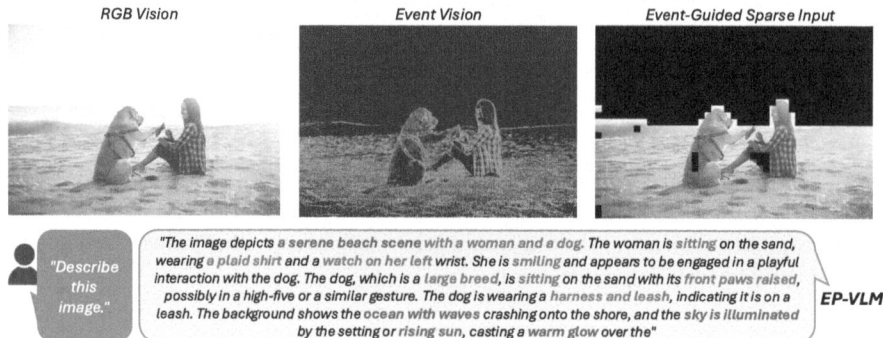

Fig. 2. Case 1: Descriptions on beach scene. The red represents the description of the subject (people/animals), and the blue represents the description of the background. (Color figure online)

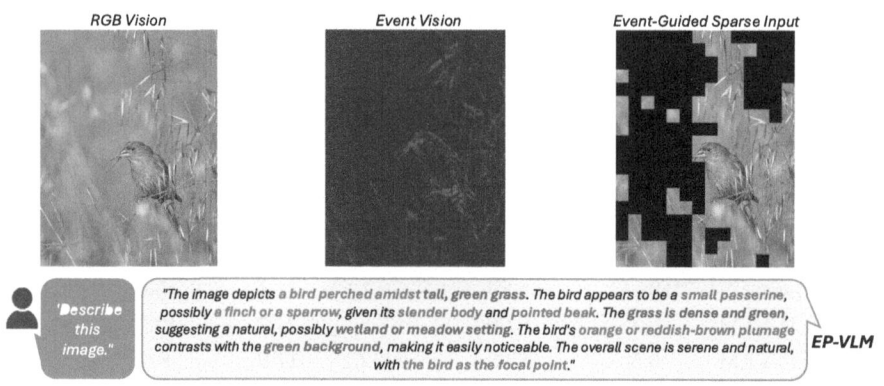

Fig. 3. Case 2: Descriptions on avian scene.

4.2 Qualitative Results

To illustrate the ability of EP-VLM to leverage event vision for efficient and accurate visual understanding, we examine qualitative case studies drawn from widely used benchmarks. The first case shows the demonstration on a complex beach scene with 50% sparse guided by event data. The second case contrasts a standard ImageNet photograph of a small bird in foliage with the corresponding n-ImageNet [26] event representation processed by EP-VLM. Together, these examples showcase how dynamic vision priors can selectively highlight salient content while suppressing redundant background information.

Turning first to the beach scene in Fig. 2, EP-VLM demonstrates a marked improvement in semantic precision and relational reasoning when guided by sparse event-based input. In the RGB demo (left), the model correctly identifies the primary actors, a woman and a dog, and the broad setting of a shoreline with waves and a glowing sky. However, the description remains somewhat generic and loosely structured, with limited emphasis on inter-object relationships. In contrast, the event-guided sparse input (right) enables EP-VLM to focus on salient motion cues and edge dynamics, yielding a richer, more structured caption. The model not only identifies the woman sitting on the sand and the dog in a high-five posture but also accurately encodes the spatial relation "woman to the right of the dog." Furthermore, EP-VLM captures fine-grained accessory details (e.g., the woman's plaid shirt and wristwatch) and contextually links these to the dog's harness and leash, reflecting a deeper scene understanding. By leveraging asynchronous event streams, the model filters out background noise, such as waves and sky illumination, and prioritizes dynamic elements, resulting in concise yet comprehensive descriptions of entities, attributes, and their spatial interplay.

Likewise, in the bird scenario in Fig. 3, the contrast between dense RGB and sparse event guidance is equally striking. Under standard ImageNet input, EP-VLM produces a correct but relatively flat caption, i.e., "a small passerine bird amidst tall green grass", noting only basic plumage contrast and habitat. When supplied with n-ImageNet event data, however, the model's description becomes far more vivid and relationally nuanced: it highlights the bird's perching action, the directional tilt of its beak toward nearby grass blades, and the interplay of light across its orange-brown feathers. The event-driven representation emphasizes micro-movements, such as head tilts and wing adjustments, allowing EP-VLM to infer behavioral context ("perched centrally within dense grass tufts in a wetland-like meadow"). This case underscores EP-VLM's capacity to translate sparse temporal cues into precise spatial and semantic relationships, mirroring the human visual system's prioritization of motion for scene interpretation.

5   Conclusion

This paper presents EP-VLM, a novel event-priori-based vision-language model that significantly enhances computational efficiency while preserving accuracy. Inspired by human visual cognition, EP-VLM leverages motion priors from event data to dynamically sparsify RGB inputs, concentrating computation on semantically salient regions identified by dynamic vision sensors. Crucially, our position-preserving tokenization strategy enables the visual encoder to process this unstructured, sparse input while maintaining accurate spatial relationships through packed rotary position embeddings. Experiments on Qwen2-VL baselines demonstrate that EP-VLM achieves a 50% reduction in FLOPs while retaining 98% accuracy on the RealWorldQA benchmark, validating that event-guided sparsification effectively eliminates redundant visual computations without compromising understanding. This work establishes event-based priors as a powerful paradigm for enabling edge-deployable VLMs, opening new pathways for efficient multimodal intelligence in resource-constrained environments.

References

1. Amir, A., et al.: A low power, fully event-based gesture recognition system. In: Proceedings of the IEEE Conference on Computer Vision and Pattern Recognition, pp. 7243–7252 (2017)
2. Anthropic: Claude 3.5 sonnet (2024). https://www.anthropic.com/news/claude-3-5-sonnet
3. Antol, S., et al.: VQA: visual question answering. In: Proceedings of the IEEE International Conference on Computer Vision, pp. 2425–2433 (2015)
4. Bai, S., et al.: Qwen2. 5-VL technical report. arXiv preprint arXiv:2502.13923 (2025)
5. Baumann, N., et al.: Enhancing autonomous driving systems with on-board deployed large language models. arXiv preprint arXiv:2504.11514 (2025)
6. Berry, M.J., Brivanlou, I.H., Jordan, T.A., Meister, M.: Anticipation of moving stimuli by the retina. Nature **398**(6725), 334–338 (1999)
7. Chamorro Hernández, W.O., Andrade-Cetto, J., Solà Ortega, J.: High-speed event camera tracking. In: Proceedings of the the 31st British Machine Vision Virtual Conference, pp. 1–12 (2020)
8. Chen, H., et al.: DB-LLM: accurate dual-binarization for efficient LLMs. arXiv preprint arXiv:2402.11960 (2024)
9. Cordone, L., Miramond, B., Thierion, P.: Object detection with spiking neural networks on automotive event data. In: 2022 International Joint Conference on Neural Networks (IJCNN), pp. 1–8. IEEE (2022)
10. Dosovitskiy, A., et al.: An image is worth 16x16 words: transformers for image recognition at scale. arXiv preprint arXiv:2010.11929 (2020)
11. Gallego, G., et al.: Event-based vision: a survey. IEEE Trans. Pattern Anal. Mach. Intell. **44**(1), 154–180 (2020)
12. Guan, Y., et al.: Intelligent virtual assistants with LLM-based process automation. arXiv preprint arXiv:2312.06677 (2023)
13. Guo, D., et al.: DeepSeek-R1: incentivizing reasoning capability in LLMs via reinforcement learning. arXiv preprint arXiv:2501.12948 (2025)
14. Guo, D., et al.: Seed1. 5-VL technical report. arXiv preprint arXiv:2505.07062 (2025)
15. Guo, J., Ouyang, W., Xu, D.: Multi-dimensional pruning: a unified framework for model compression. In: CVPR (2020)
16. Guo, J., et al.: Compressing large language models by joint sparsification and quantization. In: Forty-First International Conference on Machine Learning (2024)
17. Guo, J., Xu, D., Ouyang, W.: Multidimensional pruning and its extension: a unified framework for model compression. IEEE Trans. Neural Netw. Learn. Syst. (2023)
18. Guo, J., Zhang, W., Ouyang, W., Xu, D.: Model compression using progressive channel pruning. IEEE Trans. Circ. Syst. Video Technol. (2020)

19. He, C., Ding, Y., Guo, J., Gong, R., Qin, H., Liu, X.: DA-KD: difficulty-aware knowledge distillation for efficient large language models. In: Forty-first International Conference on Machine Learning (2025)
20. He, Y., et al.: LLMs meet multimodal generation and editing: a survey. arXiv preprint arXiv:2405.19334 (2024)
21. Huang, W., et al.: BiLLM: pushing the limit of post-training quantization for LLMs. arXiv preprint arXiv:2402.04291 (2024)
22. Huang, W., et al.: SliM-LLM: salience-driven mixed-precision quantization for large language models. arXiv preprint arXiv:2405.14917 (2024)
23. Huang, W., et al.: An empirical study of llama3 quantization: from LLMs to MLLMs. Vis. Intell. **2**(1), 36 (2024)
24. Hurst, A., et al.: GPT-4O system card. arXiv preprint arXiv:2410.21276 (2024)
25. Guo, J., Ouyang, W., Xu, D.: Channel pruning guided by classification loss and feature importance. In: AAAI (2020)
26. Kim, J., Bae, J., Park, G., Zhang, D., Kim, Y.M.: N-ImageNet: towards robust, fine-grained object recognition with event cameras. In: Proceedings of the IEEE/Cvf International Conference on Computer Vision, pp. 2146–2156 (2021)
27. Kuo, W., Cui, Y., Gu, X., Piergiovanni, A., Angelova, A.: F-VLM: open-vocabulary object detection upon frozen vision and language models. arXiv preprint arXiv:2209.15639 (2022)
28. Li, J., et al.: Integrated image-based deep learning and language models for primary diabetes care. Nat. Med. **30**(10), 2886–2896 (2024)
29. Li, Z., et al.: ARB-LLM: alternating refined binarizations for large language models. arXiv preprint arXiv:2410.03129 (2024)
30. Liu, A., et al.: DeepSeek-V3 technical report. arXiv preprint arXiv:2412.19437 (2024)
31. Liu, H., Li, C., Wu, Q., Lee, Y.J.: Visual instruction tuning. Adv. Neural. Inf. Process. Syst. **36**, 34892–34916 (2023)
32. Liu, S., et al.: EventGPT: event stream understanding with multimodal large language models. arXiv preprint arXiv:2412.00832 (2024)
33. Ma, X., Fang, G., Wang, X.: LLM-pruner: on the structural pruning of large language models. Adv. Neural. Inf. Process. Syst. **36**, 21702–21720 (2023)
34. Messikommer, N., Gehrig, D., Loquercio, A., Scaramuzza, D.: Event-based asynchronous sparse convolutional networks. In: European Conference on Computer Vision, pp. 415–431. Springer (2020)
35. Meta, A.: The llama 4 herd: the beginning of a new era of natively multimodal AI innovation (2025). https://ai.meta.com/blog/llama-4-multimodal-intelligence/. Accessed 4 July 2025
36. MrYxJ: calflops: a FLOPs and params calculate tool for neural networks (2024). https://github.com/MrYxJ/calculate-flops.pytorch
37. Mueggler, E., Rebecq, H., Gallego, G., Delbruck, T., Scaramuzza, D.: The event-camera dataset and simulator: event-based data for pose estimation, visual odometry, and slam. Int. J. Robot. Res. **36**(2), 142–149 (2017)
38. Qin, H., et al.: Accurate LoRA-finetuning quantization of LLMs via information retention. arXiv preprint arXiv:2402.05445 (2024)
39. Radford, A., et al.: Learning transferable visual models from natural language supervision. In: International Conference on Machine Learning, pp. 8748–8763. PMLR (2021)
40. Schaefer, S., Gehrig, D., Scaramuzza, D.: AEGNN: asynchronous event-based graph neural networks. In: Proceedings of the IEEE/CVF Conference on Computer Vision And Pattern Recognition, pp. 12371–12381 (2022)

41. Song, C.H., Wu, J., Washington, C., Sadler, B.M., Chao, W.L., Su, Y.: LLM-planner: few-shot grounded planning for embodied agents with large language models. In: Proceedings of the IEEE/CVF International Conference on Computer Vision, pp. 2998–3009 (2023)
42. Sun, M., Liu, Z., Bair, A., Kolter, J.Z.: A simple and effective pruning approach for large language models. arXiv preprint arXiv:2306.11695 (2023)
43. Team, G., et al.: Gemini: a family of highly capable multimodal models. arXiv preprint arXiv:2312.11805 (2023)
44. Wang, P., et al.: Qwen2-VL: enhancing vision-language model's perception of the world at any resolution. arXiv preprint arXiv:2409.12191 (2024)
45. X.AI: Grok-2 beta release (2024). https://x.ai/blog/grok-2
46. Xu, X., et al.: A survey on knowledge distillation of large language models. arXiv preprint arXiv:2402.13116 (2024)
47. Yang, A., et al.: Qwen3 technical report. arXiv preprint arXiv:2505.09388 (2025)
48. Yang, G., et al.: LLMCBench: benchmarking large language model compression for efficient deployment. In: NeurIPS (2024)
49. Yu, Z., Qu, Q., Chen, X., Wang, C.: Can large language models grasp event signals? Exploring pure zero-shot event-based recognition. In: ICASSP 2025-2025 IEEE International Conference on Acoustics, Speech and Signal Processing (ICASSP), pp. 1–5. IEEE (2025)
50. Zhou, B., et al.: TinyLLaVA: a framework of small-scale large multimodal models. arXiv preprint arXiv:2402.14289 (2024)

Prompt-Tuning Bandits: Enabling Few-Shot Generalization for Efficient Multi-task Offline RL

Finn Rietz[1,2(✉)] , Oleg Smirnov[2] , Sara Karimi[2] , and Lele Cao[2]

[1] Örebro University, Örebro, Sweden
finn.rietz@oru.se
[2] King, Microsoft Gaming, Stockholm, Sweden
{oleg.smirnov,sarakarimi,lelecao}@microsoft.com

Abstract. Prompting has emerged as the dominant paradigm for adapting large, pre-trained transformer-based models to downstream tasks. The Prompting Decision Transformer (PDT) enables large-scale, multi-task offline Reinforcement Learning (RL) pre-training by leveraging stochastic trajectory prompts to identify the target task. However, these prompts are sampled uniformly from expert demonstrations, overlooking a critical limitation: *not all prompts are equally informative for differentiating between tasks.* This limits generalization and adaptation, especially in low-data or open-world settings where sample efficiency is crucial. To address this issue, we propose a lightweight, inference-time, bandit-based prompt-tuning framework. The bandit explores and optimizes trajectory prompt selection to enhance task performance, while avoiding costly fine-tuning of the transformer backbone. Our experiments indicate not only clear performance gains due to bandit-based prompt-tuning, but also better sample complexity, scalability, and prompt space exploration compared to prompt-tuning baselines. These results highlights the importance of adaptive prompt selection mechanisms for efficient generalization in offline multi-task RL.

1 Introduction

Recent advances in Artificial Intelligence (AI) research have demonstrated the strength of large, pre-trained transformer-based foundation models in many domains, including language [2,12], vision [5,13], and reinforcement learning [10,14]. These large models leverage vast and diverse offline datasets to acquire generalizable representations that can solve many downstream tasks. A prominent strategy for leveraging these models in zero- and few-shot settings involves conditioning them on a *prompt* – a structured input that specifies the current objective. By keeping the prompt in context, the model ensures that subsequently generated tokens are aligned with the task. Consequently, the performance of a pre-trained model in a downstream task is contingent not only on

O. Smirnov, S. Karimi and L. Cao—Equal contribution.

the coverage of the pre-training data but also on the quality and informativeness of the provided prompt [6,8,11].

Building on the success of transformer-based multi-task language models, Offline Reinforcement Learning (ORL) has increasingly adopted transformer architectures, such as the Decision Transformer (DT) [4], to address sequential decision-making problems. In the multi-task setting, DT has been extended to the *Prompting Decision Transformer* (PDT) [19], which leverages *stochastic trajectory prompts*, multiple segments of expert demonstrations, to enable task-conditioned pre-training and to facilitate few-shot adaptation. These prompts serve as task descriptors that allow PDT to distinguish tasks and to generate actions aligned with the optimal policy distribution for each task. However, PDT samples these prompts uniformly at random from the demonstration dataset, overlooking a crucial limitation: not all prompts are equally informative for identifying the target task, which can lead to performance degradation and hinder generalization capabilities when uninformed sampling methods are employed. This limitation is especially problematic in applications where online exploration is costly and where adaptation to the target task must happen efficiently and robustly.

Although prompt-tuning is becoming increasingly popular to increase the few-shot performance of Large Language Models (LLMs), e.g. [3,8,11,16], prompt-tuning of RL decision transformers is still underexplored. Hu et al. [6,7] propose prompt-tuning for PDT by estimating the prompt's gradient with respect to online task return and by incrementally updating the prompt. However, performing gradient ascent directly on the prompt tokens ignores causal structures in the prompt and is not applicable in discrete settings. Yuan et al. [20] also propose a prompt-tuning approach for PDT, however, their method relies online exploration and additional data collection in the downstream tasks.

Thus, to address the limitations of PDT and prior prompt-tuning works, we introduce a simple yet effective bandit-based prompt-tuning framework that actively explores the prompt space. By formulating prompt selection as a contextual bandit problem, our method systematically identifies and exploits prompts that maximize downstream task performance, without requiring costly modifications to the pre-trained Transformer backbone. This approach is scalable, computationally efficient, and seamlessly integrates with PDT, enhancing performance while eliminating the need for additional task-specific fine-tuning. We summarize our contributions as follows:

- We introduce a bandit-based prompt-tuning approach to explore the prompt space at inference time, aiming to find the most effective prompt sequence for each downstream task.
- We validate the effectiveness of our approach in a controlled proof-of-concept environment, demonstrating that adaptive prompt selection significantly improves the performance of a pre-trained PDT model.
- We benchmark our method against two optimization-based prompt-tuning baselines and evaluate it using two bandit strategies across varying numbers of prompt segments.

– We provide analysis on exploration effectiveness and sensitivity to the initialization among different approaches.

Furthermore, ongoing work explores extending this method to more complex environments. Our findings underscore the critical role of prompt optimization in offline RL and reinforce the broader significance of prompt quality in transformer-based decision-making models.

2 Preliminaries

This section covers the background of our method. We define our learning objective in Sect. 2.1, formalize the contextual bandit problem in Sect. 2.2, and review the PDT [19] architecture in Sect. 2.3.

2.1 Offline Multi-task RL

An offline multi-task RL problem consists of a set of training tasks $\mathcal{T}^{\text{train}}$ and optionally several holdout test tasks $\mathcal{T}^{\text{test}}$. Each task $\mathcal{T}_i \in \{\mathcal{T}_1, \mathcal{T}_2, \ldots, \mathcal{T}_n,\}$ corresponds to a Markov Decision Process (MDP), defined as the tuple $\mathcal{M}_i = \langle \mathcal{S}_i, \mathcal{A}_i, r_i, d_i, \gamma_i, \mu_i^0 \rangle$. Here, $\mathcal{S}_i$ is the state space, $\mathcal{A}_i$ is the action space, $r_i : \mathcal{S}_i \times \mathcal{A}_i \to \mathbb{R}$ represents the reward function, $d_i : \mathcal{S}_i \times \mathcal{A}_i \times \mathcal{S}_i \to [0, 1]$ defines the discrete-time transition dynamics, $\gamma_i \in (0, 1]$ is the discount factor, and μ_i^0 is the initial state distribution of MDP i.

For each task $\mathcal{T}_i$, we assume access to an offline trajectory dataset $\mathcal{D}_i$. The trajectories in $\mathcal{D}_i$ can be collected using one or more policies of arbitrary quality. In addition, for PDT, we require a small set of expert demonstrations $\mathcal{P}_i$ to sample stochastic trajectory prompts from. Our goal is to exploit the available offline data to compute a generalized policy, $\pi(\mathbf{s}, \rho) \to \mathbf{a}$, capable of solving all tasks in $\mathcal{T}^{\text{train}}$. Here, ρ is a task descriptor like an index, one-hot encoding, or prompt, ensuring the policy is aware of the current task. The learning objective for the generalized policy is to maximize the expected discounted reward objective in Eq. (1) for each task $\mathcal{T}_i \in \mathcal{T}^{\text{train}}$.

$$J(\pi, i) = \mathbb{E}_{\mathbf{a}_t \sim \pi(\rho), \mathbf{s_t} \sim d_i} \left[\sum_{t=0}^{\infty} \gamma_i^t r_i(\mathbf{s}_t, \mathbf{a}_t) \right], \rho \sim \mathcal{P}_i \tag{1}$$

2.2 Contextual Multi-Armed Bandits

Multi-Armed Bandits (MABs) provide a framework for optimizing stochastic reward functions over the course of K rounds. For each round $k \in \{1, \ldots, K\}$ the bandit selects an action $a_k \in \mathcal{A}_b$ by pulling one of its arms, where $\mathcal{A}_b$ denotes the bandit's set of arms. It then perceives a stochastic reward $r_k \sim R(a_k)$ for performing that action, where R is the reward distribution. The goal is to maximize the cumulative reward $\sum_{k=1}^{K} r_k$ over the K rounds, which requires balancing exploration and exploitation of the available arms while minimizing cumulative regret [1]:

$$\text{Regret}(K) = \sum_{k=1}^{K} \left[\max_{a \in \mathcal{A}_b} \mathbb{E}[R(a)] - \mathbb{E}[r_k] \right] \tag{2}$$

Contextual Multi-Armed Bandits (CMABs) extend standard MABs by incorporating additional information (i.e. "context") $c_k \in \mathcal{C}$ observed at each round k. The stochastic reward depends on both the action and the context, $r_k \sim R(a_k \mid c_k)$, meaning a CMAB's objective is to learn a policy $\pi : \mathcal{C} \rightarrow \mathcal{A}_b$ that maximizes the expected reward objective $\mathbb{E}[\sum_{k=1}^{K} R(\pi(c_k) \mid c_k)]$. By exploiting the cross-arm features given by the context, CMABs are credited with better sample efficiency and generalization than their non-contextual counterparts [9], making them well-suited for efficient prompt-tuning.

2.3   Prompting Decision Transformer

Prompting Decision Transformer (PDT) [19] treats offline multi-task RL as a sequence learning problem by autoregressively modeling the trajectories in the available offline datasets. Trajectories consist of $(\hat{r}_t, s_t, a_t)$ triplets, with $\hat{r}_t = \sum_{t'=t}^{T} r_{t'}$ being return-to-go, needed for conditioning on optimal return. For all training tasks $\mathcal{T}^{\text{train}}$, PDT learns to model the sequence $\mathbf{x}$ in Eq. (4) by autoregressively predicting the action tokens, where $\odot$ denotes concatenation. The prompt ρ in Eq. (3) consists of J segments, each of length H, that are sampled uniformly from the expert demonstrations $\mathcal{P}_i$ for that task. Instead of relying on uninformed random sampling, we hypothesize that prompts can vary in their usefulness for describing the downstream task, based on segment composition and overlap between demonstrations for multiple tasks, and propose to optimize prompt and segment selection with a CMAB approach. As we detail in the next section, the bandit explores directly in the prompt space and learns to select the best prompt constructable from $\mathcal{P}_i$.

$$\rho = \Big(\overbrace{\hat{r}_l, s_l, a_l, \ldots, \hat{r}_{l+H}, s_{l+H}, a_{l+H}}^{\tilde{\tau}_1:\ \text{segment 1}}, \ldots, \overbrace{\hat{r}_k, s_k, a_k, \ldots, \hat{r}_{k+H}, s_{k+H}, a_{k+H}}^{\tilde{\tau}_J:\ \text{segment } J} \Big) \tag{3}$$

$$\mathbf{x} = \big(\rho \big) \odot \Big(\overbrace{\hat{r}_{t-N}, s_{t-N}, a_{t-N}, \hat{r}_{t-N+1}, s_{t-N+1}, a_{t-N+1} \ldots, \hat{r}_t, s_t, a_t}^{\tau_{N:t}\ N\ \text{most recent transitions}} \Big) \tag{4}$$

3   Method: Prompt-Tuning Contextual Bandit

We propose a contextual multi-armed bandit (CMAB) architecture to optimize the prompt selection and segment composition to improve the performance of a pre-trained PDT backbone on a downstream task $\mathcal{T}_i$. To this end, we assume access to a PDT θ^*, pre-trained until convergence on a multi-task dataset $\mathcal{D}$, a small number of expert demonstrations $\mathcal{P}_i$ to select prompts from, and a simulator $\mathcal{M}_i$ to evaluate online performance for the downstream task i.

At a high level, our approach operates as follows. For each round $k \in \{1, \ldots, K\}$, the bandit selects a prompt ρ_k from $\mathcal{P}_i$ which is prepended to the PDT's input according to Eq. (4). We then proceed by rolling out the PDT, conditioned on ρ_k, in $\mathcal{M}_i$ and take note of the achieved online return $G_k = \sum_{t=0}^{T} r_i(\mathbf{s}_t, \mathbf{a}_t) \mid \mathbf{a}_t \sim \pi(\mathbf{x}_t, \theta^*)$ for that round. Note that while $\tau_{N:t}$ in Eq. (4) is dynamically updated to reflect the last N steps in the episode, the prompt remains fixed during an entire episode. From the bandit's perspective, G_k serves as a reward for selecting prompt ρ_k, and the tuple $\langle \rho_k, G_k \rangle$ is stored for training the bandit's reward model.

We now detail our CMAB architecture and how it constructs prompts at each round k. A simple but naïve approach to bandit based prompt-tuning could be to maintain one arm per prompt constructible from the demonstrations in $\mathcal{P}_i$, however, the search space would grow *combinatorially* with the number of segments J in the prompt under this architecture. We instead propose a contextual bandit with only J arms, one for each segment in the prompt, taking the structure of the prompt space and similarity between segments into consideration. Our bandit maintains a separate reward model $\phi_j : \tilde{\tau} \rightarrow \mathbb{R}$ for each arm $j \in \{1, \ldots, J\}$, and treats prompt segments as context. Each of these reward models estimates the return achieved by the PDT for task i, when segment $\tilde{\tau} \in \mathcal{P}_i$ is placed at position j in the prompt. Thus, at each round k, our bandit predicts the reward for each segment in each position of the prompt, resulting in a prediction matrix $\mathbf{Y}$, with J columns and rows equal to $|\mathcal{P}_i|$, the number of segments in the given expert demonstration dataset. To select a prompt, the bandit can either exploit based on accumulated knowledge and $\arg\max \mathbf{Y}$ along the segments' dimension, or explore using some exploration mechanisms such as ϵ-greedy, Upper Confidence Bounds (UCB) [1], or Thompson Sampling [18]. To summarize, we propose a bandit architecture tailored to efficient prompt-tuning of PDT models and maintain linear rather then combinatorial scaling with the prompt size.

4 Experiments

This section outlines our experimental procedure. We first introduce the multi-task environment and offline dataset, then describe the baselines in Sect. 4.1 followed by results and analysis in Sect. 4.2.

Environment: We evaluate our proposed prompt-tuning bandit architecture in a 2D proof-of-concept environment. This environment features a planar 2D point agent that has to reach a goal coordinate. The state contains the agent's 2D coordinate at each step

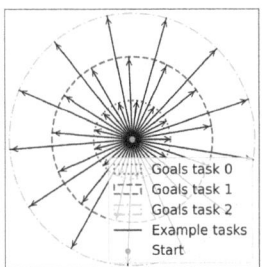

Fig. 1. Our proof-of-concept, 2D multi-task environment.

t. The action space contains two continuous actions for translating on the plane, with the step size being limited by projecting the translation vector on a unit circle with a radius of 0.1. In addition, the action space contains a binary stop action which allows the agent to terminate the episode. When selected, the episode ends, and the agent receives a sparse reward proportional to its distance from the goal. A bonus of $+10$ reward is provided (discounted for exceeding the optimal number of steps) for stopping in close proximity of the goal coordinate. To create a multi-task setting, we parameterize tasks by (r, α), the goal's radius and angle. We discretize the task sparsely using 20 discrete angles $\alpha \in \{0.1 \cdot \pi, 0.2 \cdot \pi, \ldots, 2 \cdot \pi\}$ and three discrete radii $r \in \{0.9, 1.9, 2.9\}$, yielding a total of 60 tasks (Fig. 1).

Offline Dataset and Pre-training: We collect an offline multi-task dataset by training Proximal Policy Optimization (PPO) [15] for 1M steps on each of the 60 tasks, storing the trajectories as $\mathcal{D}_i$. We extract trajectories from the top percentile from $\mathcal{D}_i$ to serve as expert demonstrations $\mathcal{P}_i$ for that task. We then train PDT, without modifications, on $\mathcal{D} = \{\mathcal{D}_1, \mathcal{D}_2, \ldots, \mathcal{D}_{60}\}$ and $\mathcal{P} = \{\mathcal{P}_1, \mathcal{P}_2, \ldots, \mathcal{P}_{60}\}$ until convergence; see [19] for details.

4.1 Baselines

We compare our proposed bandit-based prompt-tuning method, qualitative and empirically, against the following baselines.

Standard PDT [19] without prompt-tuning: This baselines reveals the possible performance gains due to prompt-tuning at inference time.

ZO-RankSGD-based prompt-tuning [6]: Closely related to our bandit-based method, this approach proposes prompt-tuning for PDT by employing ZO-RankSGD [17] to estimate the gradient of the prompt with respect to online task return G. The method samples and initial prompt $\rho_0 \sim \mathcal{P}_i$, and, at each rounds k, estimates the gradient $\hat{\nabla}_\rho G$ based on the ranking between m perturbed versions of ρ_k. The perturbed versions of the prompt are obtained as $\rho'_k = \rho_k + \epsilon \mathcal{N}(0, I_d)$, where ϵ is the noise scale, I_d is the $d \times d$ identity matrix, and $d = |\rho|$ is the length of the prompt. The prompt is then updated according to $\rho_{k+1} \leftarrow \rho_k + \eta \hat{\nabla}_\rho G$, where η is the learning rate that we anneal from 1 to 0.1 over the K rounds. Crucially, at each round k, all of the m prompt-perturbations must be evaluated with an online rollout of the PDT, meaning the sample complexity of this method is m times larger than that of our method.

Gaussian Perturbation Hill Climbing: A simple stochastic optimization approach inspired by hill climbing. Given an initial prompt $\rho \sim \mathcal{P}_i$, we iteratively perturb the sampled prompt by applying Gaussian noise. At each round k, the perturbed prompt is obtained as $\rho_k = \rho + \epsilon \mathcal{N}(0, I_d)$. We anneal ϵ from 1 to 0.1 over the K rounds. The perturbed prompt ρ_k is evaluated by rolling out the PDT. If the resulting return G_k exceeds the best return so far, we update the prompt $\rho \leftarrow \rho_k$, thereby performing hill climbing with respect to online task return directly in the prompt space.

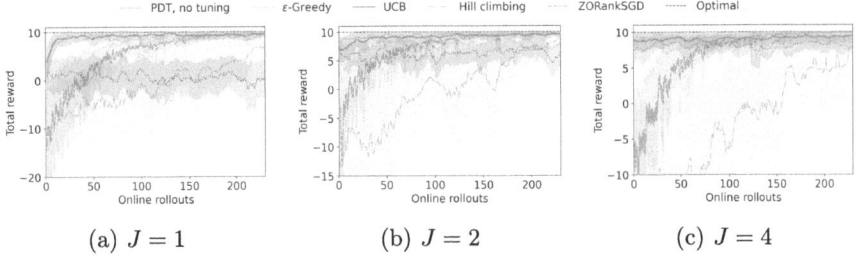

(a) $J = 1$ (b) $J = 2$ (c) $J = 4$

Fig. 2. Inference time performance gains due to prompt-tuning over 250 episodes. ZO-RankSGD performs a total of $m = 5 \times 250$ rollouts to estimate the prompt gradient 250 times, which we squash into the 0–250 range in the plot. Results are averaged over all training tasks and three seeds. To increase readability, the shaded area corresponds only to 0.25 standard deviations around the mean.

4.2 Results and Analysis

Does Bandit-Based Prompt-Tuning Improve a Frozen PDT Backbone?
We perform prompt tuning on the pre-trained PDT θ^* using 250 online rollouts on training tasks with radius $r = 2.9$. We run this experiment with $J \in \{1, 2, 4\}$, i.e., with increasingly many segments and, conversely, tokens for task identification in the prompt. We run our bandit-based prompt-tuning method with UCB [9] and ϵ-greedy exploration strategies.

Results are shown in Fig. 2, performance gains due to prompt-tuning are most prominently visible in Fig. 2a, where the prompt consists of a single segment of length $H = 3$, for a total of $J \times H \times (|\mathcal{S}| + |\mathcal{A}| + 1) = 1 \times 3 \times (2 + 3 + 1) = 18$ prompt tokens. Despite being trained to convergence on all training tasks, PDT without prompt tuning fails to achieve the optimal return. This shortfall is due to the uninformed, random prompt sampling strategy used by standard PDT which frequently selects uninformative prompts, limiting its performance. Our bandit-based prompt-tuning approach, however, quickly boosts the performance of the underlying PDT backbone to optimal levels of return by identifying high-return prompts, with no considerable difference between ϵ-greedy or UCB exploration. The other prompt-tuning baseline methods, Gaussian perturbation with hill climbing and ZO-RankSGD-based prompt-tuning, also demonstrate clear improvements over the course of the 250 online rollouts, though they are less efficient than the bandit approach. Notably, ZO-RankSGD requires $m = 5$ additional online rollouts for each prompt-gradient estimation, resulting in a total of 5×250 online rollouts. In contrast, our bandit-based approach rapidly converges, consistently selecting optimal prompts within the first few rollouts.

Additionally, we observe the following trends as prompt size increases. First, although PDT performance without prompt-tuning remains roughly constant over 250 rollouts, it scales approximately proportionally with prompt size, reducing the performance gain from prompt-tuning. In Fig. 2c, PDT achieves near-optimal return even without prompt-tuning, which implies that, in our proof-of-concept environment, exhaustive random sampling suffices for finding tokens that uniquely identify the downstream task. Interestingly, both Gaussian perturbation and the ZO-RankSGD baseline scale poorly with the prompt size. We hypothesize that this stems from their strategy of perturbing the *entire* prompt at each round, which can unnecessarily disrupt informative segments by injecting excessive noise, even when the original prompt is nearly optimal. In contrast, our bandit-based method avoids this issue by exploring prompt segments independently with each arm. This enables it to preserve high-performing segments while selectively exploring others, *without* adding unnecessary noise to effective parts of the prompt.

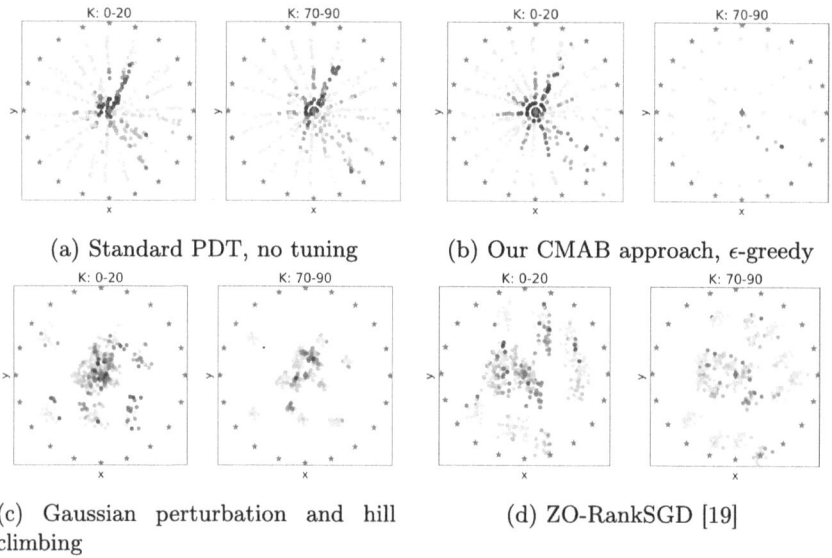

(a) Standard PDT, no tuning

(b) Our CMAB approach, ϵ-greedy

(c) Gaussian perturbation and hill climbing

(d) ZO-RankSGD [19]

Fig. 3. Spatio-temporal comparison between prompt selection approaches. Prompts are plotted by the mean spatial coordinate of the states in the prompt and colored according to the achieved return -250 -200 -150 -100 -50 0 when using that prompt. The MDP's starting state is indicated with the red diamond, and the goal states for different tasks are indicated by the red stars. K denotes the bandit rounds for each image. (Color figure online)

How Does Bandit-Based Prompt-Tuning Explore the Prompt Space?
We visualize selected prompts in the beginning (K: 0–20) and towards later stages (K: 70–90) of exploration in Fig. 3. PDT's uniform prompt selection strategy, with no difference between the early or later stages, can be seen in Fig. 3a. As shown in Fig. 3b, our bandit-based approach initially explores the entire prompt space, experiencing low- and high-performance prompts. However, in later rounds, the bandit prioritizes prompts that are closer to the goal states while avoiding the low-performance prompts near the center, as these provide less informative signals for the task.

The Gaussian perturbation method in Fig. 3c primarily explores locally. This is due to the hill climbing optimization, which finds the best-performing prompt in vicinity of the initially sampled prompt while falling short of exploring the whole prompt space. The ZO-RankSGD-based prompt-tuning in Fig. 3d similarly explore only locally, revealing a strong dependence on the initialization. Unlike incremental approaches, our bandit method is less reliant on the initially sampled prompt. Instead, it exploits segment similarities to identify the best segments in $\mathcal{P}_i$. This result highlights a key limitation of perturbation-based methods in prompt-space exploration and illustrates how our bandit approach effectively selects prompts that drive performance improvements.

5   Conclusion and Future Work

We introduce a bandit-based prompt-tuning approach that enables few-shot generalization at inference time for multi-task decision transformers. By efficiently exploring the prompt space, our approach identifies high-performing prompts for downstream tasks, avoiding exhaustive random sampling or full-model finetuning.

Our preliminary results show that the proposed contextual bandit architecture efficiently boosts a pre-trained PDT to optimal levels of performance, after only a small number of online rollouts, while uniform sampling and prior prompt-tuning approaches underperform.

We believe these findings warrant future research and are exploring the scalability of the proposed method to more complex and challenging environments and aim to present additional results at the workshop.

References

1. Auer, P., Cesa-Bianchi, N., Fischer, P.: Finite-time analysis of the multiarmed bandit problem. Mach. Learn. **47**(2 3), 235–256 (2002). https://doi.org/10.1023/A:1013689704352
2. Brown, T., et al.: Language models are few-shot learners. Adv. Neural. Inf. Process. Syst. **33**, 1877–1901 (2020)
3. Chen, L., Chen, J., Goldstein, T., Huang, H., Zhou, T.: InstructZero: efficient instruction optimization for black-box large language models. In: Proceedings of the 41st International Conference on Machine Learning, vol. 235, pp. 6503–6518 (2024)
4. Chen, L., et al.: Decision transformer: reinforcement learning via sequence modeling. Adv. Neural. Inf. Process. Syst. **34**, 15084–15097 (2021)
5. Dosovitskiy, A.: An image is worth 16x16 words: transformers for image recognition at scale. arXiv preprint arXiv:2010.11929 (2020)
6. Hu, S., Shen, L., Zhang, Y., Tao, D.: Prompt-tuning decision transformer with preference ranking. arXiv preprint arXiv:2305.09648 (2023)
7. Hu, S., Zhao, W., Lin, W., Shen, L., Zhang, Y., Tao, D.: Prompt tuning with diffusion for few-shot pre-trained policy generalization. arXiv preprint arXiv:2411.01168 (2024)

8. Lester, B., Al-Rfou, R., Constant, N.: The power of scale for parameter-efficient prompt tuning. arXiv preprint arXiv:2104.08691 (2021)

9. Li, L., Chu, W., Langford, J., Schapire, R.E.: A contextual-bandit approach to personalized news article recommendation. In: Proceedings of the 19th International Conference on World Wide Web, pp. 661–670 (2010)

10. Li, W., Luo, H., Lin, Z., Zhang, C., Lu, Z., Ye, D.: A survey on transformers in reinforcement learning. arXiv preprint arXiv:2301.03044 (2023)

11. Lin, X., et al.: Use your instinct: instruction optimization using neural bandits coupled with transformers. In: NeurIPS 2023 Workshop on Instruction Tuning and Instruction Following (2023)

12. Radford, A.: Improving language understanding by generative pre-training (2018)

13. Radford, A., et al.: Learning transferable visual models from natural language supervision. In: International Conference on Machine Learning, pp. 8748–8763. PMLR (2021)

14. Reed, S., et al.: A generalist agent. Trans. Mach. Learn. Res.

15. Schulman, J., Wolski, F., Dhariwal, P., Radford, A., Klimov, O.: Proximal policy optimization algorithms. arXiv preprint arXiv:1707.06347 (2017)

16. Shi, C., Yang, K., Yang, J., Shen, C.: Best arm identification for prompt learning under a limited budget. In: ICLR 2024 Workshop on Understanding of Foundation Model (2024)

17. Tang, Z., Rybin, D., Chang, T.H.: Zeroth-order optimization meets human feedback: provable learning via ranking oracles. arXiv preprint arXiv:2303.03751 (2023)

18. Thompson, W.R.: On the likelihood that one unknown probability exceeds another in view of the evidence of two samples. Biometrika **25**(3/4), 285–294 (1933)

19. Xu, M., et al.: Prompting decision transformer for few-shot policy generalization. In: International Conference on Machine Learning, pp. 24631–24645. PMLR (2022)

20. Yuan, H., Fu, Y., Xie, F., Lu, Z.: Pre-trained multi-goal transformers with prompt optimization for efficient online adaptation. Adv. Neural. Inf. Process. Syst. **37**, 55086–55114 (2024)

GateLIP-X: Balancing Adaptation and Generalization in CLIP for Real-World via a Training-Free Framework

Tangwei Li, Yuke Li$^{(\boxtimes)}$, Yifeng Hu, and Jialiang Ma

Netease Yidun AI Lab, Hangzhou, China
{litangwei01,liyuke,huyifeng,majialiang03}@corp.netease.com

Abstract. Vision-language models like CLIP have gained popularity due to their zero-shot ability. To improve performance on specific downstream tasks, fine-tuning methods like prompt tuning and feature adapter have shown notable progress. However, these methods inevitably encounter two challenges when deployed in the wild: (1) task-specific adaptation gains come at the cost of generalization, and (2) the training and deployment costs need to be considered. To address these issues, we propose GateLIP-X, a simple yet effective framework, comprising three key components: AutoClick-SA (AC-SA), Slim Information Enhancement (SlimInfoX), and GateModule (GM). Specifically, combined with SlimInfoX, GateLIP-X introduces GM to predict whether the test data belongs to seen or unseen classes and utilizes prior refined feature information from SlimInfoX to predict the class independently from each other. To avoid reliance on unseen-class data, AC-SA extracts seen-class-irrelevant nuisances (e.g., background regions) as pseudo-unseen samples. This design allows GateLIP-X to generalize effectively in a training-free and unseen-classes-data-free way, offering a lightweight, efficient, and low-cost solution. Extensive experiments on 11 benchmark datasets demonstrate that GateLIP-X surpasses existing state-of-the-art methods, achieving accuracy improvements ranging from 5.50% to 23.69%, while maintaining high computational efficiency. These results underscore the practical value of GateLIP-X for scalable and low-cost open-world recognition.

Keywords: Training-Free Framework · Balancing Adaptation and Generalization · Limited Resources

1 Introduction

Recently, there has been a significant advances in the field of large vision-language models (VLMs). These models, drawing on the naturally occurring supervision of internet-scale image-language pairs [21,38], have successfully

Y. Ma et al. (Eds.): IJCAI 2025, CCIS 2640, pp. 41–55, 2025.
https://doi.org/10.1007/978-981-95-0988-1_4

assimilated an encompassing corpus of vision-language correspondence knowledge and provide a way for comprehensive exploration of open-set visual concepts. These approaches not only facilitate zero-shot predictions without task-specific fine-tuning but also exhibit ease of implementation and competitive performance. However, to achieve satisfactory performance on specialized downstream tasks, VLMs still need task-specific data and fine-tuning techniques. Techniques such as prompt tuning and feature adapter [16] have been developed to aid VLMs adaptation across various applications.

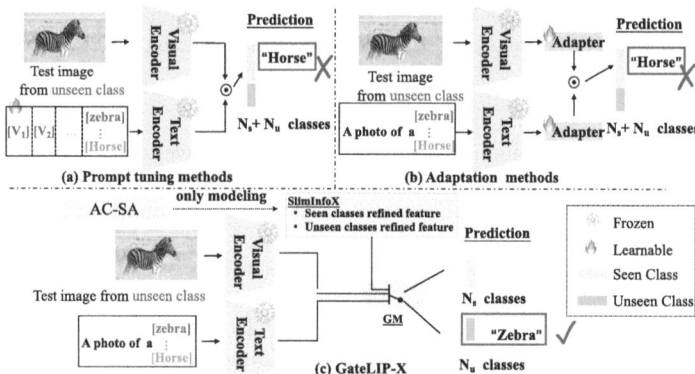

Fig. 1. Comparison of CLIP-based few-shot fine-tuning methods and GateLIP-X, including prompt tuning and feature adapter. Given an unseen class image, N_S and N_U represent the number of seen and unseen classes, respectively.

While these methodologies hold promise, they encounter substantial obstacles when confronted with real-world classification tasks. **Primarily**, these fine-tuning methodologies are effective with labeled data from seen classes [29]. Nevertheless, real-world data frequently encompasses distinct categories that are beyond the training classes, potentially undermining the model's generalization capabilities. For instance, prevalent methodologies like CLIP-based few-shot methods, as shown in Fig. 1(a) and (b), may lead to overfitting to seen-class data (like "Horse"). This results in stronger performance on seen classes but weaker results on unseen ones (like "Zebra"), which means its performance gains come at the cost of generalization: the fine-tuned models may perform worse than zero-shot models on related tasks with class variation. **Secondly**, most fine-tuning methods [36], designed for specific tasks, incorporate trainable parameters. This necessitates further training time and computational resources. Yet, when deploying the model in real-world, it is essential to provide quick and precise responses within the constraints of limited computational resources and a small number of data samples. The model should also exhibit scalability and the capacity to quickly adjust to task requirement modifications. Hence, developing fine-tuning methods that can overcome these obstacles is crucial to enhancing the effectiveness of models in real-world recognition tasks.

To address these issues, we employed CLIP, a milestone work in VLMs, and propose a simple yet innovative approach, called GateLIP-X. This approach is built upon the foundations of few-shot learning methods and maintains the classification capability in a more general and challenging in-the-wild setting where unseen classes occur on test data. Figure 1(c) provides an overview of GateLIP-X, composed of three principal elements: AutoClick-SA (AC-SA), Slim Information Enhancement (SlimInfoX), and GateModule (GM). These components serve two primary objectives: (i) to maximize the generalization capabilities of pre-trained models during fine-tuning on downstream data, and (ii) to mitigate the training and deployment costs of the model. **To emphasize generalization**, we introduce a separating data flow module, named GM, to accurately predict if an image belongs to seen or unseen classes. Depending on the outcome, we obtain the final class in two computationally different ways, which is flexible to adjust for different situations. This strategy enables the classifier to effortlessly categorize both seen and unseen classes. However, since the GM needs to complete the classification task of unseen classes, yet data for such classes is unavailable, we further propose an automatic segmentation process, called AC-SA, which is highly flexible in mining background information to serve as pseudo-unseen classes, enriching our knowledge about unseen classes. Moreover, SlimInfoX is designed to store the visual features of few-shot seen classes and their labels, which explicitly injects prior knowledge into the modeling process. **To ensure a training-free design and minimize costs**, GM and SlimInfoX function as non-parametric modules, and AC-SA is not used during inference. Additionally, SlimInfoX leverages a dimensionality reduction technique to further optimize storage efficiency and reduce resource consumption. These designs facilitate adapting the model efficiently without the need for retraining or fine-tuning.

In summary, the main contributions of GateLIP-X are as follows:

- Our work focuses on the under-explored challenge of adapting VLMs in a broader and more challenging in-the-wild setting where unseen classes occur on test data. GateLIP-X is designed to enhance performance on downstream tasks in seen classes while improving generalization on previously unseen classes. We use only a few-shot images from seen classes for modeling.
- GateLIP-X is a low-cost, effective and simple method, requiring neither extra unseen class data nor retraining. It integrates seamlessly into existing state-of-the-art (SOTA) VLMs to boost its performance in real-world setting. Our proposed SlimInfoX and GM operate without the need for training, and VLM does not require retraining. We utilize only a limited amount of seen class data while maintaining strong performance.
- Extensive experiments on 11 widely-used datasets demonstrate that GateLIP-X achieves SOTA performance. Ablation studies further validate the effectiveness of individual components. The results suggest that GateLIP-X provides significant benefits over prior techniques for realistic classification problems in the wild, proving practical value during its implementation.

2   Related Work

Vision-Language Models (VLMs). VLMs have garnered significant attention in recent years due to their ability to jointly model visual and linguistic information. The core of VLMs lies in the design of vision-language pre-training objectives that capture complex semantic correlations between modalities [28]. Pioneering works such as CLIP [21], ALIGN [12], BLIP [14], and LLaMA3.2-vision [10] adopt dual-encoder architectures trained on large-scale image-text pairs via contrastive learning, enabling robust zero-shot capabilities. Additionally, since large-scale image-text datasets are easier and more cost-effective to collect [38], they are widely used to improve the expressive power of VLMs. Besides these datasets [4, 22, 23], some studies [15, 27, 34, 35] leverage auxiliary datasets to provide richer supervision. For example, GLIP [15] incorporates Object365 [25] to extract region-level features, further enhancing model performance. Unlike prior works that focus on designing better pre-training techniques or dataset construction, we build upon the CLIP framework and explore a training-free framework to efficiently generalize from limited resources.

Downstream Adaption of VLMs. To enhance VLM performance on downstream tasks, recent research has explored two main adaptation strategies: prompt tuning [3, 41] and feature adaptation [16, 30]. Prompt tuning methods, illustrated in Fig. 1(a), include text, visual, and joint text-visual optimization. CoOp [41] replaces manual prompts with learnable context vectors, while CoCoOp [40] introduces instance-conditioned prompts to mitigate overfitting. Other works, such as VP [1] and PLOT [3] further explore learnable prompts for both images and text. Feature adaptation methods, illustrated in Fig. 1(b), such as CLIP-Adapter [8] and Tip-Adapter [39], utilize lightweight adapters to refine image or text features, either through parametric modules or by leveraging few-shot embeddings, reducing the burden of full-model fine-tuning.

However, these methods still exhibit key limitations. **Firstly**, studies have shown that performance often deteriorates in open-world settings where unseen classes emerge at test time [21, 31]. **Secondly**, most approaches necessitate an additional stage of task-specific fine-tuning with labeled training data for each downstream task [16], making them costly. In contrast, our method eliminates the need for model retraining or additional unseen data, and operates under a training-free paradigm. Thus, it is not only easier to apply, but also enhances classification accuracy in the wild setting, offering a practical and lightweight solution for real-world applications.

3   Method

3.1   Problem Definition

In this study, we aim to explore a simple yet effective approach for adapting VLMs for real-world applications. The core challenge is that models are trained on seen classes but evaluated on test sets containing both seen and unseen classes.

Formally, let the input space be $\mathcal{X}^S$ and the label space be $\mathcal{Y}^S$. The dataset used for modeling is defined as $\mathcal{D}^S = \{\boldsymbol{x}_i^S, y_i^S\}_{i=1}^{NK}$ where $\boldsymbol{x}_i \in \mathcal{X}^S$ and $y_i \in \mathcal{Y}^S$ indicate an instance and its label, respectively. This dataset comprises N seen categories, each containing K labeled samples. The unseen data is represented as $\mathcal{D}^U = \{\boldsymbol{x}_i^U, y_i^U\}$, where $\mathcal{D}^S \cap \mathcal{D}^U = \emptyset$. Consequently, the comprehensive evaluation set, which includes both seen and unseen classes, is defined as $\mathcal{D} = \mathcal{D}^S \cup \mathcal{D}^U = \{\boldsymbol{x}_i', y_i'\}_{i=1}^m$ to effectively simulate a real-world scenario, where m denotes the number of test samples. That is, the objective of this research is to develop a straightforward yet powerful approach that can make accurate and robust predictions on the combined label space $\mathcal{Y}^S \cup \mathcal{Y}^U$, without experiencing overall performance degradation due to the presence of unseen classes.

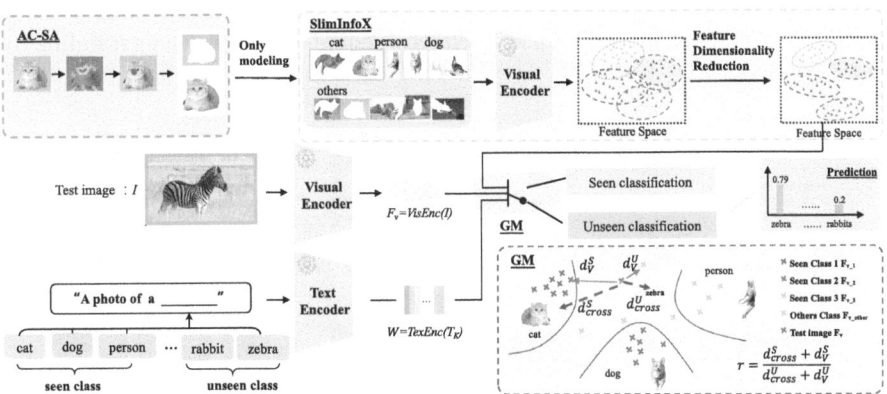

Fig. 2. The Pipeline of GateLIP-X. It is a training-free and unseen-classes-data-free way. AC-SA leverages background cues as pseudo-unseen classes, eliminating the need for actual unseen data during modeling. SlimInfoX is a lightweight module that stores reduced visual features and their one-hot labels to support class prediction. GM predicts whether an image belongs to a seen or unseen class by integrating SlimInfoX, CLIP-refined visual features, and CLIP text features. All modules operate without training.

3.2   Revisiting CLIP

CLIP consists of an image encoder VisEnc($\cdot$) and a text encoder TexEnc($\cdot$), jointly trained to extract features from both modalities. Assuming we have N candidate classes, we generate textual inputs T_N by putting all class names into the [CLASS] tags of pre-defined text templates (e.g., "Photos of [CLASS]"). For a test image I, the encoders extract a D-dimensional visual representation $F_v = \text{VisEnc}(I), F_v \in \mathbb{R}^{1 \times D}$ and textual representations $W = \text{TexEnc}(T_N), W \in \mathbb{R}^{N \times D}$. After that, the zero-shot classification logits are computed as:

$$\text{logits} = F_v W^T, \text{logits} \in \mathbb{R}^{1 \times N} \tag{1}$$

Remark 1. Our method is not limited to CLIP and can be applied to other contrastive vision-language models that promote multi-modal feature alignment.

3.3   GateLIP-X: A Training-Free and Unseen-Classes-Data-Free Way

The architecture of GateLIP-X, a training-free and unseen-classes-data-free way, is illustrated in Fig. 2. It consists of three key components: AutoClick-SA, Slim Information Enhancement, and GateModule.

AutoClick-SA (AC-SA). The direct application of CLIP-based few-shot methods [30,33,37] may incorrectly classify unseen classes due to a lack of open-set training data. Using GAN-generated pseudo-samples, which are time-consuming, as a solution is not ideal [9]. However, we observe that the background areas, not corresponding to any pre-existing classes, offer valuable insights for detecting novel class samples (see Fig. 3(a)). Thus, we propose AC-SA, a training-free and unseen-classes-data-free method that leverages background features to identify unseen classes, enhancing our understanding of unseen classes.

Fig. 3. Motivation of AC-SA. (a) Mining background regions as pseudo-unseen classes can enrich our knowledge about unseen classes. (b) Although the highest-response point (red) varies in location, the final segmentation remains consistent. (Color figure online)

We draw inspiration from SAM, a powerful segmentation model capable of segmenting arbitrary images. Among its three modes, either all instances are segmented, or interactive segmentation is desired. Nonetheless, it has been observed that in the click mode, accurate segmentation can be achieved as long as the clicked point is within the category area of the image, as shown in Fig. 3(b). Therefore, we propose an alternative to interactive manipulation by utilizing the highest response point generated by Grad-CAM as the SAM's point prompt.

Concretely, for each modeling image I with label c, after CLIP's encoding of two modalities, we get the global visual representation F_v and the textual feature w_c obtained according to the ground label of c. We name the unseen classes region as "others" class for easy understanding. Inspired by Grad-CAM [24], the heatmap is calculated by the formula $Heatmap(I) = Grad\_CAM(F_v, w_c)$, where $F_v w_c^T$ is used as the logits to compute its gradients. In this way, we can identify the regions of an image that are most activated by the given caption. We then identify the coordinates of the highest-response point in the heatmap, defined as

Point$(x, y) = $ argmax(Heatmap(I)). Based on Point(x, y), we use this coordinate as the SAM's point prompt, and the segmentation results are as follows:

$$I_{\text{others}}, I_{\text{seen}} = SA(\text{Point}(x, y)) \qquad (2)$$

where I_{seen} denotes the region of seen classes, while I_{others} denotes the regions outside the seen class regions,i.e., background, as the pseudo-unseen classes.

With this approach, AC-SA obtains unseen classes and seen classes regions without requiring any unseen classes data or training process. During inference, only the complete original test image is needed for image prediction, i.e., AC-SA is only utilized during the modeling phase.

Slim Information Enhancement (SlimInfoX). SlimInfoX aims to leverage prior knowledge not only to enhance model adaptability to downstream tasks but also to provide assistance in detecting unseen classes, while simultaneously enabling efficient feature extraction in resource-constrained environments to optimize overall system performance. At its core, SlimInfoX adopts a non-parametric strategy to construct a refined key-value cache from a training set with limited samples. In contrast to TIP-Adapter [39], SlimInfoX introduces two key innovations: **(1) Feature reduction.** The CLIP image encoder VisEnc(I) maps the input into a D-dimensional embedding. Due to contrastive learning, we have observed redundancy among features within the visual modality, meaning that not all the extracted visual features of the cache model or test image are significant for downstream tasks along the channel dimension. To address this, we calculate inter-class similarity S_i and inter-class variance V_i for the i-th channel, aiming to minimize inter-class similarity and maximize inter-class variance. Inspired by Entropy and Kullback–Leibler (KL) divergence, we further use Entropy En_i to measure the importance of each feature channel and use KL divergence KL_i to measure the difference between intra-class distribution and inter-class distribution to complete feature reduction. The feature importance indicator is calculated as:

$$F_i = \lambda_1 S_i + \lambda_2 V_i + \lambda_3 En_i + \lambda_4 KL_i \qquad (3)$$

where $\lambda_1, \lambda_2, \lambda_3, \lambda_4$ are weighting factors, and $i = 1, 2, \ldots, D$. A lower F_i value indicates higher importance. The top-Q most influential channels are selected to form the final refined feature representation $F_Q \in \mathbb{R}^{1 \times Q}$. **(2) Contains features of both seen and unseen classes.** Unlike Conventional approaches like TIP-Adapter [39] that focus solely on seen classes, SlimInfoX explicitly incorporates representations for both seen and unseen classes. Specifically, after applying AC-SA, the original training dataset $\mathcal{D}^S$ is partitioned into two subsets: one containing K instances from each of the N seen classes, and another consisting of NK images only containing background images. That is to say, the training data contains $2KN$ training samples and the entire dataset also adds an "others" class, a total of $N+1$ classes. The ground-truth label is converted into an $(N+1)$-dimensional one-hot vector. The final refined visual features and label vectors for $\mathcal{D}^S$ are represented as $F_{\text{train}} \in \mathbb{R}^{2NK \times Q}$ and $L_{\text{train}} \in \mathbb{R}^{2NK \times (N+1)}$, respectively.

Thus, SlimInfoX consists of F_{train} and L_{train}, where F_{train} are treated as keys, while L_{train} are treated their corresponding values.

GateModule (GM). GM is designed as a data flow separation module, capable of adaptively classifying images into seen or unseen classes. Previous work [18] emphasizes a multi-modal regime that fully utilizes visual and text features, which is critical for machine learning systems deployed in the open world. In addition, TIP-Adapter [39] demonstrates that leveraging visual similarity can significantly enhance adaptability in downstream tasks. Motivated by these insights, we propose GM. Its core concept is to classify images as seen or unseen classes by integrating SlimInfoX, the CLIP-encoded visual features, and the CLIP-encoded text features. This approach is a training-free way by that effectively incorporates information from both visual and textual spaces.

Let $F_v = \text{VisEnc}(I)$ be the visual feature of a test image I. We select the most influential Q channels obtained in SlimInfoX to refine F_v, denoted as $F_Q \in \mathbb{R}^{1 \times Q}$. Next, we compute the minimum distance between F_Q and the seen visual space $F_{\text{train\_seen}}$, and the minimum distance between $\text{VisEnc}(I)$ and the unseen visual space F_Q, denoted as d_V^S and d_V^U, respectively:

$$d_V^S = \min(\text{dis}(F_Q, F_{\text{train\_seen}})) \tag{4}$$

$$d_V^U = \min(\text{dis}(F_Q, F_{\text{train\_unseen}})) \tag{5}$$

where $F_{\text{train\_seen}} \in \mathbb{R}^{NK \times Q}$ is the part of F_{train} contains visual features of seen classes. $F_{\text{train\_unseen}} \in \mathbb{R}^{NK \times Q}$ is the part of F_{train} contains visual features of unseen classes. $\text{dis}(a, b)$ means the distance between a and b.

To further exploit the cross-modal space, we compute the minimum distance from $\text{VisEnc}(I)$ to the seen textual space W_{seen} and to the unseen textual space W_{unseen}, denoted as d_{cross}^S and d_{cross}^U, respectively:

$$d_{\text{cross}}^S = \min(\text{dis}(\text{VisEnc}(I), W_{\text{seen}})) \tag{6}$$

$$d_{\text{cross}}^U = \min(\text{dis}(\text{VisEnc}(I), W_{\text{unseen}})) \tag{7}$$

Here, W_{seen} and W_{unseen} represent partitions of W, containing the text features of seen and unseen classes, respectively.

It is emphasized that, during prediction, textual information for both seen and unseen classes is accessible, contrasting with the training phase where such information is solely available for seen classes. Additionally, during training, only the visual information for seen classes can be obtained. Subsequently, the distances obtained from Eqs. (4)–(7) are used to predict whether the image belongs to a seen or unseen class:

$$r = \frac{\gamma \times d_{\text{cross}}^U + d_V^U}{\gamma \times d_{\text{cross}}^S + d_V^S} \tag{8}$$

Here, γ is a hyperparameter to balance two distances from the visual space and the cross space. If $r > 1$, the image belongs to the seen class. Otherwise, it belongs to the unseen class. Finally, the overall classification logits is as follows:

$$logits = \begin{cases} \alpha A L_{\text{train}}\_\text{seen} + F_v W_{\text{seen}}^T & if \ r > 1 \\ F_v W_{\text{unseen}}^T & if \ r <= 1 \end{cases} \quad (9)$$

where the affinity matrix $A = exp(-\beta(1 - F_Q F_{\text{train}}\_\text{seen}^T))$ captures the similarities between $F_{\text{train}}\_\text{seen}$ and F_Q. $L_{\text{train}}\_\text{seen}$ is part of L_{train}, which only contains one-hot vector corresponding to the seen class. The α and β are hyperparameters controlling the influence of the affinity weighting.

Thus, GM enables data separation in a training-free way, thereby improving the downstream task adaptability while enhancing the generalization capability.

4 Experiments

Datasets. We conduct experiments for GateLIP-X on 11 widely-used datasets, involving various types of recognition tasks, including ImageNet [6], Oxford-Pets [20], Caltech101 [7], StanfordCars [13], Flowers102 [19], Food101 [2], FGV-CAircraft [17], SUN397 [32], UCF101 [26], DTD [5], and EuroSAT [11].

Evaluation Protocol. We follow the protocol in [41], where the class set of each dataset is evenly divided into 50% seen and 50% unseen classes. Under this setting, GateLIP-X models on the few-shot samples from seen classes and evaluate full class set, including both seen and unseen classes. The evaluation metric is the standard overall accuracy, denoted as *Accuracy*, which reflects the model's adaption and generalization to across both seen and unseen classes. Noting that the text features extracted by the textual encoder include information from both seen and unseen classes. This setup more accurately simulates real-world setting, where a system must classify instances from both seen and unseen classes.

Implementation Details. We compare against four representative CLIP-based baselines: CLIP [21], TIP-Adapter [39], CoOp [41], and GDA-method [30]. All baseline methods are re-trained and implemented according to the details provided in the corresponding papers. For the CLIP backbone, we utilize ResNet-50 as the visual encoder and a transformer as the textual encoder. For the pre-weights of each encoder, we follow the [21] and freeze them throughout the process. Data preprocessing follows the standard CLIP protocol [21], including random cropping, resizing, and random horizontal flip. Except for the learnable prompts in CoOp, we follow CLIP to adopt prompt ensembling especially on ImageNet and use a single handcrafted prompt on other 10 datasets. Furthermore, AC-SA just complete offline in advance. The data processed by AC-SA serves as the basis for model optimization. During inference, we use the original images which are not processed by AC-SA.

4.1 State-of-the-Art Comparison

We conduct a comprehensive quantitative evaluation of GateLIP-X across 11 benchmark datasets, comparing its performance against state-of-the-art (SOTA) approaches under varying few-shot settings (i.e., 1, 2, 4, 8, and 16 shots). As

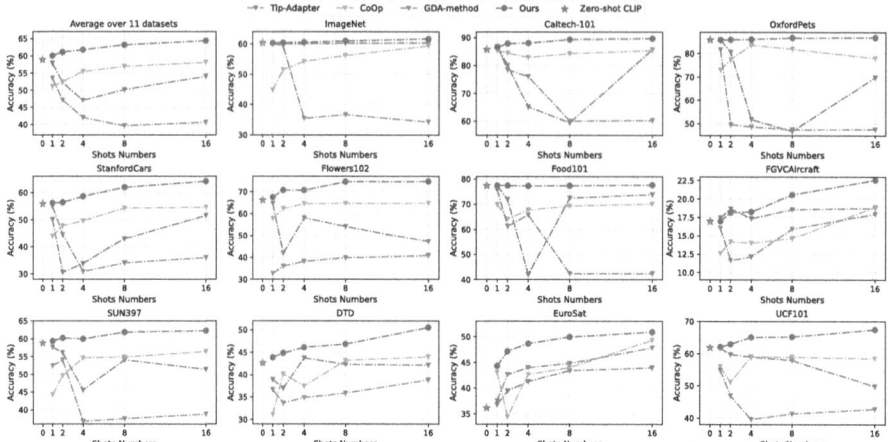

Fig. 4. Performance comparison on 11 datasets. We evaluate the performance under 1, 2, 4, 8, and 16-shot settings.

summarized in Fig. 4, GateLIP-X consistently outperforms all baseline methods, including both training-based approaches (e.g., CoOp) and training-free methods (e.g., Tip-Adapter, GDA). Notably, while existing training-free methods experience substantial performance drops as the number of shots increases, GateLIP-X maintains a stable and improving trend. For instance, the performance of GDA declines from 58.86% (1-shot) to 40.67% (16-shot), reflecting its limited generalization capability in the presence of unseen classes. In contrast, GateLIP-X achieves 64.36% accuracy in the 16-shot setting, outperforming all compared methods by margins ranging from 5.50% to 23.69% depending on the dataset and shot configuration. These results highlight GateLIP-X's ability to effectively balance adaptation and generalization. Importantly, this performance is achieved without any model retraining or the need for unseen-class data, highlighting its practicality in open-world deployment scenarios with limited resources.

4.2   Ablation Studies

AC-SA. To assess the impact of the proposed AC-SA module, we compare model performance with and without its integration. In this analysis, using Grad-CAM alone represents the model without AC-SA. Figure 5(a) provides a visual comparison between segmentation results obtained solely with Grad-CAM and those generated by AC-SA. We further illustrate the classification impact using a representative test case shown in Fig. 5(b). In this example, *american_bulldog* represents a seen class, while *russian_blue* belongs to an unseen class. Without AC-SA, the model tends to produce incorrect predictions, particularly for unseen classes. In contrast, incorporating AC-SA significantly improves prediction accuracy, suggesting its effectiveness in enhancing model performance. To further evaluate the role of AC-SA, we conducted experiments on the Oxford-

Pets dataset as an example to comprehensively analyze its influence. The results, presented in Table 1, indicate that the model incorporating AC-SA consistently outperforms the model without AC-SA under different few-shot settings, highlighting its key role in improving recognition performance in the wild setting.

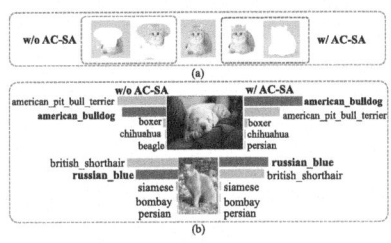

Fig. 5. Predictions from model with and without AC-SA.

Table 1. Analysis on AutoClick-SA. The experiments on the OxfordPets dataset to comprehensively analyze its influence

	1	2	4	8	16
CLIP	85.75	85.75	85.75	85.75	85.75
w/o AC-SA	85.12	85.25	85.79	86.15	86.32
w/ AC-SA	**85.71**	**85.82**	**85.98**	**86.59**	**86.70**

SlimInfoX. We investigate the impact of SlimInfoX from two perspectives: (1) varying few-shot settings and (2) the number of retained feature channels. **First**, under varying few-shot settings, we assess the performance of GateLIP-X across the 11 benchmark datasets. As shown in Fig. 4, increasing the number of cached samples consistently improves classification accuracy. This trend indicates that SlimInfoX effectively stores representative class-specific knowledge, enabling better generalization. **Second**, we study the effect of varying the number of retained feature channels Q. In the first experiment, we fix the shot number to 16 and evaluate our method on four representative datasets. The Fig. 6 (left) illustrates that performance initially improves with increasing channels, peaks between 500 and 900, then degrades. This trend suggests that SlimInfoX not only reduces storage overhead but also enhances performance by eliminating redundant or noisy features. In the second experiment, we assess the contributions of the components in Eq. (3), namely: similarity, variance, entropy, and KL divergence. Here, we fix the channel number at 512 and report the average accuracy across all datasets under varying shot numbers. Figure 6 (right) shows that omitting any criterion leads to performance drops, underscoring the necessity of each component in achieving optimal channel selection.

GM. To evaluate the contribution of the visual and textual modalities in GM, we conduct ablation experiments on the StanfordCars dataset. Specifically, we define $r = d_{\text{cross}}^U / d_{\text{cross}}^S$ to represent GM without the visual space, and $r = d_V^U / d_V^S$ to represent GM without the textual space. The results, presented in Fig. 7, indicate that the absence of either space negatively impacts performance, demonstrating that both modalities contribute complementary information essential for accurate seen/unseen class separation.

Time and Computation Efficiency. We compare the training time and computational overhead of GateLIP-X against existing methods under the 16-shot

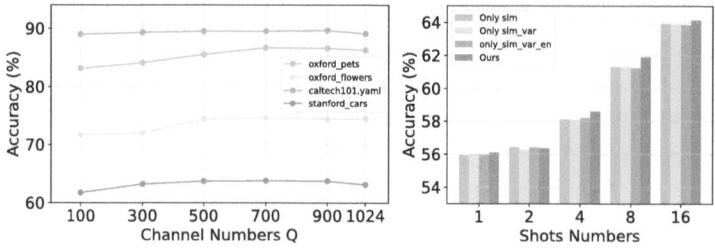

Fig. 6. Analysis on SlimInfoX.

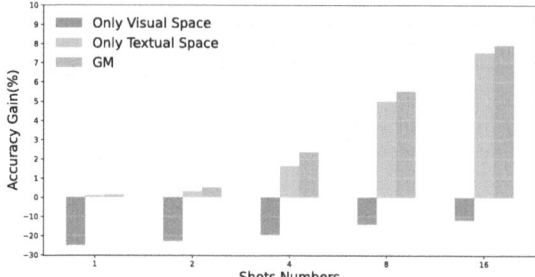

Fig. 7. Delta performance of different components for GM compared to the zero-shot baseline CLIP method.

setting on ImageNet [6]. As reported in Table 2, GateLIP-X achieves comparable or superior accuracy while operating under a training-free paradigm. Although our approach may require additional storage, the limited number of training samples makes this increase in storage requirements negligible. Furthermore, we also compare the computing overhead between our approach and the existing methods. For example, CoOp incurs significant training time and FLOPs due to gradient backpropagation through the full text encoder. In contrast, GateLIP-X requires no training, resulting in zero additional FLOPs. These characteristics make GateLIP-X a lightweight, low-cost, and efficient solution, particularly suitable for rapid updates in a resource-constrained environment.

Other Architectures. To assess the architectural generalizability of GateLIP-X, we evaluate its performance using alternative CLIP pre-trained image encoders, including ResNet-101 (RN101), ViT-B/16, and ViT-B/32. The Oxford-Pets dataset is used as a representative benchmark. As summarized in Table 3, GateLIP-X consistently outperforms CLIP across all architectures, demonstrating its can effectively integrate with diverse visual backbones without retraining or architecture-specific modifications.

Table 2. Time and Computation Efficiency. Experiments are conducted with batch size 32 on a single NVIDIA GeForce RTX 3080 GPU. The last column reports performance gains over zero-shot CLIP. "GFLOPs" are calculated during training with gradient back-propagation.

	Training	Training-Cost(h)	GFLOPs	Accuracy	Gain
CLIP	✗	0	0	58.86	0
TIP-Adapter	✗	0	0	54.04	−4.82
GDA-method	✗	0	0	40.67	−18.19
CoOP	✓	3.9	>10	58.11	−0.75
GateLIP-X	✗	0	0	**64.36**	**+5.50**

Table 3. Results on other architectures.

	RN50	RN101	VIT-B/16	VIT-B/32
CLIP	85.75	86.92	89.1	87.41
GateLIP-X	**86.70**	**87.49**	**90.99**	**87.93**

5 Conclusion

In this paper, we propose GateLIP-X, a training-free framework designed to address the often-overlooked challenge of deploying VLMs in real-world scenarios. GateLIP-X enhances VLM performance without relying on unseen class data, providing an efficient solution for balancing adaptation and generalization. GateLIP-X uniquely incorporates AC-SA during the modeling phase to extract background information to simulate unseen classes, allowing the model to continue learning even without actual unseen class data. Additionally, we design SlimInfoX to store refined visual features and their labels, thereby aiding in class prediction. Combined with SlimInfoX, the GM classifies images into either seen or unseen classes. Experiments conducted on 11 datasets demonstrate the superior performance of GateLIP-X over existing methods.

References

1. Bahng, H., Jahanian, A., Sankaranarayanan, S., Isola, P.: Exploring visual prompts for adapting large-scale models. arXiv preprint arXiv:2203.17274 **1**(3), 4 (2022)
2. Bossard, L., Guillaumin, M., Van Gool, L.: Food-101–mining discriminative components with random forests. In: Computer Vision–ECCV 2014: 13th European Conference, Zurich, Switzerland, 6–12 September 2014, Proceedings, Part VI 13, pp. 446–461. Springer (2014)
3. Chen, G., Yao, W., Song, X., Li, X., Rao, Y., Zhang, K.: Prompt learning with optimal transport for vision-language models. In: ICLR (2023)
4. Chen, X., et al.: PaLI: a jointly-scaled multilingual language-image model. arXiv preprint arXiv:2209.06794 (2022)

5. Cimpoi, M., Maji, S., Kokkinos, I., Mohamed, S., Vedaldi, A.: Describing textures in the wild. In: Proceedings of the IEEE Conference on Computer Vision and Pattern Recognition, pp. 3606–3613 (2014)
6. Deng, J., Dong, W., Socher, R., Li, L.J., Li, K., Fei-Fei, L.: ImageNet: a large-scale hierarchical image database. In: 2009 IEEE Conference on Computer Vision and Pattern Recognition, pp. 248–255. IEEE (2009)
7. Fei-Fei, L., Fergus, R., Perona, P.: Learning generative visual models from few training examples: an incremental bayesian approach tested on 101 object categories. In: 2004 Conference on Computer Vision and Pattern Recognition Workshop, p. 178. IEEE (2004)
8. Gao, P., et al.: Clip-adapter: better vision-language models with feature adapters. arXiv preprint arXiv:2110.04544 (2021)
9. Goodfellow, I., et al.: Generative adversarial networks. Commun. ACM **63**(11), 139–144 (2020)
10. Grattafiori, A., et al.: The Llama 3 herd of models (2024). https://arxiv.org/abs/2407.21783, 7
11. Helber, P., Bischke, B., Dengel, A., Borth, D.: EuroSAT: a novel dataset and deep learning benchmark for land use and land cover classification. IEEE J. Sel. Top. Appl. Earth Obs. Remote Sens. **12**(7), 2217–2226 (2019)
12. Jia, C., et al.: Scaling up visual and vision-language representation learning with noisy text supervision. In: International Conference on Machine Learning, pp. 4904–4916. PMLR (2021)
13. Krause, J., Stark, M., Deng, J., Fei-Fei, L.: 3D object representations for fine-grained categorization. In: Proceedings of the IEEE International Conference on Computer Vision Workshops, pp. 554–561 (2013)
14. Li, J., Li, D., Xiong, C., Hoi, S.: BLIP: bootstrapping language-image pre-training for unified vision-language understanding and generation. In: International Conference on Machine Learning, pp. 12888–12900. PMLR (2022)
15. Li, L.H., et al.: Grounded language-image pre-training. In: Proceedings of the IEEE/CVF Conference on Computer Vision and Pattern Recognition, pp. 10965–10975 (2022)
16. Liu, F.: Few-shot adaptation of multi-modal foundation models: a survey. Artif. Intell. Rev. **57**(10), 268 (2024)
17. Maji, S., Rahtu, E., Kannala, J., Blaschko, M., Vedaldi, A.: Fine-grained visual classification of aircraft. arXiv preprint arXiv:1306.5151 (2013)
18. Ming, Y., Cai, Z., Gu, J., Sun, Y., Li, W., Li, Y.: Delving into out-of-distribution detection with vision-language representations. Adv. Neural. Inf. Process. Syst. **35**, 35087–35102 (2022)
19. Nilsback, M.E., Zisserman, A.: Automated flower classification over a large number of classes. In: 2008 Sixth Indian Conference on Computer Vision, Graphics & Image Processing, pp. 722–729. IEEE (2008)
20. Parkhi, O.M., Vedaldi, A., Zisserman, A., Jawahar, C.: Cats and dogs. In: 2012 IEEE Conference on Computer Vision and Pattern Recognition, pp. 3498–3505. IEEE (2012)
21. Radford, A., et al.: Learning transferable visual models from natural language supervision. In: International Conference on Machine Learning, pp. 8748–8763. PMLR (2021)
22. Schuhmann, C., et al.: LAION-5B: an open large-scale dataset for training next generation image-text models. arXiv preprint arXiv:2210.08402 (2022)
23. Schuhmann, C., et al.: LAION-400M: open dataset of clip-filtered 400 million image-text pairs. arXiv preprint arXiv:2111.02114 (2021)

24. Selvaraju, R.R., Cogswell, M., Das, A., Vedantam, R., Parikh, D., Batra, D.: Grad-CAM: visual explanations from deep networks via gradient-based localization. In: Proceedings of the IEEE International Conference on Computer Vision, pp. 618–626 (2017)

25. Shao, S., et al.: Objects365: a large-scale, high-quality dataset for object detection. In: Proceedings of the IEEE/CVF International Conference on Computer Vision, pp. 8430–8439 (2019)

26. Soomro, K., Zamir, A.R., Shah, M.: UCF101: a dataset of 101 human actions classes from videos in the wild. arXiv preprint arXiv:1212.0402 (2012)

27. Tschannen, M., Mustafa, B., Houlsby, N.: Image-and-language understanding from pixels only. arXiv preprint arXiv:2212.08045 (2022)

28. Wang, X., et al.: Large-scale multi-modal pre-trained models: a comprehensive survey. Mach. Intell. Res. **20**(4), 447–482 (2023)

29. Wang, Z., Liang, J., He, R., Xu, N., Wang, Z., Tan, T.: Improving zero-shot generalization for clip with synthesized prompts. In: Proceedings of the IEEE/CVF International Conference on Computer Vision, pp. 3032–3042 (2023)

30. Wang, Z., Liang, J., Sheng, L., He, R., Wang, Z., Tan, T.: A hard-to-beat baseline for training-free clip-based adaptation. In: The Twelfth International Conference on Learning Representations (ICLR) (2024)

31. Wortsman, M., et al.: Robust fine-tuning of zero-shot models. In: Proceedings of the IEEE/CVF Conference on Computer Vision and Pattern Recognition, pp. 7959–7971 (2022)

32. Xiao, J., Hays, J., Ehinger, K.A., Oliva, A., Torralba, A.: Sun database: large-scale scene recognition from abbey to zoo. In: 2010 IEEE Computer Society Conference on Computer Vision and Pattern Recognition, pp. 3485–3492. IEEE (2010)

33. Yang, Z., Zhang, C., Li, R., Xu, Y., Lin, G.: Efficient few-shot object detection via knowledge inheritance. IEEE Trans. Image Process. **32**, 321–334 (2022)

34. Yao, L., et al.: DetCLIP: dictionary-enriched visual-concept paralleled pre-training for open-world detection. arXiv preprint arXiv:2209.09407 (2022)

35. Yu, J., Wang, Z., Vasudevan, V., Yeung, L., Seyedhosseini, M., Wu, Y.: CoCa: contrastive captioners are image-text foundation models. arXiv preprint arXiv:2205.01917 (2022)

36. Zanella, M., Ben Ayed, I.: Low-rank few-shot adaptation of vision-language models. In: Proceedings of the IEEE/CVF Conference on Computer Vision and Pattern Recognition, pp. 1593–1603 (2024)

37. Zhang, C., Song, N., Lin, G., Zheng, Y., Pan, P., Xu, Y.: Few-shot incremental learning with continually evolved classifiers. In: Proceedings of the IEEE/CVF Conference on Computer Vision and Pattern Recognition, pp. 12455–12464 (2021)

38. Zhang, J., Huang, J., Jin, S., Lu, S.: Vision-language models for vision tasks: a survey. IEEE Trans. Pattern Anal. Mach. Intell. (2024)

39. Zhang, R., et al.: Tip-adapter: training-free clip-adapter for better vision-language modeling. arXiv preprint arXiv:2111.03930 (2021)

40. Zhou, K., Yang, J., Loy, C.C., Liu, Z.: Conditional prompt learning for vision-language models. In: Proceedings of the IEEE/CVF Conference on Computer Vision and Pattern Recognition, pp. 16816–16825 (2022)

41. Zhou, K., Yang, J., Loy, C.C., Liu, Z.: Learning to prompt for vision-language models. Int. J. Comput. Vision **130**(9), 2337–2348 (2022)

QSE: Mitigating LLM Hallucinations Through Query-Adaptive Saliency-Localized Activation Editing

Kewei Liao[1], Tianbo Wang[1], and Fengxiang Yu[2](✉)

[1] State Key Laboratory of Complex and Critical Software Environment,
Beihang University, Beijing 100191, China
`{liaokewei,tianbowang}@buaa.edu.cn`
[2] Beijing Institute of Aerospace Systems Engineering, Beijing 100076, China
`yufengxiang124@163.com`

Abstract. Large Language Models (LLMs) exhibit significant capabilities and are extensively applied in diverse critical domains: advanced question-answering systems, healthcare information analysis, etc. Nevertheless, LLMs are prone to hallucination, which refers to generating outputs that are factually incorrect or unsubstantiated. This issue engenders significant reliability risks in critical applications. Inference-time activation editing has emerged as a promising strategy to mitigate hallucination without the need for model retraining. However, existing methods often employ generalized criteria for selecting attention heads and apply editing strengths that lack query-specific adaptability, therefore leading to suboptimal hallucination correction. To address these limitations, we introduce Query-adaptive Saliency-localized Activation Editing (QSE), which comprises Gradient-guided Head Saliency Localization (GSL) and Query-specific Editing Necessity Estimation (QNE), to enhance the precision and contextual adaptability of LLM activation editing. Specifically, GSL first employs a gradient-based optimization process to quantify the differential saliency of attention heads concerning factual generation, thereby pinpointing critical attention heads for precise activation editing. Subsequently, QNE comprehensively perceives the input query's knowledge semantics, and its lightweight estimator dynamically adjusts the editing strength for each head previously identified by GSL, thereby enabling highly adaptive and context-aware adjustments. Empirical evaluations on the LLaMA-3-8B-Instruct model using the TruthfulQA benchmark demonstrate that QSE achieves substantial improvements in model truthfulness, notably surpassing the baseline by 21.3% on the True*Info score.

Keywords: Large Language Models · Hallucination Mitigation · Adaptive Activation Editing

Y. Ma et al. (Eds.): IJCAI 2025, CCIS 2640, pp. 56–73, 2025.
https://doi.org/10.1007/978-981-95-0988-1_5

1   Introduction

Large Language Models (LLMs), with their remarkable capabilities in areas such as text generation [13,22], question answering [32,34], and semantic understanding [14,46], are increasingly applied in safety-critical scenarios such as medical applications [19,35,40], autonomous driving [12,39,41], etc. However, LLMs are susceptible to hallucination [17,42,45], which refers to the generation of outputs that appear plausible but are factually incorrect or unsubstantiated by verifiable world knowledge. Hallucination in these contexts poses substantial risks, particularly when LLMs are deployed in high-stakes environments. For instance, inaccurate medical guidance [3,47] from an LLM can lead to severe patient harm and diminish trust in AI-assisted systems.

The occurrence of hallucination in LLMs is attributed to multifaceted factors. These primarily involve data issues, such as flawed pre-training corpora [6,21] and knowledge boundaries [20,29]; training phase limitations, including exposure bias [25,27] and alignment challenges [11,30]; and suboptimal inference-time decoding or reasoning mechanisms [8,16]. Prevailing approaches to mitigate hallucination fall into two main categories. Training-based methods involve strategies such as training with high-quality non-hallucination data [1,15] or introducing new training objectives [22,33], and inference-time methods that aim to modify model behavior post-training, such as specialized decoding [10,18]. However, training-based methods are often constrained by excessive costs and unstable effects [7], which can limit their practical applicability.

Recently, inference-time activation editing [23,37,38,44] offers a compelling avenue to mitigate hallucination without requiring model retraining. This approach leverages the principle that concepts such as truthfulness are linearly represented within LLM activation spaces. Consequently, targeted edits along a "truthful direction" can effectively mitigate hallucinations. Specifically, these methods [23,43] compute editing vectors by distinguishing between truthful and untruthful representations, and apply these edits to particular attention heads, which are recognized to encode vital truth-related information. For example, ITI [23] first identifies these critical attention heads and steers their activations along a pre-calculated directional vector. Recognizing the limitations of employing static steering vectors, subsequent research has explored adaptive activation editing. For instance, ACT [37] acknowledging the shortcomings of a single, fixed steering vector, utilizes diverse steering vectors for different hallucination categories and adjusts the editing intensity. Similarly, SADI [14] enhances adaptability by dynamically constructing steering vectors tailored to the specific semantic context of each input from the input's own activations.

However, the saliency-agnostic head selection mechanism adopted by existing editing methods fails to accommodate the correction demands of diverse knowledge-induced query, thereby hindering the efficient mitigation of hallucinations. Specifically, existing methods typically select the top-K attention heads based on either the highest probe accuracy or the largest mean activation differences for intervention. However, such head selection mechanism fails to accurately capture the actual and query-specific saliency of individual heads that are critical for hallucination mitigation. As a result, editing less hallucination-related heads can significantly undermine intervention effectiveness. Moreover, as different queries activate distinct knowledge pathways and induce varying degrees of hallucination, the common practice in current approaches of applying uniform editing strengths across pre-selected attention heads, often combined with generalized selection criteria, fails to provide the tailored, query-specific adjustments necessary for individual heads, ultimately leading to rigid and suboptimal editing performance.

To this end, we introduce **Q**uery-adaptive **S**aliency-localized Activation **E**diting (QSE), which comprises **G**radient-guided Head **S**aliency **L**ocalization (GSL) and **Q**uery-specific Editing **N**ecessity **E**stimation (QNE), to significantly enhance the hallucination-related localization and contextual adaptability of activation editing. Specifically, GSL first localizes the most hallucination-related head to provide valuable guidance for effective hallucination mitigation. It employs a gradient-guided optimization approach to quantify the saliency of each attention head concerning factual generation, thereby precisely identifying the most critical heads for activation editing. Subsequently, QNE introduces a query-aware estimator to dynamically quantify both the necessity and the optimal magnitude of activation editing for each identified critical head based on the input query's semantics, enabling highly adaptive and context-aware adjustments. Empirical evaluations on the LLaMA-3-8B-Instruct model using the TruthfulQA benchmark demonstrate the substantial efficacy of QSE, notably achieving a True*Info score of 83.3%. We summarize our contributions as follows:

- We propose the Query-adaptive Saliency-localized Activation Editing (QSE) to significantly enhance the hallucination-related localization and contextual adaptability of activation editing.
- We introduce Gradient-guided Head Saliency Localization (GSL) to accurately identify attention heads critical for factual generation based on their learned importance.
- We devise Query-specific Editing Necessity Estimation (QNE) to dynamically modulate per-head editing strength according to input query semantics.
- Comprehensive experimental validation demonstrating significant improvements in model truthfulness achieved by QSE.

2   Related Work

2.1   Inference-Time Methods for Hallucination Mitigation

Inference-time methods for mitigating hallucination in Large Language Models (LLMs) aim to modulate model behavior post-training. One category of strategies targets the output decoding process. For instance, DoLa [10] enhances factuality by contrasting next-token logits from earlier versus later Transformer layers, leveraging differential knowledge localization. Similarly, SH2 [18] influences decoding by prompting the model to exhibit hesitation on self-identified informative input tokens and then applies contrastive decoding to the resulting output probabilities. The other primary category involves direct activation editing. A foundational approach, ITI [23], identifies truth-correlated attention heads using supervised probes and steers their activations along a pre-defined direction associated with truthfulness. Building upon this head-focused principle, TrFr [9] employs multiple orthogonal probes per head to address more complex truth representations. Diverging from an exclusive focus on attention heads, TruthX [44] uses an auto-encoder to disentangle LLM representations into semantic and truthful latent spaces, performing edits within the latter. Another distinct method, SEA [31], offers a training-free spectral projection of activations to align model behavior.

Despite the ingenuity of these varied strategies, existing activation editing methods often utilize generalized criteria for targeting model components and typically lack sufficiently dynamic, query-specific, and per-head granularity in applying editing strength, thereby limiting their precision.

2.2 Adaptive Activation Editing

Recognizing the inflexibility of static activation editing strategies, a distinct line of research has focused on adaptive mechanisms. These approaches tailor the activation editing process to specific contexts or model states, aiming for more nuanced control over LLM behavior. LITO [5], for instance, adaptively determines an optimal editing intensity on a per-query basis. It learns to select the most accurate response from generations produced under varying predefined intensity levels. SADI [38] achieves semantic adaptivity by dynamically constructing its editing direction from the current input's own activations. These activations are subsequently masked by critical model elements and appropriately scaled. ACT [37] implements adaptivity by utilizing diverse, category-specific editing directions for attention heads. It further dynamically modulates editing intensity based on the assessed truthfulness content of current activations. ASTRA [36] adaptively steers activations away from pre-identified undesired feature directions. It uses a projection mechanism between these editing vectors and current calibrated activations to selectively counteract problematic features. DRESS [28] enables adaptive activation editing by first isolating a behavior-relevant subspace. It then dynamically adjusts editing strength for each basis vector within this subspace according to the current activation's alignment with desired attributes.

While these adaptive approaches offer enhanced flexibility, key challenges remain. These include the granular, query-specific identification of crucial attention heads and the dynamic, per-head calibration of editing strength, which are vital for consistently precise truthfulness enhancements.

3 Methodology

This section elaborates on the Query-adaptive Saliency-localized Activation Editing (QSE) framework. We begin by reviewing the foundational principles of head-centric activation editing in Sect. 3.1. The QSE framework functions through the synergistic collaboration of its two core components: Gradient-guided Head Saliency Localization (GSL) and Query-specific Editing Necessity Estimation (QNE). GSL first undertakes the critical task of identifying attention heads most influential for factual generation; we detail its operational mechanism in Sect. 3.2. Building upon GSL's output, QNE leverages the input query's semantic context to dynamically calibrate the editing intensity for each GSL-identified head, with its functionality further described in Sect. 3.3. The synergistic operation of GSL and QNE culminates in the overall adaptive activation editing process of QSE. We outline this complete process in Sect. 3.4, which ensures interventions are both precisely targeted and contextually responsive.

3.1   Preliminary

Head-centric activation editing is predicated on the observation that internal LLM representations generated by informative attention heads encode concepts such as truthfulness. Therefore, by contrasting activations of truthful answers (positive samples) with untruthful answers (negative samples), a directional vector can be derived to steer the model towards more factual outputs, thereby mitigating hallucinations.

Specifically, LLMs typically employ a transformer architecture comprising N_L layers. Each layer l, where $l \in [1, N_L]$, contains N_H attention heads. During the forward pass, an input sequence is processed. The activation $z_{l,k} \in \mathbb{R}^{D_{head}}$ from the k-th attention head, for $k \in [1, N_H]$, in layer l is the focus of our editing. The dimensionality of these head activations is D_{head}. This $z_{l,k}$ represents the output of the attention mechanism within that specific head, prior to its projection back to the residual stream.

The activation editing process typically commences with a dataset $\mathcal{D}$ of query-answer pairs. Each element in $\mathcal{D}$ consists of a query Q, a corresponding truthful answer A^+, and an untruthful answer A^-. When a query Q is processed alongside A^+ or A^-, we extract the respective head activations, denoted $z_{l,k}^+$ and $z_{l,k}^-$. These are typically obtained from the final token position of the answers. A base editing direction $d_{l,k} \in \mathbb{R}^{D_{head}}$ is then computed for each head (l, k) as the mean difference:

$$d_{l,k} = \frac{1}{|\mathcal{D}|} \sum_{(Q, A^+, A^-) \in \mathcal{D}} (z_{l,k}^+ - z_{l,k}^-). \tag{1}$$

Subsequently, the primary activation editing methods select a subset of attention heads, denoted Attn_{acc}, for editing. For each head (l, k), a linear probe $f_{l,k}$ is trained to distinguish its activations $z_{l,k}^+$ from $z_{l,k}^-$. The set of selected heads Attn_{acc} comprises those heads (l, k) whose probe classification accuracy, $\text{Accuracy}(f_{l,k})$, ranks among the top K:

$$\text{Attn}_{acc} = \arg \text{TopK} \{\text{Accuracy}(f_{l,k})\}_{\forall (l,k)} \tag{2}$$

where K is the number of heads to select, and $\text{TopK}(\cdot)$ is an operator that returns the set of K heads with the highest probe accuracies. During inference, the activation $z_{l,k}$ of a target head (l, k) is shifted (Fig. 1):

$$z'_{l,k} = \begin{cases} z_{l,k} + \alpha_{\text{base}} \cdot d_{l,k}, & \text{if } (l, k) \in \text{Attn}_{\text{acc}} \\ z_{l,k}, & \text{otherwise} \end{cases} \tag{3}$$

where $z'_{l,k}$ is the edited activation, and α_{base} is a uniform base editing strength.

However, the reliance on static head selection criteria, such as identifying Attn_{acc} based on overall probe accuracies, fails to identify the attention heads most salient for a specific input query, leading to suboptimal or misdirected edits. Moreover, the application of a uniform base editing strength, α_{base}, across all queries and selected heads neglects the varying necessity and intensity of editing required by different query contexts and individual head sensitivities. In contrast, our GSL in Sect. 3.2 moves beyond such static criteria by employing gradients from a truthfulness-oriented objective $\mathcal{O}_{truth}$ to compute head-specific saliency scores $S_{l,k}$, thereby identifying a more relevant set of heads Attn_{GSL}. Subsequently, our QNE in Sect. 3.3 replaces the use of a uniform α_{base} by utilizing an estimator $\mathcal{P}_{QNE}$ to dynamically predict query-specific strengths $\{\alpha_{l,k}\}$ from query features z_Q, ensuring more nuanced, context-aware adjustments.

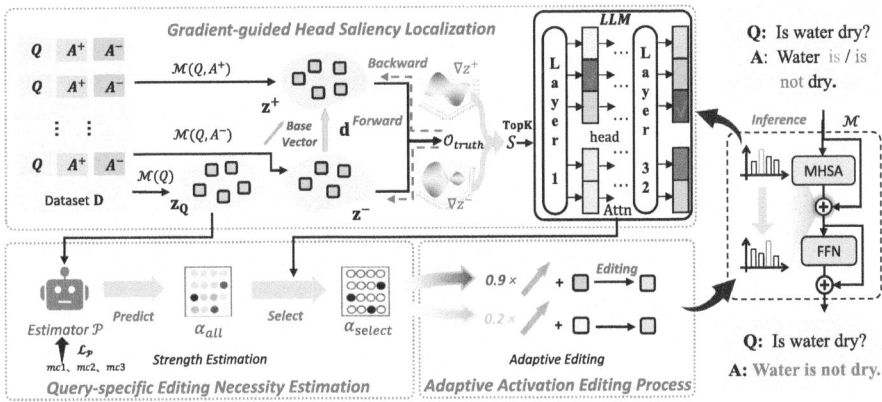

Fig. 1. An overview of the QSE framework. GSL first identifies salient heads and base editing directions. QNE's estimator then informs QSE to dynamically apply query-specific strength to these directions during inference, mitigating hallucinations.

3.2   Gradient-Guided Head Saliency Localization

To localize the valuable attention heads that significantly contribute to factuality, we propose Gradient-guided Head Saliency Localization (GSL) to precisely quantify the saliency of each attention head, thereby providing guidance for

hallucination mitigation. GSL assesses the direct influence of individual attention heads on the model's capacity to produce factual outputs by leveraging
gradient information with respect to a truthfulness-oriented objective function.
Compared with correlation-based probe accuracy or magnitude, the gradients
directly measure how actual changes in a head's activations impact this truthfulness objective, thus offering a more direct and causal measure of its functional
contribution. Consequently, GSL is able to pinpoint heads genuinely crucial for
steering LLMs towards factual consistency.

Specifically, to establish a learning target that directly reflects a head's
impact on truthfulness, GSL defines an objective function $\mathcal{O}_{\text{truth}}$, which measures
the LLM's proficiency in distinguishing truthful answers A^+ from untruthful ones
A^- for a given query Q, typically based on the model's log-likelihood scores for
these answers. By grounding the importance measure in such an objective, GSL
aims to capture a more functionally relevant notion of head contribution. The
saliency score for a specific head (l, k), denoted $S_{l,k}$, is then computed. This
score quantifies the head's impact on $\mathcal{O}_{\text{truth}}$ and is calculated as the average L2
norm of the gradients of $\mathcal{O}_{\text{truth}}$ with respect to the head's activations $z_{l,k}^+$ and
$z_{l,k}^-$:

$$
S_{l,k} = \frac{1}{|\mathcal{D}|} \sum_{(Q,A^+,A^-)\in\mathcal{D}} \left(\left\| \frac{\partial \mathcal{O}_{\text{truth}}(Q, A^+, A^-)}{\partial z_{l,k}^+} \right\|_2 + \left\| \frac{\partial \mathcal{O}_{\text{truth}}(Q, A^+, A^-)}{\partial z_{l,k}^-} \right\|_2 \right)
\tag{4}
$$

A higher saliency score $S_{l,k}$ indicates that head (l, k) exerts a more substantial influence on the model's ability to discriminate truthfulness. This gradient-
derived saliency score, therefore, provides a direct and nuanced measure of each
head's functional importance in factual generation, moving beyond indirect prox-
ies.

Based on these computed saliency scores, GSL selects the subset of attention
heads, Attn_{GSL}, for subsequent activation editing. This set comprises those heads
(l', k') that are identified by a Top-K selection mechanism operating on the
saliency scores of all heads:

$$
\text{Attn}_{\text{GSL}} = \arg \text{TopK}\{S_{l,k}\}_{\forall(l,k)}
\tag{5}
$$

where TopK is an operator that takes the collection of all attention heads paired
with their respective saliency scores $S_{l,k}$, and returns a set containing the K
head indices (l', k') corresponding to the highest saliency scores. K denotes the
number of heads selected. The heads contained in Attn_{GSL} are thus identified by
GSL as the most critical for steering towards truthfulness, forming the precise
targets for the query-adaptive editing applied by the QNE module.

3.3   Query-Specific Editing Necessity Estimation

To further account for the diverse editing necessity for different queries, we
propose Query-specific Editing Necessity Estimation (QNE), which employs a

lightweight estimator $\mathcal{P}_{\text{QNE}}$ to enable more nuanced adjustments. By fully perceiving the semantic information from the query representation z_Q that pertinent to potential hallucinations, the $\mathcal{P}_{\text{QNE}}$ can dynamically estimate query-specific editing necessity and intensity for each head in Attn_{GSL}. Therefore, QNE facilitates the robust edits against likely hallucinations while minimizing alterations for benign inputs, thereby significantly enhancing overall precision and context-awareness in hallucination mitigation.

Specifically, the parameters $\Theta_{\mathcal{P}}$ of the estimator $\mathcal{P}_{\text{QNE}}$ are trained to optimize the LLM's truthfulness discrimination capabilities, typically evaluated on a multiple-choice task such as TruthfulQA. This training objective is vital as it directly aligns the learned mapping from z_Q to editing strengths with the goal of enhancing factual accuracy in the LLM's responses. The optimization specifically aims to maximize a composite score derived from metrics analogous to MC1, MC2, and MC3. These metrics are computed based on the LLM's log-likelihood scores for candidate answers, evaluated as if edited by strengths that $\mathcal{P}_{\text{QNE}}$ (with parameters $\Theta_{\mathcal{P}}$) would hypothetically predict during an auxiliary forward pass in the training loop. Let $Score(A_{\text{cand}}|Q, \Theta_{\mathcal{P}})$ denote the log-likelihood of a candidate answer A_{cand} for query Q, given the editing strengths that would be applied based on $\Theta_{\mathcal{P}}$. Let $\mathcal{A}_Q^+$ be the set of true reference answers, $\mathcal{A}_Q^-$ be the set of false reference answers, and $A_Q^{*+} \in \mathcal{A}_Q^+$ be the single best true answer for query Q. The internal scoring functions are:

$$mc1_Q(\Theta_{\mathcal{P}}) = \sigma \left(\frac{Score(A_Q^{*+}|Q, \Theta_{\mathcal{P}}) - \max_{A_j \in \mathcal{A}_Q^-} Score(A_j|Q, \Theta_{\mathcal{P}})}{\tau} \right) \quad (6)$$

$$mc2_Q(\Theta_{\mathcal{P}}) = \sum_{A_j \in \mathcal{A}_Q^+} \text{softmax}(\{Score(A_i|Q, \Theta_{\mathcal{P}}) \mid A_i \in \mathcal{A}_Q^+ \cup \mathcal{A}_Q^-\})_j \quad (7)$$

$$mc3_Q(\Theta_{\mathcal{P}}) = \text{mean}_{A_i \in \mathcal{A}_Q^+} \left(\sigma \left(\frac{Score(A_i|Q, \Theta_{\mathcal{P}}) - \max_{A_j \in \mathcal{A}_Q^-} Score(A_j|Q, \Theta_{\mathcal{P}})}{\tau} \right) \right) \quad (8)$$

The joint optimization using these metrics $(mc1_Q, mc2_Q, mc3_Q)$ guides $\mathcal{P}_{\text{QNE}}$ to learn editing strengths that collectively enhance the LLM's ability to identify and prioritize truthful information comprehensively and robustly. The loss function $\mathcal{L}_{\mathcal{P}}$ for training $\mathcal{P}_{\text{QNE}}$ is the negative expectation of a weighted sum of these scores over a validation set $\mathcal{D}_{\text{val}}$:

$$\mathcal{L}_{\mathcal{P}}(\Theta_{\mathcal{P}}) = -\mathbb{E}_{Q \sim \mathcal{D}_{\text{val}}}[w_1 \cdot mc1_Q(\Theta_{\mathcal{P}}) + w_2 \cdot mc2_Q(\Theta_{\mathcal{P}}) + w_3 \cdot mc3_Q(\Theta_{\mathcal{P}})] \quad (9)$$

This objective directly tunes $\mathcal{P}_{\text{QNE}}$ to learn the function that maps query representations to editing strengths which markedly enhance the LLM's truthfulness discrimination capabilities.

3.4 Adaptive Activation Editing Process

The QSE framework integrates the outputs of GSL and QNE to perform targeted and adaptive activation editing during LLM inference. The process for a new input query Q is as follows. First, the query's hidden representation z_Q, which encapsulates its semantic information relevant to potential hallucinations, is extracted from a designated layer of the LLM. This representation z_Q is then provided to the trained QNE estimator, $\mathcal{P}_{\mathrm{QNE}}$. As detailed in Sect. 3.3, $\mathcal{P}_{\mathrm{QNE}}$ is trained to map z_Q to query-specific editing strengths. During inference, it yields the strengths $\{\alpha_{l,k}\}$ for each head (l,k) within the set of salient heads:

$$\{\alpha_{l,k}\}_{(l,k)\in \mathrm{Attn}_{\mathrm{GSL}}} = \mathcal{P}_{\mathrm{QNE}}(h_Q; \Theta_{\mathcal{P}}) \tag{10}$$

Subsequently, for each attention head (l,k) in the LLM, its current activation $z_{l,k}$ is edited only if it belongs to the set $\mathrm{Attn}_{\mathrm{GSL}}$. The base editing direction $d_{l,k}$ (computed as per Eq. (1)) is retrieved. The edited activation $z'_{l,k}$ is then computed using the dynamically predicted query-specific strength $\alpha_{l,k}$ corresponding to that head:

$$z'_{l,k} = \begin{cases} z_{l,k} + \alpha_{l,k} \cdot d_{l,k}, & \text{if } (l,k) \in \mathrm{Attn}_{\mathrm{GSL}} \\ z_{l,k}, & \text{otherwise} \end{cases} \tag{11}$$

These edited head activations $z'_{l,k}$ are then utilized by the LLM for its subsequent computations and eventual token generation. This adaptive process targets only salient heads identified by GSL and applies query-specific strengths determined by QNE. Such an approach allows QSE to make precise and contextually appropriate adjustments, thereby steering the LLM towards more truthful outputs.

4   Experiments

To rigorously evaluate the effectiveness of our proposed QSE framework in mitigating Large Language Model hallucinations, we conducted comprehensive experiments on standard benchmarks.

4.1   Experimental Setup

Benchmarks and Metrics. Our primary evaluation centered on the TruthfulQA benchmark [26], a standard dataset designed to test an LLM's propensity to generate common falsehoods. TruthfulQA comprises two main evaluation tracks: open-ended generation and multiple-choice question answering.

For the open-ended generation task, model performance was evaluated using: True (%), indicating the percentage of truthful responses; Info (%), representing the percentage of informative responses; and True*Info (%), the product of True and Info, serving as the principal composite metric. Evaluations of truthfulness and informativeness were conducted using an LLaMA-2-7B model fine-tuned by Allen AI [2], a common substitute for the original GPT-3 based judges.

For the multiple-choice task, we employed three accuracy metrics: MC1 (%), MC2 (%), and MC3 (%). MC1 measures the accuracy where the model assigns the highest probability to the single best answer. MC2 evaluates if the normalized probability sum for all correct answers exceeds that of incorrect ones. MC3 determines if all correct answers are ranked higher than all incorrect ones.

Baseline and Comparative Methods. All experiments utilized the LLaMA-3-8B-Instruct model as the foundational LLM. The QSE framework was benchmarked against Baseline and a suite of contemporary truthfulness enhancement techniques. These include training-based methods such as SFT [24] and prompting strategies like FSP [4]. We also compared QSE with several inference-time editing approaches. Among these are decoding strategies like DoLa [10] and SH2 [18]. Additionally, we considered activation engineering methods including TruthX [44], LITO [5], SEA [31] and ITI [23]. Furthermore, we included TrFr [9], which uses orthogonal probes, as comparative methods based on the results reported in Table 1.

Implementation Details. Our QSE framework was implemented on the LLaMA-3-8B-Instruct model. For training the QSE components and for validation, we primarily utilized the TruthfulQA dataset. We adhered to the data splitting protocol from prior studies [23, 24], employing a 2-fold cross-validation scheme. Specifically, half of the TruthfulQA questions, comprising 408 samples, were allocated for the training and validation phases; this set was further randomly divided in a 3:1 ratio for these respective purposes. The remaining half of TruthfulQA was reserved for testing. For the GSL module, the number of salient heads selected for the set Attn_{GSL}, denoted as K in Eq. (5), was set to 96. The estimator within the QNE module, $\mathcal{P}_{\text{QNE}}$, is an MLP with a hidden layer dimensionality of 256. For training $\mathcal{P}_{\text{QNE}}$, we employed the AdamW optimizer. The learning rate was set to 1×10^{-4}, and the batch size was 1. Unless otherwise specified, the base editing directions $d_{l,k}$, as defined in Eq. (1), were computed using the Mass Mean Shift approach. The temperature parameter τ utilized in Eqs. (6) and (8) was set to 1. The weights w_1, w_2, w_3 in the QNE loss function (Eq. (9)) were each set to 1.0.

4.2 Experimental Results

The empirical evaluations conducted on the TruthfulQA benchmark, utilizing LLaMA-3-8B-Instruct as the base model, underscore the substantial efficacy of our proposed QSE framework in enhancing LLM truthfulness. As detailed in Table 1, QSE not only significantly outperforms the baseline model but also demonstrates clear advantages over both general activation editing techniques and existing adaptive activation editing methodologies across open-ended generation and multiple-choice tasks.

Performance on Open-Ended Generation: In the open-ended generation task, QSE achieved a True*Info score of 83.3%. This marks a profound improvement of 21.3 absolute points over the Baseline (62.0%) and also surpasses general activation editing methods like ITI (69.0%) and TruthX (64.9%) by a significant margin. Notably, this superior True*Info score results from QSE achieving a high True score of 92.3% while maintaining excellent informativeness at 90.2%. When compared against existing adaptive methods such as SADI which achieved

Table 1. Comparison of QSE with SOTA methods on the TruthfulQA benchmark, implemented on LLaMA-3-8B-Instruct. The best results are in **bold**. Each numerical result is reported as the average over multiple runs.

Methods	Open-ended Generation			Multiple-Choice		
	True*Info (↑)	True (↑)	Info (↑)	MC1 (↑)	MC2 (↑)	MC3 (↑)
Baseline	62.0	69.5	89.2	39.1	58.6	29.5
SFT	69.5	71.2	97.6	39.3	56.6	30.6
FSP	66.4	67.4	98.4	41.4	59.2	29.6
Decoding-based Methods						
DoLa	71.8	73.2	**98.0**	40.6	59.3	31.8
SH2	62.3	71.9	86.7	32.2	56.5	31.9
Editing-based Methods						
TruthX	64.9	71.8	90.3	42.8	61.2	32.2
LITO	52.6	84.6	62.3	40.4	58.3	29.6
SEA	72.3	81.8	88.4	42.8	61.1	33.3
ITI	69.0	79.8	86.4	41.1	61.1	31.7
TrFr	73.2	82.0	89.3	41.5	60.0	30.8
ACT	72.6	79.6	91.2	42.2	62.1	32.1
ASTRA	63.7	71.2	89.5	40.5	59.1	30.2
SADI	72.5	80.1	90.5	43.1	62.6	32.4
Ours	**83.3**	**92.3**	90.2	**49.6**	**67.8**	**38.8**

a True*Info score of 72.5%, QSE still exhibits a clear lead. This enhanced performance is primarily attributed to QSE's unique dual-module mechanism. GSL enables a more informed initial targeting of attention heads critical to truthfulness through its gradient-guided learning of head saliency. Subsequently, QNE refines the activation editing by dynamically adjusting the editing strength for these selected heads based on the specific input query. This approach contrasts with methods that often apply uniform activation editing or adaptive techniques lacking such fine-grained, per-head, query-specific strength modulation.

Performance on Multiple-Choice Tasks: QSE's advantages are also prominent in the multiple-choice tasks (Table 1). It attained an MC1 score of 49.0%, substantially higher than the Baseline (39.1%). QSE also outperformed general activation editing methods like ITI (41.1%) and TruthX (42.8%), as well as adaptive methods like LITO (40.4%). This considerable improvement over the Baseline in MC1 indicates a significantly enhanced capability of the QSE-edited model to correctly identify and assign the highest probability to the best answer. Consistent gains were also observed for MC2 (67.8%) and MC3 (38.8%) metrics. The superior performance in these discriminative tasks further highlights the precision of QSE. By identifying critical heads based on their learned saliency via GSL, and then tailoring the editing intensity for these heads according to the query via QNE, QSE facilitates more accurate internal representation and evaluation of factual correctness. This leads to more reliable answer selection.

In summary, the experimental results robustly validate QSE's effectiveness. Its ability to learn head-specific saliency via GSL and then dynamically adapt editing strength per-query via QNE allows it to address the limitations of both static and less granular adaptive activation editing methods. This leads to substantial improvements in LLM truthfulness without compromising informativeness, showcasing the significant contribution of QSE's head-adaptive activation editing strategy.

5 Analysis

To further investigate the efficacy and inner workings of our proposed Query-adaptive Saliency-localized Activation Editing framework, this section presents a series of detailed analyses. We first conduct an ablation study to assess the distinct contributions of QSE's core modules, GSL and QNE. Additionally, we delve into an analysis of attention head behavior under QSE's adaptive activation editing paradigm.

5.1 Ablation Study

To assess the individual contributions of QSE's core components and the influence of key hyperparameters, we conducted targeted ablation studies. These analyses separately investigated the impact of the GSL module and the QNE module. We also examined the effect of varying the number of selected heads, K, for activation editing.

Module Contribution Analysis. To validate GSL and QNE's necessity, we evaluated QSE variants with these modules selectively deactivated. The results, presented in Table 2, reveal that deactivating either module leads to a notable decline in truthfulness metrics compared to the full QSE framework. For instance, omitting GSL forces reliance on a default or simpler head selec-

Table 2. The ablation study of two modules in QSE.

GSL	QNE	True*Info	True	MC1
Baseline		62.0	69.5	39.1
✓		80.2	87.9	46.8
	✓	70.1	78.6	40.1
✓	✓	**83.3**	**92.3**	**49.6**

tion method. This causes the True*Info score to drop from 83.3% for the full QSE to 70.1%. Similarly, omitting QNE reverts the process to using a uniform editing strength across queries. This reduces the True*Info score to 80.2%. These findings clearly demonstrate that GSL's precise, saliency-based head identification and QNE's dynamic, query-adaptive strength modulation are individually crucial. Their synergy is vital for QSE's superior performance in mitigating hallucinations, as each addresses a distinct limitation of prior methods.

Impact of Edited Head Count. To investigate the influence of the number of edited heads, we varied K_{select} from 16 up to 96, targeting the top saliency heads identified by the GSL module. Our findings, illustrated in Fig. 2, show a consistent positive correlation between K_{select} and performance improvement on key metrics. For instance, the MC1 score progres-

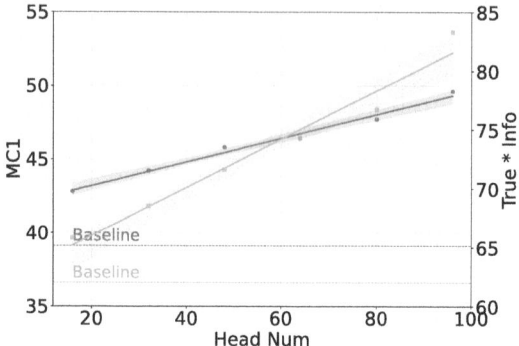

Fig. 2. MC1 and True*Info scores achieved by QSE with different numbers of edited heads.

sively increased from 42.8% ($K_{select} = 16$) to 45.8% ($K_{select} = 48$), and reached a peak of 49.6% at $K_{select} = 96$. A similar trend was observed for the True*Info score, which rose from 65.8% ($K_{select} = 16$) to 83.3% at $K_{select} = 96$ in this specific parameter sweep. This trend underscores the efficacy of the GSL module in accurately ranking head importance and confirms that intervening on a sufficiently large set of these high-saliency heads is vital for maximizing truthfulness enhancements. However, it is also important to note that while increasing the number of edited heads generally leads to better truthfulness performance, it concurrently results in a corresponding increase in the computational overhead during inference.

5.2   Attention Head Analysis

To gain deeper insights into how QSE interacts with the internal mechanisms of the LLM, particularly its attention heads, we analyze two key aspects. First, we examine the distribution of head saliency scores as identified by GSL. Second, we investigate the adaptive nature of the editing strengths applied by QNE. These analyses help elucidate the underpinnings of QSE's effectiveness.

Distribution of Learned Head Saliency. To understand which attention heads are predominantly identified by GSL as critical for truthfulness, we visualized the distribution of the learned head saliency scores, $S_{l,k}$. This visualization, presented in Fig. 3, reveals distinct head saliency patterns across all layers and head indices. The heatmap demonstrates a non-uniform distribution. Notably higher saliency scores are concentrated in specific layers, frequently the middle to upper layers of the LLM. Certain head indices within these layers consistently exhibit greater saliency. This observation aligns with findings suggesting that different layers and heads in LLMs specialize in processing different types of information. Middle-to-upper layers are often implicated in more complex semantic processing and reasoning relevant to factual accuracy. The GSL module, through its gradient-guided analysis, effectively captures these architectural nuances. It pinpoints heads that are most influential in the pathway to generating truthful or, conversely, untruthful statements. Such targeted identification by GSL allows QSE to focus its activation editing on these pivotal junctures. This targeted approach significantly contributes to its enhanced precision and efficiency compared to less discriminate head selection strategies.

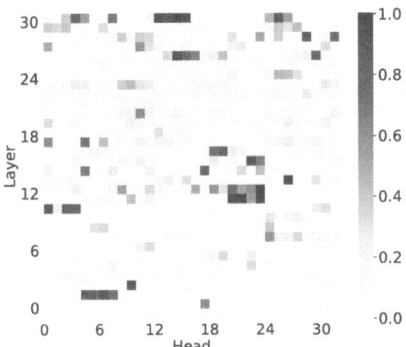

Fig. 3. Distribution of learned head saliency scores across all layers and attention heads.

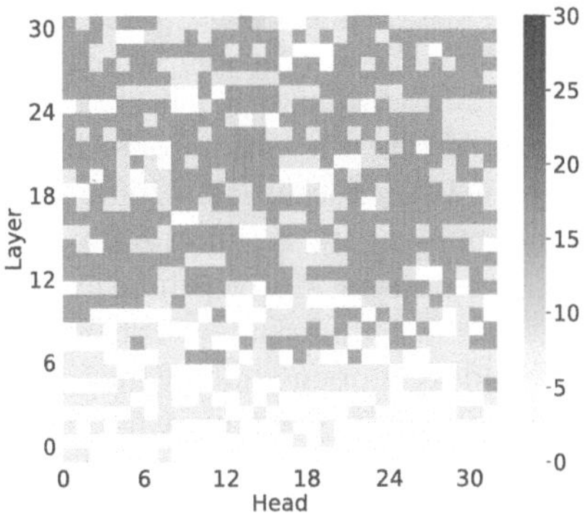

Fig. 4. Distribution of average query-adaptive editing strengths across all layers and attention heads.

Adaptive Editing Strength per Head. To illustrate the dynamic and query-specific nature of the activation editing applied by QSE, we analyzed the average predicted editing strengths, $\alpha_{l,k}$. These strengths are determined by the QNE module for the selected salient heads in Attn_{GSL}. Figure 4 presents a heatmap visualizing these average strengths across different attention heads and layers. The visualization clearly shows substantial variability in the average editing strengths applied to different heads, both within the same layer and across layers. This heterogeneity indicates that the QNE module does not apply a uniform correction. Instead, QNE learns to assign distinct editing magnitudes to individual heads based on the input query's characteristics. For instance, heads identified by GSL as highly salient might receive stronger or weaker editing depending on the specific query context. This reflects a nuanced understanding by QNE of when and how intensely to modulate a particular head's activity. This capacity for query-adaptive, per-head strength modulation is a core tenet of QSE. It enables fine-grained adjustments that correct potential hallucinations effectively while minimizing unnecessary perturbations to the LLM's representations, thereby preserving overall generation quality and informativeness.

6   Limitation and Future Work

While our proposed Query-adaptive Saliency-localized Activation Editing framework demonstrates significant advancements in enhancing Large Language

Model truthfulness, we acknowledge several limitations and avenues for future research.

The efficacy of the gradient-guided head saliency scores computed by GSL is inherently linked to the formulation and representativeness of the objective function $\mathcal{O}_{\text{truth}}$ used for gradient computation. Different objective formulations might yield varied saliency landscapes. Furthermore, training the QNE module's estimator, $\mathcal{P}_{\text{QNE}}$, relies on the availability and quality of query-answer datasets. These datasets must be suitable for deriving the internal MC1, MC2, and MC3 scores, despite the estimator's direct optimization for downstream truthfulness metrics. Its generalization to vastly different query types or domains not well-represented in its training data also warrants further investigation. Additionally, our current study primarily focuses on truthfulness enhancement as evaluated on benchmarks like TruthfulQA. Extending the QSE framework to effectively address open-ended generation tasks, where discrete answer scoring is less straightforward, presents a notable challenge. Concurrently managing multiple behavioral dimensions, such as harmlessness and helpfulness alongside truthfulness, also poses complex but important future research directions.

Future work will proceed along several directions. First, we plan to explore more sophisticated gradient-based metrics and alternative learning paradigms for discerning head saliency. This aims for an even more robust and nuanced identification of critical heads for activation editing. Second, developing techniques to reduce data dependency for training the QNE estimator, $\mathcal{P}_{\text{QNE}}$, would enhance the practical utility of QSE. Such techniques might include semi-supervised learning or the design of more data-efficient objective functions.

7   Conclusion

This paper introduced Query-adaptive Saliency-localized Activation Editing, a novel inference-time activation editing framework. QSE is designed to mitigate hallucinations in Large Language Models (LLMs) by enhancing the precision and adaptability of internal activation editing. QSE achieves its adaptability through the synergy of its core modules, GSL and QNE. GSL employs a gradient-guided mechanism to ascertain the saliency of individual attention heads for factual generation. Building on this, QNE dynamically predicts per-head editing strengths tailored to the specific semantics of input queries. Extensive empirical evaluations on the LLaMA-3-8B-Instruct model using the TruthfulQA benchmark demonstrate that QSE significantly improves model truthfulness. These improvements are evident across both open-ended generation and multiple-choice tasks, where QSE outperforms existing static and adaptive activation editing techniques. By enabling more targeted and contextually-aware modifications of LLM activations, QSE offers a promising advancement. This contributes towards the development of more reliable and trustworthy AI systems.

References

1. Abbas, A., Tirumala, K., Simig, D., Ganguli, S., Morcos, A.S.: SemDeDup: data-efficient learning at web-scale through semantic deduplication. arXiv preprint arXiv:2303.09540 (2023)

2. Allen AI: Finetuning llama-2 to judge the truthfulness and informativeness for truthfulqa (2024). https://huggingface.co/allenai/truthfulqa-truth-judge-llama2-7B

3. Alber, D.A., et al.: Medical large language models are vulnerable to data-poisoning attacks. Nat. Med., 1–9 (2025)

4. Bai, Y., et al.: Training a helpful and harmless assistant with reinforcement learning from human feedback. arXiv preprint arXiv:2204.05862 (2022)

5. Bayat, F.F., Liu, X., Jagadish, H., Wang, L.: Enhanced language model truthfulness with learnable intervention and uncertainty expression. In: Findings of the Association for Computational Linguistics ACL 2024, pp. 12388–12400 (2024)

6. Bender, E.M., Gebru, T., McMillan-Major, A., Shmitchell, S.: On the dangers of stochastic parrots: Can language models be too big? In: Proceedings of the 2021 ACM Conference on Fairness, Accountability, and Transparency, pp. 610–623 (2021)

7. Casper, S., et al.: Open problems and fundamental limitations of reinforcement learning from human feedback. Trans. Mach. Learn. Res. (2023)

8. Chen, X., Li, M., Gao, X., Zhang, X.: Towards improving faithfulness in abstractive summarization. Adv. Neural. Inf. Process. Syst. **35**, 24516–24528 (2022)

9. Chen, Z., et al.: Truth forest: toward multi-scale truthfulness in large language models through intervention without tuning. In: Proceedings of the AAAI Conference on Artificial Intelligence, vol. 38, pp. 20967–20974 (2024)

10. Chuang, Y.S., Xie, Y., Luo, H., Kim, Y., Glass, J.R., He, P.: DoLa: decoding by contrasting layers improves factuality in large language models. In: The Twelfth International Conference on Learning Representations (2023)

11. Cotra, A.: Why AI alignment could be hard with modern deep learning. Cold Takes (2021)

12. Cui, C., et al.: A survey on multimodal large language models for autonomous driving. In: Proceedings of the IEEE/CVF Winter Conference on Applications of Computer Vision, pp. 958–979 (2024)

13. Dathathri, S., et al.: Plug and play language models: a simple approach to controlled text generation. arXiv preprint arXiv:1912.02164 (2019)

14. De Curtò, J., De Zarza, I., Calafate, C.T.: Semantic scene understanding with large language models on unmanned aerial vehicles. Drones **7**(2), 114 (2023)

15. Gunasekar, S., et al.: Textbooks are all you need. arXiv preprint arXiv:2306.11644 (2023)

16. Holtzman, A., Buys, J., Du, L., Forbes, M., Choi, Y.: The curious case of neural text degeneration. arXiv preprint arXiv:1904.09751 (2019)

17. Huang, L., et al.: A survey on hallucination in large language models: principles, taxonomy, challenges, and open questions. ACM Trans. Inf. Syst. **43**(2), 1–55 (2025)

18. Kai, J., Zhang, T., Hu, H., Lin, Z.: SH2: self-highlighted hesitation helps you decode more truthfully. In: Findings of the Association for Computational Linguistics: EMNLP 2024, pp. 4514–4530 (2024)

19. Karabacak, M., Margetis, K.: Embracing large language models for medical applications: opportunities and challenges. Cureus **15**(5) (2023)

20. Katz, D.M., Bommarito, M.J., Gao, S., Arredondo, P.: GPT-4 passes the bar exam. Phil. Trans. R. Soc. A **382**(2270), 20230254 (2024)
21. Lee, K., et al.: Deduplicating training data makes language models better. arXiv preprint arXiv:2107.06499 (2021)
22. Lee, N., et al.: Factuality enhanced language models for open-ended text generation. Adv. Neural. Inf. Process. Syst. **35**, 34586–34599 (2022)
23. Li, K., Patel, O., Viégas, F., Pfister, H., Wattenberg, M.: Inference-time intervention: eliciting truthful answers from a language model. Adv. Neural Inf. Process. Syst. **36** (2024)
24. Li, Y., Wei, Z., Jiang, H., Gong, C.: DESTEIN: navigating detoxification of language models via universal steering pairs and head-wise activation fusion. arXiv preprint arXiv:2404.10464 (2024)
25. Li, Z., Zhang, S., Zhao, H., Yang, Y., Yang, D.: BatGPT: a bidirectional autoregressive talker from generative pre-trained transformer. arXiv preprint arXiv:2307.00360 (2023)
26. Lin, S., Hilton, J., Evans, O.: TruthfulQA: measuring how models mimic human falsehoods. In: Proceedings of the 60th Annual Meeting of the Association for Computational Linguistics (Volume 1: Long Papers), pp. 3214–3252 (2022)
27. Liu, B., Ash, J., Goel, S., Krishnamurthy, A., Zhang, C.: Exposing attention glitches with flip-flop language modeling. Adv. Neural. Inf. Process. Syst. **36**, 25549–25583 (2023)
28. Ma, X., et al.: Dressing up LLM: efficient stylized question-answering via style subspace editing. arXiv preprint arXiv:2501.14371 (2025)
29. Onoe, Y., Zhang, M.J., Choi, E., Durrett, G.: Entity cloze by date: what LMs know about unseen entities. arXiv preprint arXiv:2205.02832 (2022)
30. Perez, E., et al.: Discovering language model behaviors with model-written evaluations. In: Findings of the Association for Computational Linguistics: ACL 2023, pp. 13387–13434 (2023)
31. Qiu, Y., Zhao, Z., Ziser, Y., Korhonen, A., Ponti, E.M., Cohen, S.B.: Spectral editing of activations for large language model alignment. Adv. Neural Inf. Process. Syst. (2024)
32. Shao, Z., Yu, Z., Wang, M., Yu, J.: Prompting large language models with answer heuristics for knowledge-based visual question answering. In: Proceedings of the IEEE/CVF Conference on Computer Vision and Pattern Recognition, pp. 14974–14983 (2023)
33. Shi, W., et al.: In-context pretraining: Language modeling beyond document boundaries. arXiv preprint arXiv:2310.10638 (2023)
34. Singhal, K., et al.: Toward expert-level medical question answering with large language models. Nature Med., 1–8 (2025)
35. Thirunavukarasu, A.J., Ting, D.S.J., Elangovan, K., Gutierrez, L., Tan, T.F., Ting, D.S.W.: Large language models in medicine. Nat. Med. **29**(8), 1930–1940 (2023)
36. Wang, H., Wang, G., Zhang, H.: Steering away from harm: an adaptive approach to defending vision language model against jailbreaks. arXiv preprint arXiv:2411.16721 (2024)
37. Wang, T., et al.: Adaptive activation steering: a tuning-free LLM truthfulness improvement method for diverse hallucinations categories. In: Proceedings of the ACM on Web Conference 2025, pp. 2562–2578 (2025)
38. Wang, W., Yang, J., Peng, W.: Semantics-adaptive activation intervention for LLMs via dynamic steering vectors. arXiv preprint arXiv:2410.12299 (2024)
39. Wen, L., et al.: DiLu: a knowledge-driven approach to autonomous driving with large language models. arXiv preprint arXiv:2309.16292 (2023)

40. Yang, R., et al.: Large language models in health care: development, applications, and challenges. Health Care Sci. **2**(4), 255–263 (2023)
41. Yang, Z., Jia, X., Li, H., Yan, J.: LLM4Drive: a survey of large language models for autonomous driving. arXiv preprint arXiv:2311.01043 (2023)
42. Ye, H., Liu, T., Zhang, A., Hua, W., Jia, W.: Cognitive mirage: a review of hallucinations in large language models. arXiv preprint arXiv:2309.06794 (2023)
43. Yin, F., Ye, X., Durrett, G.: LoFiT: localized fine-tuning on LLM representations. Adv. Neural. Inf. Process. Syst. **37**, 9474–9506 (2024)
44. Zhang, S., Yu, T., Feng, Y.: TruthX: alleviating hallucinations by editing large language models in truthful space. In: Proceedings of the 62nd Annual Meeting of the Association for Computational Linguistics (Volume 1: Long Papers), pp. 8908–8949 (2024)
45. Zhang, Y., et al.: Siren's song in the AI ocean: a survey on hallucination in large language models. arXiv preprint arXiv:2309.01219 (2023)
46. Zhang, Z., et al.: Semantics-aware BERT for language understanding. In: Proceedings of the AAAI Conference on Artificial Intelligence, vol. 34, pp. 9628–9635 (2020)
47. Zhou, H., et al.: A survey of large language models in medicine: progress, application, and challenge. arXiv preprint arXiv:2311.05112 (2023)

Meta-learning with Heterogeneous Tasks

Zhaofeng Si[1] , Shu Hu[2] , Kaiyi Ji[1] , and Siwei Lyu[1] ($\boxtimes$)

[1] State University of New York at Buffalo, Buffalo, NY 14260, USA
{zhaofeng,kaiyiji,siweilyu}@buffalo.edu
[2] Purdue University, West Lafayette, IN 47907, USA
hu968@purdue.edu

Abstract. Meta-learning is a general approach to equip machine learning models with the ability to handle few-shot scenarios when dealing with many tasks. Most existing meta-learning methods work based on the assumption that all tasks are of equal importance. However, real-world applications often present heterogeneous tasks characterized by varying difficulty levels, noise in training samples, or being distinctively different from most other tasks. In this paper, we introduce a novel meta-learning method designed to effectively manage such heterogeneous tasks by employing rank-based task-level learning objectives, _Heterogeneous Tasks Robust Meta-learning_ (HeTRoM). HeTRoM is proficient in handling heterogeneous tasks, and it prevents easy tasks from overwhelming the meta-learner. The approach allows for an efficient iterative optimization algorithm based on bi-level optimization, which is then improved by integrating statistical guidance. Our experimental results demonstrate that our method provides flexibility, enabling users to adapt to diverse task settings and enhancing the meta-learner's overall performance.

Keywords: Meta-learning · Few-shot learning · Robustness · Rank-based loss

1 Introduction

Deep neural network models trained with supervised learning have made significant progress in computer vision, in many cases surpassing human abilities. Conventional supervised learning needs a large number of training samples, but in real-world situations such as image classification [27], models must tackle multiple tasks that arise during the learning process, each with only a few samples available. This scenario is often referred to as _few-shot_ learning. Meta-learning, or learning to learn, has been proposed as a solution to few-shot learning. In particular, optimization-based meta-learning methods introduce a meta-model [11,17], whose parameters can be fine-tuned for individual tasks using a few gradient descent update steps. In this way, the meta-model can use the knowledge gained from previous training tasks to enable the learning model to adapt rapidly to new tasks during meta-testing.

Y. Ma et al. (Eds.): IJCAI 2025, CCIS 2640, pp. 74–94, 2025.
https://doi.org/10.1007/978-981-95-0988-1_6

Current meta-learning methods often implicitly assume that all tasks are more or less equal in importance. However, in real-world applications, tasks are often heterogeneous in the level of learning difficulty, data quality, and domain consistency. We use image retrieval as an example to demonstrate the situation, Fig. 1. Specifically, we can identify three types of tasks: (a) Harder tasks, which are tasks with ambiguous contexts (row 1: wolf vs. husky) are more challenging for the model; (b) Noisy tasks: tasks with corrupted labels (row 3, first sample mislabeled as "boxer" and the query mislabeled as "lion") are more prone to errors; and (c) Outlier tasks that are considerably different from most training tasks (row 3 birds vs. row 1-2 airplanes). We can often differentiate these tasks using the task-level losses on actual multi-task meta-learning tasks, as shown in the bottom row of Fig. 1. It shows a histogram that outlines the distribution of task-level losses by conducting fast adaptation using a MAML [11] trained meta-model on clean tasks from Mini-ImageNet, noisy (tasks derived from Mini-ImageNet but with labels randomly flipped), and outlier tasks with classes from Tiered-ImageNet that do not overlap with those in Mini-ImageNet tasks.

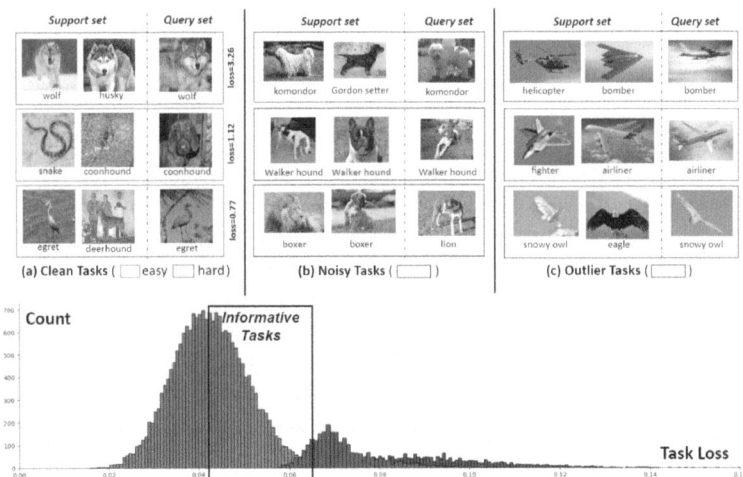

Fig. 1. *Heterogeneous tasks in meta-learning for image retrieval on real-world datasets (Mini-ImageNet and Tiered-ImageNet).* (**Top**) *Three different types of tasks based on their difficulty.* (**Bottom**) *Histograms of losses can be used to differentiate three types of tasks. The displayed histogram is derived from real-world datasets, the details are provided in texts.*

The heterogeneity introduces challenges for the meta-training step. Several works have concentrated on improving the effectiveness of meta-learning algorithms at the task level to address challenges posed by varying task difficulties [10,25] and tasks with noise [21,24]. However, limited works studied the effects of outlier tasks (also known as Out-of-Distribution tasks in [21]) in meta-learning and the method of handling multiple heterogeneous tasks concurrently. A substantial body of literature has addressed the development of robust meta-learning algorithms to mitigate the impact of corrupted labels [21,24,29]. Nevertheless, these works predominantly concentrate on sample-level noise, with limited attention directed to examining robustness at task level.

In this paper, we introduce the _Heterogeneous Tasks Robust Meta-learning_ (HeTRoM) method to address the problem posed by the heterogeneous tasks in meta-learning. The core component of HeTRoM is a new rank-based task-level loss that enables the dynamical selection of tasks in the meta-training step. Specifically, the HeTRoM loss controls the cut-off range in the ranked individual task losses, which reduces the influence of tasks whose losses are either too small (easy tasks) or too large (noisy tasks and outlier tasks). The hyper-parameters determining the range can be obtained based on a log-normal model of the distribution of the individual task losses. We show that the HeTRoM objective can be formulated as a bi-level optimization problem and efficiently solved with a stochastic gradient-based algorithm to update the meta-model. Experimental evaluations on two benchmark datasets underscore the effectiveness and robustness of HeTRoM.

2   Related Works

As the most representative optimization-based approach, Model Agnostic Meta-learning (MAML) [11] learns an initialization such that a gradient descent procedure starting from the initial model can achieve fast adaptation. In the following years, a large number of works on various MAML variants have been proposed [12,13].

Another group of meta-regularization approaches has been proposed for improving the bias for a regularized empirical risk minimization problem [1,5]. In addition, there is a common embedding-based framework in few-shot learning [6,22]. The goal of this framework is to learn a shared embedding model that can be used for all tasks. Task-specific parameters are then learned for each task based on the embedded features.

There exists a body of literature dedicated to investigating the robustness of optimization-based meta-learning. Some of these studies concentrate on addressing noise at the sample level within few-shot tasks. [21,24]. For example, Eigen-Reptile [9] is a method that derives the updating direction of the meta-model by calculating the main direction of fast adaptation, which mitigates the impact of corrupted data within tasks.

There are also several works focusing on task-level robustness [10,21,23,30]. [30] propose to use an adaptive task scheduler (ATS) to decide the next tasks to be used while training to avoid the effect of tasks with corrupted labels. Nest-edMAML [21] uses a weighted sum of instances or tasks in meta-training for handling Out-of-Distribution (OOD) tasks or noisy data, where the weights are updated through a nested bi-level optimization approach. While this re-weighting approach can reduce the effect of corrupted samples and tasks, it cannot eliminate them entirely. [23] focus on improving the robustness of metric-based meta-learning, which is not within the scope of this paper, as we concentrate on optimization-based meta-learning.

3   Background

Meta-learning is commonly formulated as an optimization problem [17]. Let $\{\mathcal{T}_i\}_{i=1}^{n}$ be a collection of n tasks. Each task $\mathcal{T}_i$ has a specific loss function $\mathcal{L}(\phi, w_i; \xi)$ in sample ξ, where ϕ are the parameters of the shared embedding model for all tasks and w_i are the task-specific parameters. We aim to learn the optimal parameters ϕ that work well for all tasks, and each task uses the optimized ϕ to adapt its specific parameters w_i minimizing $\mathcal{L}(\phi, w_i; \xi)$. For instance, if the learning task is solved with a series of deep neural network models, w_i may correspond to the parameters of the final layer within a neural network, while the parameters of the preceding layers are represented by ϕ. For simplicity, we denote $\mathbf{w} = (w_1, ..., w_n)$ as the collection of task-specific parameters. The objective function of meta-learning is given by

$$\min_{\phi} L_{\mathcal{D}}(\phi, \mathbf{w}^*) = \frac{1}{n} \sum_{i=1}^{n} \ell_i(\phi)$$
$$\text{s.t.} \quad \mathbf{w}^* = \arg\min_{\mathbf{w}} \mathcal{L}_{\mathcal{S}}(\phi, \mathbf{w}) := \frac{1}{n} \sum_{i=1}^{n} \mathcal{L}_{\mathcal{S}_i}(\phi, w_i), \tag{1}$$

where $\ell_i(\phi) = \frac{1}{|\mathcal{D}_i|} \sum_{\xi \in \mathcal{D}_i} \mathcal{L}(\phi, w_i^*; \xi)$ and $\mathcal{L}_{\mathcal{S}_i}(\phi, w_i) = \frac{1}{|\mathcal{S}_i|} \sum_{\xi \in \mathcal{S}_i} \mathcal{L}(\phi, w_i; \xi)$. This is a bi-level optimization problem [8, 19], which can be solved in two stages. In the inner learning stage, the base learner of each task $\mathcal{T}_i$ searches the minimizer w_i^* of its loss over a support set $\mathcal{S}_i$. In the outer learning stage, the meta-learner evaluates the minimizers w_i^* on a held-out query set $\mathcal{D}_i$ and optimizes ϕ across all tasks.

As we mentioned in the Introduction, most existing meta-learning methods assume all tasks have equal influence on the meta-model. However, in real-world applications, tasks are often heterogeneous in terms of learning difficulty, data quality, and consistency. In the following experiments, we show the influence of heterogeneous tasks on meta-learning.

Influences of the Majority Tasks. *Setting*: We train two meta-models, one using all tasks in each mini-batch of size 16 for updating meta-model parameters (traditional learning), and the other using only the top-8 tasks with the highest individual task losses (hard task mining). We evaluate both models by fast adaptation to all training tasks and testing them on the same test dataset. The distributions of task query losses and the test accuracy are presented in Fig. 2(a). *Analysis*: Using hard task mining during meta-training leads to lower task losses compared to using all tasks, indicating that easy tasks dominate training. Moreover, training with "hard" tasks improves the generalization of the meta-model, as demonstrated by the increased testing accuracy.

Sensitive to Noisy Tasks. *Setting*: We generate two training sets: clean and noisy, where 60% of the tasks contain samples with flipped labels. Then, we

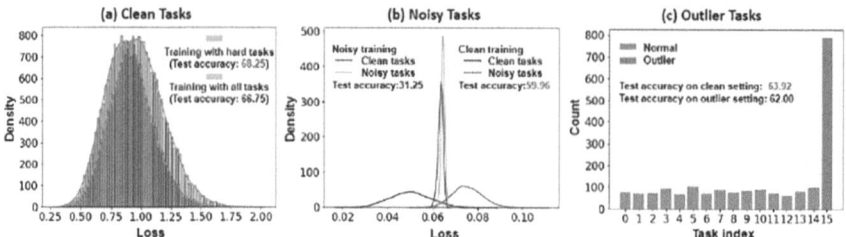

Fig. 2. *Behavior analysis of meta-learning. (a) The loss distributions of training tasks with models trained with all tasks and hard tasks, respectively. (b) The loss distributions of clean and noisy tasks with models trained with a clean dataset ("Clean training") and a noisy dataset ("Noisy training"), respectively. (c) The frequency of each task index with the highest loss throughout the training process, where the outlier task is assigned index 15 in each iteration. "Test accuracy" (%) is obtained by testing on a separate clean test set.* (Color figure online)

trained two meta-models on these two datasets separately and conducted fast adaptation on all clean tasks and noisy tasks respectively in the noisy training set. The distributions of training task losses together with test accuracy are shown in Fig. 2(b). *Analysis*: When trained with a noisy dataset, there is a significant overlap between the task loss distributions of noisy and clean tasks (yellow and green lines, respectively). However, when trained with a clean dataset, there is a clear separation between the two distributions, indicating that the meta-model trained with the noisy dataset cannot effectively distinguish between noisy and clean tasks. Additionally, training with noisy datasets results in higher clean task losses than clean training (blue line), while clean training results in higher noisy task losses than noisy training (red line). These illustrate the susceptibility of meta-learning to noisy tasks and how it can harm the meta-model's generalization ability, as indicated by the decline in test accuracy.

Vulnerability to the Outlier Tasks. *Setting*: Two categories with multiple classes from the Tiered-ImageNet [26] dataset were randomly chosen as the target and outlier categories. Two meta-models were trained, the first one using 16 tasks randomly sampled from the target category as clean tasks in each iteration of the mini-batch, and the second one using 15 tasks from the target category (indexed 0 to 14) and 1 task from the outlier category (indexed as 15) in each iteration of the mini-batch. For the second one, we track the task with the highest loss in each iteration by recording its task index, and the frequency of each task index being the highest throughout the training process is plotted. The test accuracy of both models is also reported in Fig. 2(c). *Analysis*: The task from the outlier category frequently has the highest loss in each batch. Meta-learning is also vulnerable to outlier tasks, as evidenced by the lower test accuracy compared to the model trained without outliers.

4 Method

HeTRoM is based on a simple observation that hard, noisy, or outlier tasks are usually associated with large task-level losses during meta-training, while most tasks have relatively small losses throughout the training process. A similar observation can be made at the sample level in [20, 29]. As illustrated in Sect. 3, our findings also show that this phenomenon exists widely at the task level. Let $\mathbb{L} := \{\ell_1(\phi), ..., \ell_n(\phi)\}$ be a set of all task losses on their corresponding query dataset. We also denote $\ell_{[i]}(\phi)$ as the i-th largest individual task loss after sorting the elements in set $\mathbb{L}$ (ties can be broken in any consistent way). With two integers k and m, $0 \leq m < k \leq n$, the HeTRoM loss is given by:

$$\min_{\phi} \mathcal{L}_{\mathcal{D}}(\phi, \mathbf{w}^*) = \frac{1}{k-m} \sum_{i=m+1}^{k} \ell_{[i]}(\phi)$$

$$\text{s.t.} \quad \mathbf{w}^* = \arg\min_{\mathbf{w}} \mathcal{L}_{\mathcal{S}}(\phi, \mathbf{w}) := \frac{1}{n} \sum_{i=1}^{n} \mathcal{L}_{\mathcal{S}_i}(\phi, w_i). \tag{2}$$

The HeTRoM loss is a generalization of ranked ranges in supervised learning [16]. It is equivalent to a dynamic task selection method that filters imperfect tasks based on their individual task losses. Specifically, it selects tasks with small losses, which are more likely to be normal tasks, and drops the top-m tasks with large. It also excludes tasks with small losses (*i.e.*, top-k to top-n losses), which are the majority of tasks that are normal and potentially redundant. Conventional meta-learning is a special case of HeTRoM with $k = n$ and $m = 0$.

4.1 Algorithm

The ranking operation in HeTRoM can be eliminated using the following result.

Theorem 1. *Denote* $[a]_+ = \max\{0, a\}$ *as the hinge function. Equation (2) is equivalent to*

$$\min_{\phi, \lambda} \max_{\hat{\lambda}} \hat{\mathcal{L}}_{\mathcal{D}}(\phi, \mathbf{w}^*) = \frac{1}{k-m} \sum_{i=1}^{n} \hat{\mathcal{L}}(\phi, w_i^*, \lambda, \hat{\lambda})$$

$$:= \left[[\ell_i(\phi) - \lambda]_+ - [\ell_i(\phi) - \hat{\lambda}]_+ + \frac{k}{n}\lambda - \frac{m}{n}\hat{\lambda} \right]$$

$$\text{s.t.} \quad \mathbf{w}^* = \arg\min_{\mathbf{w}} \mathcal{L}_{\mathcal{S}}(\phi, \mathbf{w}) := \frac{1}{n} \sum_{i=1}^{n} \mathcal{L}_{\mathcal{S}_i}(\phi, w_i), \tag{3}$$

If the optimal of ϕ *and* $\mathbf{w}^*$ *are achieved,* $(\ell_{[k]}(\phi), \ell_{[m]}(\phi))$ *can be the optimum solutions of* $(\lambda, \hat{\lambda})$.

The proof of Theorem 1 can be found in Appendix B. A bi-level optimization procedure [18] can be used to solve (3). Specifically, in each iteration j, we sample a batch of N tasks $\{\mathcal{T}_i\}_{i=1}^{N}$, and then each sampled task $\mathcal{T}_i$ conducts D steps of inner-loop updates as

$$w_{i,j}^t = w_{i,j}^{t-1} - \alpha \nabla_w \mathcal{L}_{\mathcal{S}_i}(\phi_j, w_{i,j}^{t-1}), \quad t = 1, ..., D \tag{4}$$

where α is the inner-loop step size, $w_{i,j}^t$ is the task $\mathcal{T}_i$'s parameter at iteration j in step t, and $\nabla_w \mathcal{L}_{\mathcal{S}_i}$ is the gradient of $\mathcal{L}_{\mathcal{S}_i}$ with respect to (w.r.t.) w. Then, we need to update λ and $\hat{\lambda}$ together with the meta-model to keep track of the ranked range of task losses on the query set from top-m to top-k. To optimize the minimax problem in upper-level objective of Eq. (3), we use single gradient steps to update λ and $\hat{\lambda}$ simultaneously using their (sub)gradients given by

$$
\begin{aligned}
\partial_\lambda \hat{\mathcal{L}}(\phi_j, w_{i,j}^D, \lambda_j, \hat{\lambda}_j) &= \frac{k}{N} - \mathbb{I}_{[\ell_i(\phi_j, w_{i,j}^D) > \lambda_j]}, \\
\partial_{\hat{\lambda}} \hat{\mathcal{L}}(\phi_j, w_{i,j}^D, \lambda_j, \hat{\lambda}_j) &= \mathbb{I}_{[\ell_i(\phi_j, w_{i,j}^D) > \hat{\lambda}_j]} - \frac{m}{N}
\end{aligned}
\tag{5}
$$

where $\ell_i(\phi_j, w_{i,j}^D)$ is the task $\mathcal{T}_i$'s loss on its query set using iteration j's meta-model parameters ϕ_j and task parameter $w_{i,j}^D$, and $\mathbb{I}_{[A]}$ is an indicator function, which returns 1 if the condition A is true. Finally, we adopt the stable iterative differentiation (ITD)-based approach [14] to efficiently approximate the gradient of $\hat{\mathcal{L}}_{\mathcal{D}}(\phi, \mathbf{w}^*)$ w.r.t. ϕ (which refers to as the hyper-gradient because of the implicit dependence of $\mathbf{w}^*$ on ϕ). In specific, we first evaluate the upper-level function over the inner-loop output $w_{i,j}^D$, and compute the hyper-gradient estimate as

$$
\text{Hg}(\phi_j) := \frac{1}{k-m} \frac{\partial \sum_{i=1}^N \hat{\mathcal{L}}(\phi_j, w_{i,j}^D, \lambda_j, \hat{\lambda}_j)}{\partial \phi_j}
\tag{6}
$$

by conducting back-propagation over inner-loop trajectory w.r.t. ϕ_j. Following [11,19], the first-order hyper-gradient approximation $\frac{1}{k-m} \sum_{i=1}^N \partial_\phi \hat{\mathcal{L}}(\phi_j, w_{i,j}^D, \lambda_j, \hat{\lambda}_j)$ is employed to avoid the computation cost introduced by computing implicit derivative $\frac{\partial w_{i,j}^D}{\partial \phi_i}$ that contains second-order model information with a large model size. We show the entire optimization procedure of our method in Algorithm 1.

In practice, we follow the results obtained from Theorem 1 and initialize λ and $\hat{\lambda}$ through adaptation on a batch of randomly sampled tasks. Then, we sort the loss on the corresponding query sets and assign the k-th loss and m-th loss values to λ and $\hat{\lambda}$, respectively.

4.2 Statistic Guided Learning

The values of hyper-parameters k and m are important to the overall performance of the model trained by Algorithm 1. We describe three practical measures to find their values.

Warm-Up. Based on Theorem 1, we can determine how many task losses exceed the values of λ and $\hat{\lambda}$ by analyzing the values of k and m. Specifically, we use the conventional meta-learning approach to "warm up" the model based on Eq. (1) for a few iterations by training on the training data, which may contain noisy or outlier tasks. This procedure is similar to Algorithm 1. In particular, we have no λ and $\hat{\lambda}$ that need to be updated but we update meta-parameter ϕ using $\phi_{j+1} = \phi_j - \beta\overline{\text{Hg}}(\phi_j)$, where $\overline{\text{Hg}}(\phi_j) := \frac{1}{N} \frac{\partial \sum_{i=1}^N \ell_i(\phi_j, w_{i,j}^D)}{\partial \phi_j}$.

Algorithm 1. Optimization procedure of HeTRoM

1: **Input:** Total iteration number J; inner-loop iteration number D; batch size N; stepsizes α, β, γ, initial meta-parameter ϕ_0; initial task-specific parameter w_0; hyper-parameters k, m; $\lambda_0, \hat{\lambda}_0$.

2: **for** $j = 0, 1, 2, ..., J$ **do**

3:     Sample a batch of tasks $\{\mathcal{T}_i\}_{i=1}^N$

4:     **for** each task $\mathcal{T}_i$ in $\{\mathcal{T}_i\}_{i=1}^N$ **do**

5:         Initialize task-specific parameter as $w_{i,j}^0 = w_0$

6:         **for** $t = 1, 2, ..., D$ **do**

7:             Update $w_{i,j}^t = w_{i,j}^{t-1} - \alpha \nabla_w \mathcal{L}_{\mathcal{S}_i}(\phi_j, w_{i,j}^{t-1})$

8:         **end for**

9:     **end for**

10:     $\begin{pmatrix} \lambda_{j+1} \\ \hat{\lambda}_{j+1} \end{pmatrix} \leftarrow \begin{pmatrix} \lambda_j \\ \hat{\lambda}_j \end{pmatrix} - \frac{\gamma}{k-m} \begin{pmatrix} \sum_{i=1}^N \partial_\lambda \hat{\mathcal{L}}(\phi_j, w_{i,j}^D, \lambda_j, \hat{\lambda}_j) \\ -\sum_{i=1}^N \partial_{\hat{\lambda}} \hat{\mathcal{L}}(\phi_j, w_{i,j}^D, \lambda_j, \hat{\lambda}_j) \end{pmatrix}$ based on equation (5)

11:     Update meta-parameter $\phi_{j+1} = \phi_j - \beta \mathrm{Hg}(\phi_j)$ based on equation (6)

12: **end for**

Identification. After the "warm-up", we fast adapt the meta-model with parameters ϕ_{j+1} to all training tasks $\{\mathcal{T}_i\}_{i=1}^n$ using D steps of the inner-loop for each of them. Then we obtain the new trained task-specific parameters $\{\tilde{w}_i^D\}_{i=1}^n$. Next, we calculate all training task losses on their corresponding query sets so that we get $\{\ell_i(\phi_{j+1}, \tilde{w}_i^D)\}_{i=1}^n$. A histogram based on $\{\ell_i(\phi_{j+1}, \tilde{w}_i^D)\}_{i=1}^n$ is used to describe the training behaviors of all tasks. We can use different distributions to fit the histogram. However, in practice, the log-normal distribution can be a better fit. In addition, it is also popular to use log-normal distribution to fit training loss as [15] in machine learning. Therefore, we take a log of all task losses as $\overline{\mathbb{L}} := \{\log \ell_i(\phi_{j+1}, \tilde{w}_i^D)\}_{i=1}^n$ and use their mean $\mathrm{Mean}(\overline{\mathbb{L}})$ and standard deviation $\mathrm{Std}(\overline{\mathbb{L}})$ as the descriptor for the statistic of task losses. In order to identify potential easy tasks and noisy or outlier tasks, we must define the thresholds that differentiate them from others. Specifically, we define the thresholds as:

$$\lambda^* = \exp(\mathrm{Mean}(\overline{\mathbb{L}}) - \rho_1 \mathrm{Std}(\overline{\mathbb{L}})), \tag{7}$$

$$\hat{\lambda}^* = \exp(\mathrm{Mean}(\overline{\mathbb{L}}) + \rho_2 \mathrm{Std}(\overline{\mathbb{L}})), \tag{8}$$

where ρ_1 and ρ_2 are hyper-parameters. In practice, we find that setting them within the range $[1, 3]$ yields good results.

Distillation. After we get the thresholds, we continue to train the meta-model obtained from the warm-up procedure. Thus, the meta-model parameters should be ϕ_{j+1}. Then, we use the thresholds to select tasks to update the meta-model parameters dynamically. In particular, tasks with their losses fall into $[\lambda^*, \hat{\lambda}^*]$ are regarded as useful tasks that benefit learning. The learning procedure is also similar to Algorithm 1. However, in the upper-level loop, we only need to use the following gradient to update meta-model parameters ϕ:

$$\widetilde{\mathrm{Hg}}(\phi_{j+1}) := \frac{1}{|\mathcal{S}_\ell|} \frac{\partial \sum_{\ell_i \in \mathcal{S}_\ell} \ell_i}{\partial \phi_{j+1}} \tag{9}$$

Table 1. *Test accuracy (%) on Mini-ImageNet and Tiered-ImageNet. For the clean setting, we report the average accuracy with 95% confidence intervals. The best results are shown in **Bold**. Gray indicates our methods outperform baseline methods in the same setting.*

Dataset	Model	Method	Clean		Noisy (5-ways 5-shots)			Outlier (3-ways 5-shots)		
			5-ways 5-shots	5-ways 1-shot	Fixed	1-step	2-step	ratio = 0	ratio = 0.1	ratio = 0.3
Mini-ImageNet	CNN4	MAML [11]	63.11 ± 0.91	48.70 ± 1.75	60.25	55.20	30.30	78.05	77.44	77.29
		ATS [30]	61.60 ± 0.69	50.75 ± 0.73	59.89	60.09	59.50	71.09	70.80	69.84
		Eigen-Reptile [9]	69.85 ± 0.85	53.25 ± 0.45	63.47	61.78	49.63	69.56	69.50	67.95
		HeTRoM (Ours)	**70.45 ± 0.71**	59.75 ± 1.28	**68.75**	67.30	61.45	**81.25**	78.96	**80.63**
		sg-HeTRoM (Ours)	70.08 ± 1.07	**60.50 ± 2.03**	67.58	**68.00**	**67.67**	79.86	**79.17**	78.12
	ResNet12	MAML [11]	69.54 ± 0.38	58.60 ± 0.42	64.50	58.25	44.75	79.30	77.78	77.29
		HeTRoM (Ours)	**75.35 ± 0.82**	**60.50 ± 2.32**	**71.25**	64.50	54.33	**87.35**	**86.21**	**80.77**
		sg-HeTRoM (Ours)	71.87 ± 1.93	59.38 ± 1.84	70.13	**67.25**	**59.75**	86.18	85.50	80.01
Tiered-ImageNet	CNN4	MAML [11]	66.25 ± 0.19	50.98 ± 0.26	34.50	31.25	31.50	63.92	62.83	62.00
		ATS[30]	60.44 ± 0.76	43.25 ± 0.84	58.72	57.12	49.06	48.69	48.64	48.02
		Eigen-Reptile [9]	57.36 ± 0.19	42.24 ± 0.18	56.05	53.37	52.16	59.01	57.17	55.41
		HeTRoM (Ours)	**71.25 ± 0.57**	58.50 ± 1.07	**68.75**	66.00	67.75	67.07	66.75	**65.50**
		sg-HeTRoM (Ours)	70.80 ± 1.74	**58.75 ± 0.98**	68.67	**69.33**	66.83	**69.17**	**69.37**	64.17
	ResNet12	MAML [11]	71.24 ± 0.43	58.58 ± 0.49	67.00	68.25	54.63	65.83	61.33	51.67
		HeTRoM (Ours)	**72.25 ± 1.29**	**61.25 ± 0.82**	69.17	64.88	67.75	66.25	**65.00**	58.75
		sg-HeTRoM (Ours)	71.25 ± 0.74	58.75 ± 1.64	**69.33**	**70.25**	**68.25**	**67.08**	64.17	**59.16**

where $\mathcal{S}_\ell = \mathbb{I}_{[\lambda^* \leq \ell_i(\phi_{j+1}, w_{i,j}^D) \leq \hat{\lambda}^*]}$ is the set containing task losses that fall between λ^* and $\hat{\lambda}^*$.

The illustrative figure of this algorithm Fig. 4 and the corresponding Algorithm 2 are available in Appendix C. We call this approach statistic-guided HeTRoM (sg-HeTRoM). The significance of the thresholds can be more clearly understood as follows: λ^* and $\hat{\lambda}^*$ can be regarded as the optimal values of λ and $\hat{\lambda}$. In each iteration of the distillation process, we eliminate the impact of noisy or outlier tasks on the meta-parameter updates by using the upper bound $\hat{\lambda}^*$ of the task losses. Additionally, we enhance the meta-model's generalization ability by potentially removing overly simple tasks based on the lower bound λ^*, which is akin to a hard task mining strategy.

5   Experiments

5.1   Experimental Settings

Datasets. We conduct our experiments in a few-shot classification setting, where two widely recognized datasets are used for few-shot classification: Mini-ImageNet [28], and Tiered-ImageNet [26]. Both are subsets of the ILSVRC-12 dataset [27]. Mini-ImageNet comprises 100 classes, with each class containing 600 images of 84×84 pixel dimensions. The dataset is divided into three subsets: 64 classes for training, 16 for validation, and 20 for testing. On the other hand, Tiered-ImageNet is a more substantial dataset, containing 779,165 images annotated across 608 classes. These classes are further grouped into 34 categories. This dataset is split at the category level, with 20 categories used for training, 6 for validation, and 8 for testing.

Baselines. We showcase the effectiveness of our approach by contrasting it with recent optimization-based meta-learning methods **aiming at enhancing the robustness to heterogeneous tasks** of meta-training, such as ATS [30] and Eigen-Reptile [9], Consequently, we do not directly compare our method with strategies that solely aim at boosting the meta-model's performance [3,4,10]. NestedMAML [21] is not included in our comparison, as the original paper neither provides source code nor records performance on prevalent datasets like Mini-ImageNet and Tiered-ImageNet. Moreover, we examine the impact of our HeTRoM loss on the issues previously mentioned in the context of representation-based meta-learning methods. Importantly, our investigation is conducted without relying on training tracks, as is the case in [2]. As a result, we benchmark our method against the MAML approach, which is widely acknowledged as a prevalent method in meta-learning. We do not compare with the most recent optimization-based meta-learning methods because our approach is versatile and can readily incorporate these methods. The detailed information on implementation can be found in Appendix D.

5.2   Results

Performance on Clean Tasks. We report the overall results (accuracy on the testing set) based on clean tasks in Table 1. Specifically, we use the HeTRoM loss and the statistically driven method to filter out non-informative and easy tasks during training dynamically. We achieve a significant improvement in performance over the MAML method, with a $[1.9\%, 11.8\%]$ margin. In addition, our method outperforms two robust meta-learning methods ATS and Eigen-Reptile on both datasets and two different few-shot settings (*i.e.*, 5-ways 5-shots and 5-ways 1-shot).

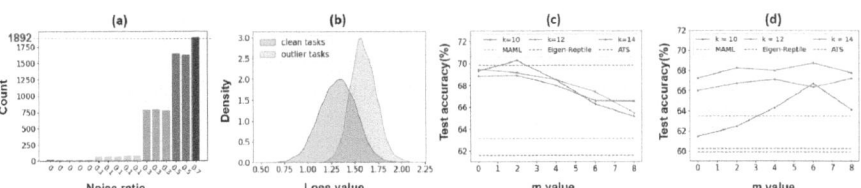

Fig. 3. (a) Frequency of the noise ratio for each task in a mini-batch being excluded by $\hat{\lambda}$ during meta-training. (b) Loss distribution of clean and outlier tasks when conducting fast adaptation with a trained meta-model. (c) Test accuracy with varying k and m in clean task setting. (d) Test accuracy with varying k and m in fixed noisy task setting.

Performance on Noisy Tasks. Table 1 also shows the results of all methods on noisy task settings of 5-ways 5-shots classification. It is clear that all methods experience a significant decrease in performance in the presence of noise compared to the clean task scenario, but our methods still perform better than the others. As we move from Mini-ImageNet to Tiered-ImageNet, the variety of tasks increases and MAML loses its generalization ability. This may be attributed to the fact that the number of easy tasks has increased significantly. On the other hand, ATS and Eigen-Reptile perform relatively well but still show a decreasing trend. In contrast, our methods consistently maintain stable or even better performance, indicating their robustness to the diversity of tasks in the presence of noisy tasks.

We then analyze in detail how HeTRoM works to enhance the robustness of MAML in a noisy task scenario under the *fixed* setting. We can keep track of the noise ratio for each task within a mini-batch since each task is indexed and fixed with one noisy ratio. This means that we can record the frequency of the noise ratio for each task excluded by $\hat{\lambda}$ (*i.e.*, identified as a noisy task) during meta-training. Figure 3(a) displays this information. Our HeTRoM method can identify noisy tasks during meta-training, as demonstrated by the higher frequency of exclusion of tasks with a higher noise ratio. Clean tasks are rarely excluded, providing valuable information for training. Note that we do not require our method to exclude noisy tasks precisely in each iteration, which is not practical for an efficient method.

Performance on Outlier Tasks. Table 1 presents a comparison of our methods with other approaches on the outlier tasks setting of 3-ways 5-shots. We can observe that the performance of MAML shows a decreasing trend when increasing the ratio of outlier tasks. ATS and Eigen-Reptile fail to achieve competitive performance with MAML on both datasets, while our method demonstrates superior performance compared to MAML by a substantial margin. This can be attributed to the effective filtering of outlier tasks and too-easy tasks. To provide additional validation for the efficacy of removing outlier tasks during meta-training using our approach, we randomly sample 10,000 tasks from the Mini-ImageNet dataset (considered as clean) and the Tiered-ImageNet dataset (considered as outlier) respectively. A meta-model trained by our method performs fast adaptation on all these tasks, and the distribution of task losses is depicted in Fig. 3(b). The results exhibit a clear trend wherein the task loss of outlier tasks tends to be larger than that of clean tasks, justifying the use of loss as a criterion for identifying outlier tasks.

Table 2. Test accuracy (%) on Mini-ImageNet when incorporated with MetaOptNet [22]. **Bold** indicates best results for each setting.

Architecture	Setting	Clean	Noisy		
			Fixed	1-step	2-step
CNN4	w/o HeTRoM	69.61 ± 0.38	67.36 ± 0.38	67.06 ± 0.39	63.35 ± 0.36
	w/HeTRoM	$\mathbf{69.91 \pm 0.37}$	$\mathbf{67.65 \pm 0.39}$	$\mathbf{69.23 \pm 0.38}$	$\mathbf{65.23 \pm 0.38}$
ResNet12	w/o HeTRoM	78.63 ± 0.46	76.76 ± 0.40	75.18 ± 0.40	72.40 ± 0.38
	w/HeTRoM	$\mathbf{78.97 \pm 0.34}$	$\mathbf{78.61 \pm 0.35}$	$\mathbf{78.45 \pm 0.35}$	$\mathbf{75.95 \pm 0.36}$

Performance of sg-HeTRoM Method. From Table 1, we can also observe the performance comparison between models trained with HeTRoM and sg-HeTRoM. The results indicate no significant performance gap between two methods. Moreover, both methods outperform all baselines, highlighting the effectiveness of leveraging statistical information to identify informative tasks and filter out noisy and outlier tasks. Furthermore, using a large model ResNet12 leads to improved performance in most settings. Nevertheless, our method still outperforms MAML.

Incorporating with SOTA Meta-learning Method. To ascertain the efficacy of our approach in conjunction with other state-of-the-art (SOTA) methodologies, we integrated our method with MetaOptNet [22] in both clean task and noisy task settings using Mini-ImageNet dataset. The results are shown in Table 2. It is evident from the results that the performance of MetaOptNet experiences a significant decline when confronted with noisy tasks. In contrast, our method demonstrates a mitigating effect on this performance degradation, particularly noteworthy in experiments with larger model (ResNet 12 in Table 2).

Table 3. Test accuracy on MiniImageNet compared with TIM.

Model	Method	Clean		60% noisy samples	
		5w5s	5w1s	5w5s	5w1s
ResNet18	TIM w/o HeTRoM	79.11 ± 0.14	59.53 ± 0.21	73.56 ± 0.21	$\mathbf{57.21 \pm 0.21}$
	TIM w HeTRoM	$\mathbf{80.16 \pm 0.14}$	$\mathbf{61.03 \pm 0.20}$	$\mathbf{74.48 \pm 0.16}$	57.20 ± 0.20
WideResNet28-10	TIM w/o HeTRoM	$\mathbf{82.81 \pm 0.13}$	62.59 ± 0.20	74.02 ± 0.16	57.37 ± 0.21
	TIM w HeTRoM	82.68 ± 0.14	$\mathbf{63.35 \pm 0.20}$	$\mathbf{74.28 \pm 0.16}$	$\mathbf{57.49 \pm 0.21}$

Incorporating with SOTA Few-Shot Learning Method. In addition to SOTA meta-learning techniques, our sg-HeTRoM method is readily adaptable to other few-shot learning approaches with various training paradigms. We apply our sg-HeTRoM method at the sample level to integrate with TIM [7], with the results presented in Table 3. To be specific, we apply the same model settings as in [7], and use the clean and 2-step random noisy setting as in Sect. 5.1. In implementing our sg-HeTRoM approach at the sample level, we continue to adhere to the Warm-up, Identification, and Distillation framework specified in Sect. 4.2, with the adaptation that the Identification phase is executed at the sample level. The results demonstrate that incorporating our method allows TIM to attain comparable or even superior performance across different model architectures in both clean and noisy environments, underscoring the effectiveness of our approach when combined with SOTA methods.

Meta-learning with Extreme Few Tasks. In real-world scenarios, users may face challenges accessing a substantial number of tasks for training the meta-model. We conducted experiments under the constraint of a limited task set (specifically, 100 tasks in this setting) during training, and the outcomes are presented in Table 4. The results reveal a noteworthy performance decline for MAML compared to the experiments detailed in Table 1, rendering it impractical in such constrained settings. In contrast, our method demonstrates appropriate performance, with particularly noteworthy efficacy in noisy settings.

Table 4. *Test accuracy (%) on Mini-ImageNet and Tiered-ImageNet using CNN4 architecture with 100 training tasks. The best results are shown in* **Bold** *for each setting.* Gray *indicates our methods outperform baseline methods in the same setting.*

Dataset	Method	Clean		Noisy (5-ways 5-shots)			Outlier (3-ways 5-shots)		
		5w5s	5w1s	Fixed	1-step	2-step	ratio = 0	ratio = 0.1	ratio = 0.3
	MAML	48.72	42.25	41.00	41.85	38.95	65.83	65.33	64.58
Mini-ImageNet	HeTRoM (Ours)	**59.90**	46.25	**59.45**	**59.15**	**58.25**	75.42	72.50	71.25
	sg-HeTRoM (Ours)	58.94	**46.50**	57.60	57.25	56.75	**79.41**	**78.75**	**77.08**
	MAML	56.10	46.25	52.85	52.60	47.85	59.41	58.50	57.40
Tiered-ImageNet	HeTRoM (Ours)	**62.75**	**49.50**	**62.10**	**61.65**	**61.65**	59.75	59.50	59.42
	sg-HeTRoM (Ours)	61.75	47.25	60.89	61.25	60.10	**64.79**	**62.58**	**62.17**

Time Complexity Analysis. The time complexity of our method is comparable to MAML [11], requiring only the maintenance of two extra scalar variables thus ensuring efficiency relative to other SOTA methods, which typically require additional computations (*e.g.*, weight calculation in [30]). In Table 5 we display the average iteration time of our method and baseline methods, showing that our method can achieve better efficiency.

5.3 Discussion

k **and** m **in Clean Setting.** We analyze the effect on training with a variety of k and m in the clean task setting. As common settings, we conduct meta-training on the original Mini-ImageNet dataset with k chosen from $\{10, 12, 14\}$, and m chosen from $\{0, 2, 4, 6, 8\}$. The results are shown in Fig. 3(c). The experimental results suggest two key findings: firstly, the best performance for each k is achieved with a small m value (*e.g.*, $m = 2$), and performance diminishes with increasing k, indicating that easy tasks mainly influence meta-learning. Secondly, increasing m for a fixed k results in performance declines, underscoring the beneficial effect of incorporating hard tasks in training.

Table 5. *Average iteration time of our method and baseline methods.*

Methods	MAML	ATS	Eigen-Reptile	Ours
Time	1.22 s	2.68 s	3.59 s	1.36 s

k **and** m **in Noisy Setting.** We study the impact of hyper-parameters in the noisy task settings by conducting experiments in *fixed* noisy setting with a variety of k and m on Mini-ImageNet. The results are shown in Fig. 3(d). As m increases, there is a clear trend of improved performance, which can be attributed to the exclusion of more corrupted tasks from training, given the fact that the majority of tasks in a mini-batch are affected by varying levels of noise in *fixed* noise setting. Additionally, a larger value of k generally leads to higher performance, as it includes more clean tasks during training. Moreover, there is a clear range of k and m that our method outperforms the compared methods.

ρ_1 **and** ρ_2 **in Outlier Setting.** We conducted experiments on the Tiered-ImageNet dataset with the outlier setting (ratio $= 0.1$) using sg-HeTRoM to study the impact of hyper-parameters ρ_1 and ρ_2 in Eq. (7), which determine the thresholds for identifying easy tasks and outlier tasks. The results are presented in Table 6. We observe that sg-HeTRoM is not overly sensitive to ρ_1 and ρ_2. If we set $\rho_2 = \infty$, changing the value of ρ_1 does not seem to affect the performance significantly. This could be because the outlier tasks significantly impact meta-learning more than the easy tasks. However, when we set $\rho_1 = \infty$, and ρ_2 varies, there is a visible fluctuation in the performance. This implies that ρ_2 is useful in mitigating the effect of outlier tasks.

Table 6. *Effect of ρ_1 and ρ_2 on sg-HeTRoM in outlier task setting. $\rho_1 = \infty$ means no lower bound for task selection, and $\rho_2 = \infty$ means no upper bound for task selection.*

	$\rho_1 = 1$	$\rho_1 = 2$	$\rho_1 = 3$	$\rho_1 = \infty$
$\rho_2 = 1$	67.50	69.17	67.29	68.54
$\rho_2 = 2$	68.33	68.75	**69.37**	67.61
$\rho_2 = 3$	67.08	65.83	67.50	67.92
$\rho_2 = \infty$	67.08	66.77	67.67	67.37

6 Conclusion

Meta-learning provides a solution to handle few-shot scenarios when dealing with many tasks. Existing optimization-based meta-learning methods operate on the premise that all tasks are equally important. However, this assumption is often challenged in real-world scenarios where tasks are inherently heterogeneous, characterized by varying levels of difficulty, noisy training samples, or a significant divergence from the majority of tasks. In response to these challenges, we have developed a novel meta-learning approach that proficiently manages these heterogeneous tasks using rank-based task-level learning objectives. A key advantage of our method is its ability to handle outlier tasks effectively, and it prevents an over-representation of similar tasks in influencing the meta-learner. Our method also employs an efficient iterative optimization algorithm grounded in bi-level optimization. Our experimental evaluations demonstrate the flexibility of our approach, as it enables users to adapt to a variety of task settings and improves the overall performance of the meta-learner.

We plan to enhance our method in several ways in the future. Firstly, we aim to expand it to online meta-learning, where the model adjusts and learns in a real-time, sequential manner with the incoming data flow. Secondly, we intend to investigate its theoretical guarantees, including optimization error and generalization bound. Thirdly, we will test the effectiveness of our methods for other applications where meta-learning is helpful, such as object detection, speech recognition, and NLP.

Appendix

A   Settings for the Experiments in Section 3

Influence of Majority Tasks. In this setting, we use CNN4 as a backbone and train 2 meta-models on the Mini-ImageNet dataset with a mini-batch of size 16. During the meta-training phase, the two meta-models are updated iteratively using the entire mini-batch of tasks (traditional learning) and tasks with the top-8 highest losses (hard task mining) in each iteration. After 2000 iterations of training, we perform fast adaptation on all the training tasks and examine the distribution of task losses on the query set. Additionally, the test accuracy of both meta-models on the same test dataset is presented in Fig. 2(a).

Sensitive to Noisy Tasks. In this setting, we utilize two distinct datasets: clean dataset and noisy dataset. The clean dataset consists of 20,000 tasks generated from the original Mini-ImageNet dataset, while the noisy dataset involves corrupting 60% of the tasks by randomly flipping all labels within each task. We train two separate meta-models on these datasets and subsequently perform fast adaptation on all tasks within the noisy dataset. Next, we separate the task losses of clean tasks (40% of all tasks) and noisy tasks (60% of all tasks) and show their respective distribution in Fig. 2(b). Note that the test accuracy shown in the figure corresponds to the performance evaluation conducted on the same clean test dataset.

Vulnerable to Outlier Task. As described in Sect. 5.1, the Tiered-ImageNet dataset is divided into categories, each containing a series of classes. In this setting, we choose two categories as target category and outlier category respectively. Two meta-models were trained, the first one using 16 tasks randomly sampled from the target category as clean tasks in each iteration of the mini-batch, and the second one using 15 tasks from the target category (indexed from 0 to 14) and 1 task from the outlier category (indexed as 15) in each iteration of the mini-batch. During training, we monitor the behavior of meta-training involving outlier tasks by recording the index of tasks with the highest task loss within the mini-batch in each iteration. Then we plot the frequency of each task index being the highest throughout the training process, which is shown in Fig. 2(c) together with the test accuracy of these two models on the same test dataset.

B   Proof of Theorem 1

To prove Theorem 1, we first introduce the following lemma.

Lemma 1. *([16]) For a set of task losses* $\mathbb{L} = \{\ell_1(\phi), ..., \ell_n(\phi)\}$, *and* $\ell_{[i]}$ *denotes the i-th largest loss after sorting the elements in* $\mathbb{L}$, *we have*

$$\sum_{i=1}^{k} \ell_{[i]}(\phi) = min_{\lambda \in \mathbb{R}}\{k\lambda + \sum_{i=1}^{n}[\ell_i(\phi) - \lambda]_+\}.$$

Furthermore, $\ell_{[k]}(\phi) \in \arg\min_{\lambda \in \mathbb{R}}\{k\lambda + \sum_{i=1}^{n}[\ell_i(\phi) - \lambda]_+\}.$

Proof. We know $\sum_{i=1}^{k} \ell_{[i]}(\phi)$ is the solution of

$$\max_{\mathbf{p}} \mathbf{p}^\top \mathbb{L}, \ \text{s.t.} \mathbf{p}^\top \mathbf{1} = k, 0 \leq \mathbf{p} \leq 1.$$

We apply Lagrangian to this equation and get

$$L = -\mathbf{p}^\top \mathbb{L} - \mathbf{v}^\top \mathbf{p} + \mathbf{u}^\top (\mathbf{p} - 1) + \lambda(\mathbf{p}^\top \mathbf{1} - k),$$

where $\mathbf{u} \geq \mathbf{0}$, $\mathbf{v} \geq \mathbf{0}$, $\lambda \in \mathbb{R}$ are Lagrangian multipliers. Taking its derivative w.r.t $\mathbf{p}$ and set it to 0, we have $v = \mathbf{u} - \mathbb{L} + \lambda\mathbf{1}$. Substituting it back to Lagrangian, we have

$$\min_{\mathbf{u},\lambda} \mathbf{u}^\top \mathbf{1} + k\lambda, \text{s.t.} \mathbf{u} \geq \mathbf{0}, \mathbf{u} + \lambda\mathbf{1} - \mathbb{L} \geq \mathbf{0}.$$

This means

$$\sum_{i=1}^{k} \ell_{[i]}(\phi) = \min_{\lambda}\left\{k\lambda + \sum_{i=1}^{n}[\ell_i(\phi) - \lambda]_+\right\}. \tag{B.1}$$

Furthermore, we can see that $\lambda = \ell_{[i]}(\phi)$ is always one optimal solution for Eq. B.1. So

$$\ell_{[k]}(\phi) \in \arg\min_{\lambda}\left\{k\lambda + \sum_{i=1}^{n}[\ell_i(\phi) - \lambda]_+\right\}.$$

Theorem B.1. *(Theorem 1 restated) Denote* $[a]_+ = \max\{0, a\}$ *as the hinge function. Equation (2) is equivalent to*

$$\min_{\phi,\lambda} \max_{\hat{\lambda}} \hat{\mathcal{L}}_\mathcal{D}(\phi, \mathbf{w}^*) = \frac{1}{k - m} \sum_{i=1}^{n} \hat{\mathcal{L}}(\phi, w_i^*, \lambda, \hat{\lambda})$$

$$:= \left[[\ell_i(\phi) - \lambda]_+ - [\ell_i(\phi) - \hat{\lambda}]_+ + \frac{k}{n}\lambda - \frac{m}{n}\hat{\lambda}\right]$$

$$\text{s.t.} \ \ \mathbf{w}^* = \arg\min_{\mathbf{w}} \mathcal{L}_\mathcal{S}(\phi, \mathbf{w}) := \frac{1}{n} \sum_{i=1}^{n} \mathcal{L}_{\mathcal{S}_i}(\phi, w_i), \tag{B.2}$$

If the optimal of ϕ and $\hat{\mathbf{w}}^*$ are achieved, $(\ell_{[k]}(\phi), \ell_{[m]}(\phi))$ *can be the optimum solutions of* $(\lambda, \hat{\lambda})$.

Proof. From Lemma 1 and upper-level formulation in (2), we have

$$\min_{\phi} \mathcal{L}_{\mathcal{D}}(\phi, \mathbf{w}^*) = \frac{1}{k-m} \min_{\phi} \sum_{i=m+1}^{k} \ell_{[i]}(\phi)$$

$$= \frac{1}{k-m} \min_{\phi} \left[\sum_{i=1}^{k} \ell_{[i]}(\phi) - \sum_{i=1}^{m} \ell_{[i]}(\phi) \right]$$

$$= \frac{1}{k-m} \min_{\phi} \left[\min_{\lambda \in \mathbb{R}} \left\{ k\lambda + \sum_{i=1}^{n} [\ell_i(\phi) - \lambda]_+ \right\} \right.$$

$$\left. - \min_{\hat{\lambda} \in \mathbb{R}} \left\{ m\hat{\lambda} + \sum_{i=1}^{n} [\ell_i(\phi) - \hat{\lambda}]_+ \right\} \right]$$

$$= \frac{1}{k-m} \min_{\phi,\lambda} \max_{\hat{\lambda}} \sum_{i=1}^{n} \left[[\ell_i(\phi) - \lambda]_+ - [\ell_i(\phi) - \hat{\lambda}]_+ \right.$$

$$\left. + \frac{k}{n}\lambda - \frac{m}{n}\hat{\lambda} \right].$$

According to Lemma 1, if the optimal parameter ϕ^* is achieved, we have $\lambda = \ell_{[k]}(\phi^*)$ and $\hat{\lambda} = \ell_{[m]}(\phi^*)$. Since $k > m$, it is obvious that $\hat{\lambda} > \lambda$.

C   The Algorithm of sg-HeTRoM

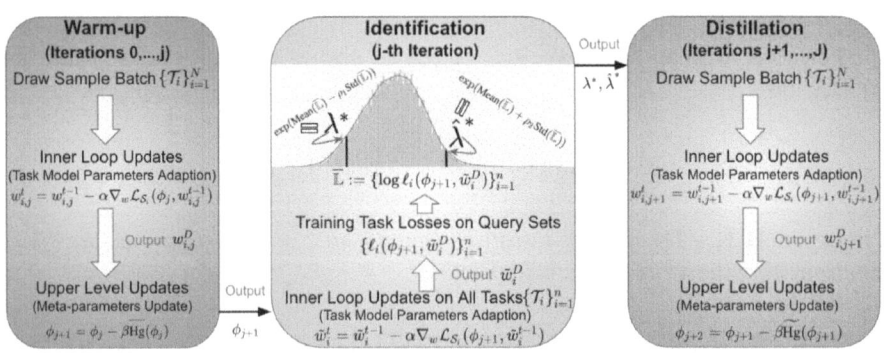

Fig. 4. Illustration of statistic-guided learning for solving HeTRoM.

In this section we provide comprehensive illustration of sg-HeTRoM method mentioned in Sect. 4.2, as in Fig. 4 and Algorithm 2.

Algorithm 2. Optimizing procedure of sg-HeTRoM

1: **Input:** Warmup iteration number P; total iteration number J; inner-loop iteration number D; batch size N; stepsize α, β, γ, initial meta-parameter ϕ_0; initial task-specific parameter w_0; warmup flag $flag = 1$; hyperparameters ρ_1, ρ_2.

2: **for** $j = 0, 1, 2, ..., J$ **do**

3:     Sample a batch of tasks $\{\mathcal{T}_i\}_{i=1}^N$

4:     **for** each task $\mathcal{T}_i$ in $\{\mathcal{T}_i\}_{i=1}^N$ **do**

5:         Initialize task-specific parameter as $w_{i,j}^0 = w_0$

6:         **for** $t = 1, 2, ..., D$ **do**

7:             Update $w_{i,j}^t = w_{i,j}^{t-1} - \alpha \nabla_w \mathcal{L}_{\mathcal{S}_i}(\phi_j, w_{i,j}^{t-1})$

8:         **end for**

9:     **end for**

10:     **if** $flag == 1$ **then**

11:         Calculate hypergradient of $L_{\mathcal{D}}(\phi, \mathbf{w}^*)$ w.r.t. ϕ: $\overline{\text{Hg}}(\phi_j) = \frac{1}{N} \frac{\partial \sum_{i=1}^N \ell_i(\phi_j, w_{i,j}^D)}{\partial \phi_j}$

12:         Update meta-parameter $\phi_{j+1} = \phi_j - \beta \overline{\text{Hg}}(\phi_j)$

13:         **if** $j == P$ **then**

14:             **for** each task $\mathcal{T}_i$ in the training set of all tasks $\{\mathcal{T}_i\}_{i=1}^n$ **do**

15:                 Initialize task-specific parameter as $\tilde{w}_i^0 = w_0$

16:                 **for** $t = 1, 2, ..., D$ **do**

17:                     Update $\tilde{w}_i^t = \tilde{w}_i^{t-1} - \alpha \nabla_w \mathcal{L}_{\mathcal{S}_i}(\phi_{j+1}, \tilde{w}_i^{t-1})$

18:                 **end for**

19:             **end for**

20:             Calculate log of all training task losses on their query set: $\overline{\mathbb{L}} = \{\log \ell_i(\phi_{j+1}, \tilde{w}_i^D)\}_{i=1}^n$

21:             Calculate+. $\begin{pmatrix} \hat{\lambda}^* \\ \hat{\lambda}^* \end{pmatrix} \leftarrow \begin{pmatrix} \exp(\text{Mean}(\overline{\mathbb{L}}) - \rho_1 \text{Std}(\overline{\mathbb{L}})) \\ \exp(\text{Mean}(\overline{\mathbb{L}}) + \rho_2 \text{Std}(\overline{\mathbb{L}})) \end{pmatrix}$

22:             $flag \leftarrow 0$

23:         **end if**

24:     **else**

25:         Update meta-parameter $\phi_{j+1} = \phi_j - \beta \widetilde{\text{Hg}}(\phi_j)$ based on Eq. (9)

26:     **end if**

27: **end for**

D   Implementation Details

Network Architecture. In this study, we employ two distinct network architectures, namely 4-layer CNN (CNN4) and ResNet12. CNN4 comprises four convolutional layers with a feature dimension of 64, each followed by a ReLU activation layer and max pooling. On the other hand, ResNet12 consists of four residual blocks, each containing three convolutional layers, along with batch normalization and ReLU activation.

Training Configuration. We conduct our experiments in a few-shot classification setting. Two types of neural network backbones are used for meta-training: a 4-layer CNN (CNN4) and ResNet12. Our proposed method is trained using a mini-batch ADAM algorithm with a batch size of 16. The total iterations J are set to 2000, with inner-loop iterations D at 10. The initial learning rates are

$\alpha = 0.05$, $\beta = \gamma = 0.002$. All our experiments are conducted using the PyTorch platform with two NVIDIA RTX A6000 GPUs. We construct our loss function based on the cross-entropy loss for the tasks. In line with [16], we conduct a grid search to select the values of k and m. We select ρ_1 and ρ_2 from the set $\{1, 2, 3\}$. The results we present, including a 95% confidence interval, are based on five random runs. Unless stated otherwise, all experiments are conducted based on Algorithm 1.

Learning Rate Strategy for Training ResNet12 Model. Throughout the meta-training process of the ResNet12 model, the initial individual task losses are high but undergo a significant decrease as training progresses. In order to ensure that our thresholds, λ and $\hat{\lambda}$, are able to adapt to the changing scale of task losses, we introduce a scaling factor for the learning rate γ, denoted as δ. This scaling factor starts with a large value at the beginning of meta-training and linearly decreases over time, ultimately reaching 0 at the end of training. This procedure is denoted as $\gamma_i = i\delta\gamma_0/J$, where γ_i denotes the learning rate of λ and $\hat{\lambda}$ at i-th iteration, and γ_0 is the base learning rate. In our experiments, we set $\gamma_0 = \beta = 0.003$ and the scaling factor $\delta = 1000$.

The Generation of Clean Tasks. We designate the original Mini-ImageNet and Tiered-Imagenet datasets as clean datasets, from which we extract tasks for conducting experiments in the clean task setting. Our experiments focus on two few-shot classification tasks: 5-ways 5-shots, and 5-ways 1-shot. In both tasks, the "way" number refers to the number of classes in the task and the "shot" number indicates the number of examples sampled from each class.

The Generation of Noisy Tasks. we consider three generation settings for noisy tasks: fixed, 1-step random, and 2-step random. (a) In the *fixed* setting, we assign a specific noise probability for each of the tasks in a batch and then change the label of each sample to another randomly chosen label in each task according to the preset probability. For example, consider a batch of 16 tasks, where the first five tasks have no noise, the next five tasks have 10% noise each, the following three tasks have 30% noise each, the 14th and 15th tasks have 50% noise each, and the 16th task has 70% noise in each. This setting can help us track the noise in each batch to show the process of eliminating noisy tasks from training. (b) In *1-step random* setting, for each task, we randomly choose its noise probability from $\{0\%, 10\%, 20\%, 30\%, 40\%\}$. (c) In *2-step random*, following [30], we first randomly select 60% of tasks from all training tasks and set their noise probability to 80%.

The Generation of Outlier Tasks. (a) For the Tiered-ImageNet dataset, we consider the preset categories in Tiered-ImageNet as different domains and randomly select two categories: one is designated as the target category, and the other as the outlier category. We split all classes in each category into separate training and test parts with a 7:3 ratio. During the training phase, we randomly select a portion (*i.e.*, 10%, 30%) of tasks as outlier tasks, whose samples are extracted from the training part of the outlier category. Samples from other tasks are taken from the training part of the target category. During the test phase, all tasks are sampled from the test part of the target category. (b) For Mini-ImageNet dataset, we cross-reference the classes in Mini-ImageNet with the classes in Tiered-ImageNet to determine the category to which each class in Mini-ImageNet belongs. This allows us to identify the categories included in Mini-ImageNet, and the remaining categories in Tiered-ImageNet are considered outlier categories. In training phase, we sample a portion (*i.e.*, 10%, 30%) of tasks from outlier categories as outlier tasks, while the remaining tasks are sampled from Mini-ImageNet. During test phase, we exclusively evaluate the model's performance on Mini-ImageNet.

References

1. Alquier, P., Pontil, M., et al.: Regret bounds for lifelong learning. In: Artificial Intelligence and Statistics (AISTATS), pp. 261–269 (2017)
2. Antoniou, A., Edwards, H., Storkey, A.: How to train your MAML. arXiv preprint arXiv:1810.09502 (2018)
3. Baik, S., Choi, J., Kim, H., Cho, D., Min, J., Lee, K.M.: Meta-learning with task-adaptive loss function for few-shot learning. In: Proceedings of the IEEE/CVF International Conference on Computer Vision, pp. 9465–9474 (2021)
4. Baik, S., Choi, M., Choi, J., Kim, H., Lee, K.M.: Meta-learning with adaptive hyperparameters. Adv. Neural. Inf. Process. Syst. **33**, 20755–20765 (2020)
5. Balcan, M.F., Khodak, M., Talwalkar, A.: Provable guarantees for gradient-based meta-learning. In: International Conference on Machine Learning (ICML), pp. 424–433 (2019)
6. Bertinetto, L., Henriques, J.F., Torr, P., Vedaldi, A.: Meta-learning with differentiable closed-form solvers. In: International Conference on Learning Representations (ICLR) (2018)
7. Boudiaf, M., Masud, Z., Rony, J., Dolz, J., Piantanida, P., Ayed, I.: Transductive information maximization for few-shot learning. arxiv. arXiv preprint arXiv:2008.11297 (2020)
8. Bracken, J., McGill, J.T.: Mathematical programs with optimization problems in the constraints. Oper. Res. **21**(1), 37–44 (1973)
9. Chen, D., Wu, L., Tang, S., Yun, X., Long, B., Zhuang, Y.: Robust meta-learning with sampling noise and label noise via eigen-reptile. In: International Conference on Machine Learning, pp. 3662–3678. PMLR (2022)
10. Collins, L., Mokhtari, A., Shakkottai, S.: Task-robust model-agnostic meta-learning. Adv. Neural. Inf. Process. Syst. **33**, 18860–18871 (2020)
11. Finn, C., Abbeel, P., Levine, S.: Model-agnostic meta-learning for fast adaptation of deep networks. In: International Conference on Machine Learning, pp. 1126–1135. PMLR (2017)
12. Finn, C., Rajeswaran, A., Kakade, S., Levine, S.: Online meta-learning. In: International Conference on Machine Learning (ICML), pp. 1920–1930 (2019)
13. Grant, E., Finn, C., Levine, S., Darrell, T., Griffiths, T.: Recasting gradient-based meta-learning as hierarchical bayes. In: International Conference on Learning Representations (ICLR) (2018)
14. Grazzi, R., Franceschi, L., Pontil, M., Salzo, S.: On the iteration complexity of hypergradient computation. In: International Conference on Machine Learning, pp. 3748–3758. PMLR (2020)

15. Holland, M.J.: Flexible risk design using bi-directional dispersion. In: International Conference on Artificial Intelligence and Statistics, pp. 1586–1623. PMLR (2023)
16. Hu, S., Ying, Y., Lyu, S., et al.: Learning by minimizing the sum of ranked range. Adv. Neural. Inf. Process. Syst. **33**, 21013–21023 (2020)
17. Huisman, M., van Rijn, J.N., Plaat, A.: A survey of deep meta-learning. Artif. Intell. Rev. **54**(6), 4483–4541 (2021). https://doi.org/10.1007/s10462-021-10004-4
18. Ji, K., Yang, J., Liang, Y.: Bilevel optimization: nonasymptotic analysis and faster algorithms. arXiv preprint arXiv:2010.07962 (2020)
19. Ji, K., Yang, J., Liang, Y.: Bilevel optimization: convergence analysis and enhanced design. In: International Conference on Machine Learning, pp. 4882–4892. PMLR (2021)
20. Jiang, L., Zhou, Z., Leung, T., Li, L.J., Fei-Fei, L.: MentorNet: learning data-driven curriculum for very deep neural networks on corrupted labels. In: International Conference on Machine Learning, pp. 2304–2313. PMLR (2018)
21. Killamsetty, K., Li, C., Zhao, C., Chen, F., Iyer, R.: A nested bi-level optimization framework for robust few shot learning. In: Proceedings of the AAAI Conference on Artificial Intelligence, vol. 36, pp. 7176–7184 (2022)
22. Lee, K., Maji, S., Ravichandran, A., Soatto, S.: Meta-learning with differentiable convex optimization. In: IEEE Conference on Computer Vision and Pattern Recognition (CVPR) (2019)
23. Liang, K.J., Rangrej, S.B., Petrovic, V., Hassner, T.: Few-shot learning with noisy labels. In: Proceedings of the IEEE/CVF Conference on Computer Vision and Pattern Recognition, pp. 9089–9098 (2022)
24. Liu, C., Wang, Z., Sahoo, D., Fang, Y., Zhang, K., Hoi, S.C.: Adaptive task sampling for meta-learning. In: Computer Vision–ECCV 2020: 16th European Conference, Glasgow, UK, 23–28 August 2020, Proceedings, Part XVIII 16, pp. 752–769. Springer (2020)
25. Liu, X., Lyu, Y., Jing, L., Zeng, T., Yu, J.: Not all tasks are equal: a parameter-efficient task reweighting method for few-shot learning. In: Joint European Conference on Machine Learning and Knowledge Discovery in Databases, pp. 421–437. Springer (2023)
26. Ren, M., et al.: Meta-learning for semi-supervised few-shot classification. arXiv preprint arXiv:1803.00676 (2018)
27. Russakovsky, O., et al.: ImageNet large scale visual recognition challenge. Int. J. Comput. Vision **115**, 211–252 (2015)
28. Vinyals, O., Blundell, C., Lillicrap, T., Wierstra, D., et al.: Matching networks for one shot learning. Adv. Neural Inf. Process. Syst. **29** (2016)
29. Wang, Z., Hu, G., Hu, Q.: Training noise-robust deep neural networks via meta-learning. In: Proceedings of the IEEE/CVF Conference on Computer Vision and Pattern Recognition, pp. 4524–4533 (2020)
30. Yao, H., et al.: Meta-learning with an adaptive task scheduler. Adv. Neural. Inf. Process. Syst. **34**, 7497–7509 (2021)

DIN: Dynamical Interaction Network for Multi-station Multi-variable Weather Prediction

Chujie Xu[1], Yinkai Liu[2], Yajun Gao[1], Xiaotong Zhu[1], Yudie Wang[1], Yong Han[2], and Yan Wu[3(✉)]

[1] State Key Laboratory of Complex and Critical Software Environment, Beihang University, Beijing 100191, China
{chujie_xu,yajungao,hiutungzyu,yudiewang}@buaa.edu.cn
[2] School of Computer Science and Engineering, Beihang University, Beijing 100191, China
{greatherobrine,hanyong}@buaa.edu.cn
[3] Beijing Academy of Science and Technology, Beijing 100089, China
wuyanbh@buaa.edu.cn

Abstract. Multi-station multi-variable weather prediction delivers crucial meteorological forecasts for distributed geographical locations, with significant implications for human activities. Existing methods often overlook the underlying physical dynamics governing atmospheric processes and fail to capture complex interdependencies between weather variables, limiting their predictive accuracy. To address these limitations, we propose the Dynamical Interaction Network (DIN), which integrates physical processes with data-driven learning through two synergistic modules. The spatiotemporal dynamical modeling module captures multiscale atmospheric processes by integrating local dynamics, cross-regional patterns, and temporal evolution. The higher-order cross-variable interaction module learns the complex dependencies among meteorological variables by using convolutions to simulate differential operators. Extensive experiments on the Global Wind/Temp dataset demonstrate that DIN achieves state-of-the-art performance.

Keywords: Weather prediction · Spatiotemporal dynamics · Cross-variable interaction

1 Introduction

Accurate weather prediction is of paramount importance for early warning systems [32], disaster prevention [1], and socio-economic planning [8]. The task of multi-station multi-variable weather prediction focuses on jointly forecasting multiple meteorological factors at spatially distinct observation points over time [23,40]. Existing methods often take into account the complexity of weather systems and carefully design network architectures to model temporal dependencies [28,30,37,39] and spatial relationships [9,18,31,33]. For example, Wang et al. [27] proposed past-decomposable-mixing and future-multipredictor-mixing blocks to effectively disentangle and integrate multiscale temporal patterns. Wu et al. [29] proposed transforming one-dimensional time series into two-dimensional tensors to effectively model complex intraperiod and interperiod patterns. On the other hand, Tang et al. [24] proposed a simple paradigm for distilling spatial representations from graph neural networks to improve scalability in large-scale spatiotemporal prediction tasks. Wu et al. [31] constructed a multiscale tree structure that considers cross-correlation between stations.

Although these methods have shown promise in modeling historical weather patterns, there are two key limitations. First, most models operate in a purely data-driven manner, without considering the physical laws that govern atmospheric processes. This omission restricts their ability to generalize beyond training distributions and increases the risk of physically implausible predictions. Second, most models handle meteorological variables independently, without considering the inherent interdependencies among them. This simplification overlooks the coupled nature of weather systems—for example, wind speed and temperature influence each other through complex thermodynamic processes—and results in fragmented forecasts that fail to capture holistic system behavior.

To address these limitations, we propose a novel Dynamical Interaction Network (DIN) for multi-station multi-variable weather prediction. The DIN adopts an encoder-decoder architecture with two key components: spatiotemporal dynamical modeling and high-order cross-variable interaction modules. The spatiotemporal dynamical modeling holistically integrates local dynamical modeling to capture fine-grained physical processes within specific regions, cross-regional spatial modeling to represent large-scale atmospheric patterns, and temporal modeling to interpret the evolution of weather systems over time. The high-order cross-variable interaction employs convolutional operations to simulate differential processes, learning higher-order relationships between diverse meteorological variables and explicitly modeling their mutual influences, thereby achieving more accurate and physically consistent predictions.

Our main contributions can be summarized as follows:

- We propose a novel Dynamical Interaction Network for multi-station multi-variable weather prediction, which incorporates spatiotemporal dynamics and cross-variable interactions to enhance prediction accuracy.
- We propose the spatiotemporal dynamical modeling module that captures multi-scale atmospheric processes by integrating local physical dynamics, cross-regional patterns, and temporal evolution.
- We propose the high-order cross-variable interaction module that learns the complex dependencies among meteorological variables by using convolutions to simulate differential operators.
- Extensive experiments on the Global Wind/Temp dataset demonstrate that the proposed method achieves state-of-the-art performance.

2   Related Work

Existing deep learning-based weather prediction methods generally focus on temporal or spatial relationships. In this section, we introduce related work on these two aspects separately. Section 2.1 presents the weather prediction methods with the temporal modeling, and Sect. 2.2 presents the weather prediction methods with the spatial modeling.

2.1   Weather Prediction with the Temporal Modeling

Due to the significant advantages of deep learning, an increasing number of deep weather prediction methods [5,10,22,30,37,38] based on time series prediction demonstrate impressive performance. Classic time series models such as RNN [22], LSTM [10], and GRU [5] have shown good prediction performance. Since the advance of the Transformer [25] for natural language processing, numerous works have adopted it for time series prediction. Informer [37] refines the quadratic complexity of the attention mechanism and improves its ability to capture long-term dependencies between the outputs and the inputs. AutoFormer [30] improves the long-term prediction performance by combining sequence decomposition with the attention mechanism. However, the efficacy of Transformers for time series has been contested. For instance, Zeng et al. [35] argue that the permutation-invariance property in Transformers may lead to the loss of temporal information in time series. Subsequently, other MLP-based architectures showed efficacy in the time series prediction task [7,27]. However, time-series prediction methods are limited to individual weather station analysis [30,37,38], ignoring the spatiotemporal relationship between different stations.

2.2   Weather Prediction with the Spatial Modeling

Some spatiotemporal prediction methods [2,21,26,36] consider gridded data such as satellite radar for weather prediction. For example, large meteorological models, such as Pangu [3], GraphCast [17], and Neural GCM [16], have demonstrated remarkable performance in medium to long-term global forecasting. However, their enormous model sizes pose significant challenges for real-world deployment, especially in resource-constrained settings, necessitating efficient model compression techniques such as pruning and quantization [12–15]. Furthermore, these models generally operate on coarse-grained gridded inputs and are unable to deliver fine-grained forecasts for specific ground stations, which limits their application in localized weather-sensitive scenarios.

Other spatiotemporal prediction methods [18,20,31] consider multiple weather stations and focus on modeling spatial correlations between them to improve forecasting accuracy. Lin et al. [18] construct graph neural networks that utilize conditional local convolutional modeling of correlation between stations. Ma et al. [20] propose the HiSTGNN model, a hierarchical spatiotemporal graph neural network designed to capture multi-scale spatiotemporal dependencies using a hierarchical graph structure and multi-layer graph convolutional

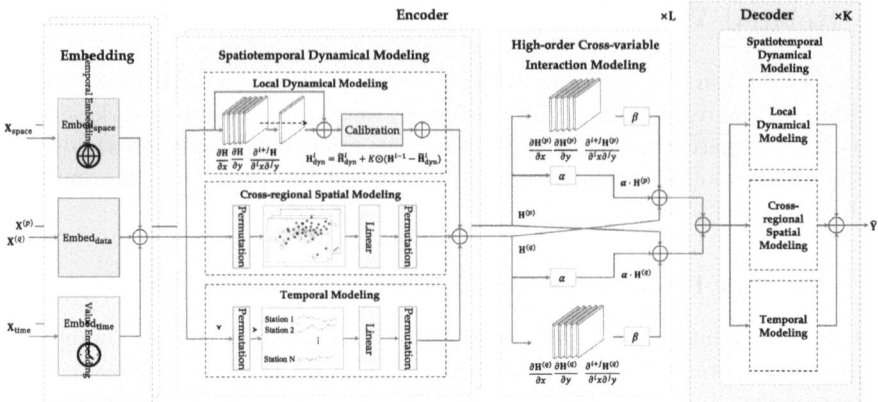

Fig. 1. The overall architecture of DIN.

networks. Wu et al. [31] construct a tree-based multiscale structure that considers cross-correlation between stations, enhancing the forecasting performance. Although previous studies have achieved satisfactory results, most spatiotemporal prediction methods do not consider the physical processes of weather systems or the complex relationships among different variables.

3 Methodology

In this section, we present the proposed Dynamical Interaction Network (DIN) for multi-station multi-variable weather prediction. Section 3.1 defines the problem setting. Section 3.2 introduces the overall architecture of the model. Section 3.3 introduces the spatiotemporal dynamical modeling module to capture local dynamics, regional spatial dependencies, and temporal evolution. Section 3.4 describes the high-order cross-variable interaction module, designed to model complex dependencies among meteorological variables. Finally, Sect. 3.5 specifies the training objective for network parameter optimization.

3.1 Problem Formulation

We formulate the multi-station multi-variable weather prediction task as a spatiotemporal forecasting problem. Let $\mathbf{X} \in \mathbb{R}^{N \times T \times V}$ denote the meteorological data, where N is the number of stations, T is the number of time steps, and V is the number of variables. Given an input sequence $\mathbf{X} \in \mathbb{R}^{N \times T_{\text{in}} \times V}$, the goal is to predict the future sequence $\hat{\mathbf{Y}} \in \mathbb{R}^{N \times T_{\text{out}} \times V}$. Formally, the model learns a mapping function:

$$f : \mathbb{R}^{N \times T_{\text{in}} \times V} \rightarrow \mathbb{R}^{N \times T_{\text{out}} \times V}, \quad \hat{\mathbf{Y}} = f(\mathbf{X}). \tag{1}$$

3.2   Overall Architecture

As illustrated in Fig. 1, our framework adopts a multi-branch architecture composed of three sequential stages: embedding, encoding, and decoding.

In the embedding stage, we account for the significant variability among different meteorological variables and the local similarity of weather patterns across neighboring stations. To this end, each variable is processed independently, and the N stations are grouped into R spatial regions to facilitate the extraction of local features. Specifically, for each variable q in $\mathbf{X}$, the input sequence $\mathbf{X}^{(q)} \in \mathbb{R}^{N \times T_{\text{in}}}$ is reshaped into $\tilde{\mathbf{X}}^{(q)} \in \mathbb{R}^{R \times T_{\text{in}} \times \frac{N}{R}}$ by partitioning the N stations. Then, by integrating both temporal and spatial information, the input is projected into a latent embedding space as follows:

$$\mathbf{H}_{\text{emb}}^{(q)} = \text{Embed}_{\text{data}}(\tilde{\mathbf{X}}^{(q)}) + \text{Embed}_{\text{space}}(\mathbf{X}_{\text{space}}) + \text{Embed}_{\text{time}}(\mathbf{X}_{\text{time}}), \qquad (2)$$

where $\mathbf{X}_{\text{space}} \in \mathbb{R}^{N \times 3}$ encodes the longitude, latitude, and elevation of each station, and $\mathbf{X}_{\text{time}} \in \mathbb{R}^{T_{\text{in}} \times 4}$ encodes the year, month, day, and hour for each time step. All embedding layers Embed.$(\cdot)$ are implemented via linear projections, with appropriate broadcasting along spatial and temporal dimensions to ensure consistent tensor shapes.

In the encoding stage, a stack of encoder layers is applied to extract spatiotemporal features of intra-variable and inter-variable dependencies. Each encoder layer integrates two key modules: Spatiotemporal Dynamical Modeling (SDM) and High-order Cross-variable Interaction (HCI). Formally, The operation of l-th encoding layer can be expressed as:

$$\mathbf{H}_{\text{enc}}^l = \text{Encoder}^l(\mathbf{H}_{\text{enc}}^{l-1}) = \text{SDM} \circ \text{HCI}(\mathbf{H}_{\text{enc}}^{l-1}), \qquad (3)$$

where $\mathbf{H}_{\text{enc}}^l$ denotes the output of the l-th encoder layer and $\mathbf{H}_{\text{enc}}^0$ is defined as $\mathbf{H}_{\text{emb}}$.

In the decoding stage, a stack of decoder layers transforms the encoded representations into future predictions. Each decoder layer focuses on modeling spatiotemporal dynamics via the SDM module:

$$\mathbf{H}_{\text{dec}}^l = \text{Decoder}^l(\mathbf{H}_{\text{dec}}^{l-1}) = \text{SDM}(\mathbf{H}_{\text{dec}}^{l-1}), \qquad (4)$$

where $\mathbf{H}_{\text{dec}}^l$ denotes the output of the l-th decoder layer and $\mathbf{H}_{\text{dec}}^0$ is defined as the output of the last encoder layer $\mathbf{H}_{\text{enc}}^L$. The output of the last decoder layer is linearly mapped to obtain the final prediction result $\hat{\mathbf{Y}}$.

The following sections provide a detailed description of the proposed SDM and HCI modules.

3.3   Spatiotemporal Dynamical Modeling

Accurately modeling the evolution of complex weather systems requires capturing both fine-grained local dynamics and large-scale spatiotemporal dependencies. To this end, we propose the SDM module, which comprises three complementary components: local dynamical modeling, cross-regional spatial modeling, and temporal modeling.

Weather systems often exhibit complex and nonlinear behavior at the local scale, driven by physical processes that can be approximated using partial differential equations (PDEs). Motivated by this, we adopt a generalized PDE-based formulation to implement local dynamical modeling. Specifically, we first project the hidden representation onto a 2D spatial domain, and then compute its evolution as:

$$\tilde{\mathbf{H}}^l_{\text{dyn}} = \mathbf{H}^{l-1} + \Phi(\mathbf{H}^{l-1}) = \mathbf{H}^{l-1} + \sum_{i,j:i+j\leq k} c_{i,j} \frac{\partial^{i+j}\mathbf{H}^{l-1}}{\partial x^i \partial y^j}, \tag{5}$$

where each term in the summation represents a spatial derivative of order up to k, and the coefficients $c_{i,j}$ are learnable parameters. This generic class of linear PDEs allows the model to flexibly approximate various local dynamics such as diffusion, advection, or more complex patterns.

To implement the operator $\Phi(\mathbf{H}^{l-1})$, we follow the previous work [11] and employ a convolutional neural network. Each convolutional filter is regularized using a kernel moment loss, which constrains the filters to approximate the behavior of specific differential operators. This formulation allows the convolutional kernels to act as discrete counterparts to continuous spatial derivatives, enabling the network to emulate the underlying physical processes encoded in the PDE structure. Details of the kernel moment loss are provided in Sect. 3.5.

However, pure PDE-based approximations may not fully capture time-dependent deviations caused by external influences or unmodeled factors. To address this, we introduce a time-dependent correction coefficient K that adaptively adjusts the PDE output based on the discrepancy between the predicted and actual features:

$$\mathbf{H}^l_{\text{dyn}} = \tilde{\mathbf{H}}^l_{\text{dyn}} + K \odot (\mathbf{H}^{l-1} - \tilde{\mathbf{H}}^l_{\text{dyn}}), \tag{6}$$

where K uses a network to learn. This correction mechanism enables the model to maintain robustness against modeling errors and temporal shifts in local dynamics.

While local dynamical modeling focuses on short-range dependencies, large-scale weather patterns are often driven by long-range interactions across geographically distant regions. To capture these cross-regional spatial dependencies, we employ a linear layer along the spatial axis:

$$\mathbf{H}^l_{\text{spatio}} = \text{Linear}(\mathbf{H}^{l-1}). \tag{7}$$

This component provides a global perspective that complements the local PDE-based dynamics, enabling the model to represent large-scale meteorological phenomena such as pressure systems and jet streams that span across regions.

To explicitly capture the temporal evolution of features, we incorporate a separate temporal modeling branch, which applies a linear transformation along the time axis:

$$\mathbf{H}^l_{\text{temporal}} = \text{Linear}(\mathbf{H}^{l-1}). \tag{8}$$

This allows the model to encode feature trajectories over time, independent of spatial dynamics, and supports learning temporal dependencies such as periodicity and transitions.

The final output of the SDM module aggregates the contributions from all three components:

$$\mathbf{H}^l = \mathbf{H}^l_{\text{dyn}} + \mathbf{H}^l_{\text{spatio}} + \mathbf{H}^l_{\text{temporal}}. \tag{9}$$

This integration ensures that the updated hidden representation captures a comprehensive view of spatiotemporal dynamics, accounting for both localized physical processes and broader atmospheric evolution across space and time.

3.4   High-Order Cross-Variable Interaction

Weather prediction involves multiple interrelated meteorological variables, such as temperature, wind, humidity, and pressure. These variables do not evolve in isolation; instead, their dynamic behaviors are governed by complex interactions that are often nonlinear and spatially varying. To better capture these inter-variable dependencies, we introduce a high-order cross-variable interaction mechanism that models both direct relationships between variables and their shared spatial dynamics.

For each variable q, we model its interaction with another variable p by incorporating both the raw representation and its higher-order spatial derivatives. The update rule is defined as:

$$\mathbf{H}^{(q)} \leftarrow \mathbf{H}^{(q)} + \alpha \cdot \mathbf{H}^{(p)} + \beta \cdot \sum_{i,j:i+j\leq k} c_{i,j} \frac{\partial^{i+j}\mathbf{H}^{(p)}}{\partial x^i \partial y^j}, \tag{10}$$

where $\mathbf{H}^{(q)}$ and $\mathbf{H}^{(p)}$ denote the representations of variables q and p, respectively. The term $\alpha \cdot \mathbf{H}^{(p)}$ captures the low-order direct influence of p on q. In contrast, the term $\beta \cdot \sum_{i,j:i+j\leq k} c_{i,j} \frac{\partial^{i+j}\mathbf{H}^{(p)}}{\partial x^i \partial y^j}$ involving the mixed partial derivatives of $\mathbf{H}^{(p)}$ models higher-order spatial variations shared across variables. The high-order term is also implemented using a convolutional neural network, and the filters are constrained through a kernel moment loss to approximate specific derivative orders. The coefficients α and β are learnable parameters, enabling the model to adaptively balance the strength of direct and high-order influences.

This mechanism enables the model to capture both the direct cross-variable influence and the shared fine-grained spatial dynamics, leading to more accurate and physically consistent weather predictions.

3.5   Training Objective

The overall training objective combines two components: a prediction loss that ensures accurate forecasting, and a kernel moment loss that regularizes the convolutional filters to approximate specific differential operators.

Prediction Loss. The model is trained by minimizing the Mean Squared Error (MSE) between predictions and ground-truth weather observations:

$$\mathcal{L}_{\text{pred}} = \frac{1}{NT} \sum_{n=1}^{N} \sum_{t=1}^{T} \left(\hat{\mathbf{Y}}_t^{(n)} - \mathbf{Y}_t^{(n)} \right)^2, \tag{11}$$

where $\hat{\mathbf{Y}}_t^{(n)}$ and $\mathbf{Y}_t^{(n)}$ denote the predicted and true weather variables for sample n at time t, respectively. N is the number of training samples and T is the prediction horizon.

Kernel Moment Loss. To ensure that the learned convolutional filters accurately approximate the desired differential operators, we employ a kernel moment loss $\mathcal{L}_{\text{moment}}$ following [11, 19]. For each filter $\mathbf{w}$ of size $k \times k$ designed to approximate the partial derivative $\frac{\partial^{i+j}}{\partial x^i \partial y^j}$, we compute its moment matrix $\mathbf{M}(\mathbf{w}_{i,j}^k)$ and compare it to a target moment matrix $\Delta_{i,j}^k$ and penalize deviations from the target $\Delta_{i,j}^k$:

$$\mathcal{L}_{\text{moment}} = \sum_{i \leq k} \sum_{j \leq k} \left\| \mathbf{M}(\mathbf{w}_{i,j}^k) - \Delta_{i,j}^k \right\|_F, \tag{12}$$

The combined training objective is then given by:

$$\mathcal{L} = \mathcal{L}_{\text{pred}} + \lambda \mathcal{L}_{\text{moment}}, \tag{13}$$

where λ is a weighting hyperparameter that balances the prediction accuracy and physical consistency of the learned filters. This hybrid objective enables the model to simultaneously achieve high forecasting performance while adhering to fundamental physical principles.

4   Experiments

In this section, we present a comprehensive evaluation of our proposed DIN on the Global Wind/Temp dataset. Section 4.1 outlines the experimental settings, including data description, implementation details, and evaluation metrics. Section 4.2 highlights the superior performance of our model compared to state-of-the-art baselines. Section 4.3 provides an ablation study to verify the effectiveness of key components.

4.1   Experimental Settings

Data Description. The Global Wind/Temp dataset [31] contains hourly wind speed and temperature data from 3,850 stations worldwide between 1 January 2019 and 31 December 2020. For experimental purposes, the dataset is typically further partitioned into training, validation, and test sets in chronological order adhering to a 7:1:2 ratio. The standard forecasting task involves predicting meteorological conditions for the subsequent 24-h period (24 steps) based on observations from the preceding 48-h period (48 steps).

Table 1. Performance comparison on Global Wind/Temp dataset

Category	Model	Conference/Journal	Wind		Temp	
			MSE	MAE	MSE	MAE
MLP-based	DLinear	AAAI 2023	3.959	1.364	8.837	2.033
CNN-based	UniRepLKNet	CVPR 2024	3.865	1.301	7.602	1.832
Transformer-based	Informer	AAAI 2021	4.929	1.576	33.326	4.415
	Autoformer	NerulIPS 2021	4.687	1.465	10.142	2.250
	FEDformer	ICML 2022	4.750	1.503	11.054	2.405
	Corrformer	Nat. Mach. Intell. 2023	3.889	1.304	7.709	1.888
GNN-based	StemGNN	NeurlIPS 2020	4.066	1.389	13.926	2.746
	FourierGNN	NeurlIPS 2023	3.897	1.332	8.106	1.921
	HiSTGNN	Inf. Sci. 2023	3.750	1.313	7.469	1.863
	DIN (Ours)	–	**3.739**	**1.299**	**6.801**	**1.769**

Implementation Details. The experimental setup was implemented using PyTorch 2.1.0 framework on an NVIDIA GeForce RTX 2080 Ti GPU. The Adam optimizer was employed with a learning rate of 0.0001 while retaining default parameters for other hyperparameters ($\beta_1 = 0.9, \beta_2 = 0.999, \epsilon = 1e-8$). Training was conducted with a batch size of 1 for a total of 10 epochs. The Mean Squared Error (MSE) was utilized as the loss function. To prevent overfitting and ensure training efficiency, an early stopping mechanism was incorporated, which monitors the validation loss and terminates training if there is no improvement for 3 consecutive epochs. Additionally, in the experiments, the number of encoder layers and decoder layers was set to 2 and 1, respectively. The loss balancing coefficient λ was set to 0.01.

Evaluation Metrics. To compare the performance of our proposed approach and the baseline models, we employ two widely recognized evaluation metrics: Mean Squared Error (MSE) and Mean Absolute Error (MAE).

4.2 Performance Comparison

Our proposed DIN is thoroughly evaluated against a range of baseline models built upon diverse architectural paradigms, including:

- MLP-based model: DLinear [35];
- CNN-based model: UniRepLKNet [6];
- Transformer-based models: Informer [37], Autoformer [30], FEDformer [38], and Corrformer [31];
- GNN-based models: StemGNN [4], FourierGNN [34], and HiSTGNN [20].

Table 2. Ablation Study on the Effectiveness of the SDM Module

TM	CSM	LDM	Wind (MSE)	Temp (MSE)
✓			3.857	7.540
✓	✓		3.836	7.201
✓	✓	✓	**3.739**	**6.801**

Table 3. Ablation Study on the Effectiveness of the HCI Module

Interaction	Equation	Wind (MSE)	Temp (MSE)
No Interaction	–	3.761	6.933
Direct interaction	$\mathbf{H}^{(q)} \leftarrow \mathbf{H}^{(q)} + \alpha \cdot \mathbf{H}^{(p)}$	3.761	6.894
HCI	Equation (10)	**3.739**	**6.801**

As shown in Table 1, the proposed DIN achieves state-of-the-art performance on both wind speed and temperature prediction tasks using the Global Wind/Temp dataset. For wind speed prediction, DIN attains an MSE of 3.7391 and an MAE of 1.2987, matching or exceeding the performance of leading baseline models. For temperature prediction, DIN demonstrates superior results with an MSE of 6.8013 and an MAE of 1.7687, outperforming all baseline models across various architectural categories. These improvements highlight the model's strong capability in capturing complex spatiotemporal dependencies and underlying physical dynamics within multivariate, multi-station meteorological data.

4.3   Ablaction Study

To verify the effectiveness of key components in our framework, we conducted comprehensive ablation studies.

As shown in Table 2, the first analysis evaluates the contributions of the components of spatial-temporal dynamical modeling. Using only temporal modeling (TM) yields baseline performance, while incorporating cross-regional spatial modeling (CSM) largely reduces temperature prediction errors, demonstrating the necessity of capturing large-scale weather interactions. However, the improvement in wind speed prediction results remains insignificant. By further incorporating local dynamical modeling (LDM), the model achieves optimal results, with an MSE of 6.801 for temperature and 3.739 for wind speed. This confirms that localized dynamics effectively complements spatiotemporal pattern extraction. Overall, these results underscore the critical role of jointly modeling temporal evolution, large-scale spatial dependencies, and local dynamics for accurately representing complex weather systems.

In Table 3, we investigate the role of low-order direct interaction and high-order cross-variable interaction (HCI). Specifically, a naive fusion of raw cross-variable representations yields limited improvement in meteorological variable prediction. In contrast, our full model, which integrates higher-order spatial derivatives, achieves the lowest MSE values (6.801 for temperature and 3.739 for wind speed). These results confirm that high-order mixed partial derivatives effectively capture nonlinear cross-variable dependencies by modeling shared spatial variations, thereby enhancing predictive accuracy.

The collective results highlight the critical role of both SDM and HCI in achieving accurate weather forecasting. These findings offer valuable insights into the key architectural choices that underpin the model's ability to capture complex spatiotemporal dynamics and physics-informed interdependencies within weather systems.

4.4   Conclusion

In this paper, we propose a novel Dynamical Interaction Network (DIN) for accurate multi-station multi-variable weather prediction which incorporates physical insights with data-driven learning. By integrating a SDM module to capture multi-scale atmospheric processes by integrating local physical dynamics, cross-regional patterns, and temporal evolution, alongside a HCI module to model the complex dependencies among meteorological variables by using convolutions to simulate differential operators. Extensive experimental evaluations on the Global Wind/Temp benchmark demonstrate that our approach achieves state-of-the-art forecasting performance, significantly outperforming existing methods across multiple meteorological variables.

References

1. Akhyar, A.: Deep artificial intelligence applications for natural disaster management systems: a methodological review. Ecol. Ind. **163**, 112067 (2024)
2. de Bezenac, E., Pajot, A., Gallinari, P.: Deep learning for physical processes: incorporating prior scientific knowledge. In: International Conference on Learning Representations (2018)
3. Bi, K., Xie, L., Zhang, H., Chen, X., Gu, X., Tian, Q.: Accurate medium-range global weather forecasting with 3d neural networks. Nature **619**(7970), 533–538 (2023)
4. Cao, D., et al.: Spectral temporal graph neural network for multivariate time-series forecasting. Adv. Neural. Inf. Process. Syst. **33**, 17766–17778 (2020)
5. Dey, R., Salem, F.M.: Gate-variants of gated recurrent unit (GRU) neural networks. In: 2017 IEEE 60th International Midwest Symposium on Circuits and Systems (MWSCAS), pp. 1597–1600. IEEE (2017)
6. Ding, X., et al.: UniRepLKNet: a universal perception large-kernel convnet for audio video point cloud time-series and image recognition. In: Proceedings of the IEEE/CVF Conference on Computer Vision and Pattern Recognition, pp. 5513–5524 (2024)
7. Ekambaram, V., Jati, A., Nguyen, N., Sinthong, P., Kalagnanam, J.: TSMixer: lightweight MLP-mixer model for multivariate time series forecasting. In: Proceedings of the 29th ACM SIGKDD Conference on Knowledge Discovery and Data Mining, pp. 459–469 (2023)

8. Fan, C., Xu, J., Natarajan, B.Y., Mostafavi, A.: Interpretable machine learning learns complex interactions of urban features to understand socio-economic inequality. Comput.-Aided Civ. Infrastruct. Eng. **38**(14), 2013–2029 (2023)

9. Feng, Y., Wang, Q., Xia, Y., Huang, J., Zhong, S., Liang, Y.: Spatio-temporal field neural networks for air quality inference. In: Proceedings of the Thirty-Third International Joint Conference on Artificial Intelligence, pp. 7260–7268 (2024)

10. Graves, A., Graves, A.: Long short-term memory. Supervised sequence labelling with recurrent neural networks, pp. 37–45 (2012)

11. Guen, V.L., Thome, N.: Disentangling physical dynamics from unknown factors for unsupervised video prediction. In: Proceedings of the IEEE/CVF Conference on Computer Vision and Pattern Recognition, pp. 11474–11484 (2020)

12. Guo, J., et al.: Compressing large language models by joint sparsification and quantization. In: Forty-First International Conference on Machine Learning (2024)

13. Guo, J., Xu, D., Ouyang, W.: Multidimensional pruning and its extension: a unified framework for model compression. IEEE Trans. Neural Netw. Learn. Syst. (2023)

14. Guo, J., Zhang, W., Ouyang, W., Xu, D.: Model compression using progressive channel pruning. IEEE Trans. Circ. Syst. Video Technol. (2020)

15. He, C., Ding, Y., Guo, J., Gong, R., Qin, H., Liu, X.: DA-KD: difficulty-aware knowledge distillation for efficient large language models. In: Forty-First International Conference on Machine Learning (2025)

16. Kochkov, D., et al.: Neural general circulation models for weather and climate. Nature, 1–7 (2024)

17. Lam, R., et al.: Learning skillful medium-range global weather forecasting. Science **382**(6677), 1416–1421 (2023)

18. Lin, H., Gao, Z., Xu, Y., Wu, L., Li, L., Li, S.Z.: Conditional local convolution for spatio-temporal meteorological forecasting. In: Proceedings of the AAAI Conference on Artificial Intelligence, vol. 36, pp. 7470–7478 (2022)

19. Long, Z., Lu, Y., Dong, B.: PDE-Net 2.0: learning PDEs from data with a numeric-symbolic hybrid deep network. J. Comput. Phys. **399**, 108925 (2019)

20. Ma, M., et al.: HiSTGNN: hierarchical spatio-temporal graph neural network for weather forecasting. Inf. Sci. **648**, 119580 (2023)

21. Ma, Y., et al.: SeeMore: a spatiotemporal predictive model with bidirectional distillation and level-specific meta-adaptation. SCIENCE CHINA Inf. Sci. **67**(8), 1–25 (2024)

22. Medsker, L.R., Jain, L., et al.: Recurrent neural networks. Des. Appl. **5**(64–67), 2 (2001)

23. Rasp, S., et al.: WeatherBench 2: a benchmark for the next generation of data-driven global weather models. J. Adv. Model. Earth Syst. **16**(6), e2023MS004019 (2024)

24. Tang, J., Wei, W., Xia, L., Huang, C.: EasyST: a simple framework for spatio-temporal prediction. In: Proceedings of the 33rd ACM International Conference on Information and Knowledge Management, pp. 2220–2229 (2024)

25. Vaswani, A., et al.: Attention is all you need. Adv. Neural Inf. Process. Syst. **30** (2017)

26. Verma, Y., Heinonen, M., Garg, V.: ClimODE: climate and weather forecasting with physics-informed neural ODEs. arXiv preprint arXiv:2404.10024 (2024)

27. Wang, S., et al.: TimeMixer: decomposable multiscale mixing for time series forecasting. In: The Twelfth International Conference on Learning Representations (2024)

28. Wang, Y., Han, Y., Guo, Y.: Self-adaptive extreme penalized loss for imbalanced time series prediction. In: Proceedings of the Thirty-Third International Joint Conference on Artificial Intelligence, pp. 5135–5143 (2024)
29. Wu, H., Hu, T., Liu, Y., Zhou, H., Wang, J., Long, M.: TimesNet: temporal 2D-variation modeling for general time series analysis. In: The Eleventh International Conference on Learning Representations (2023)
30. Wu, H., Xu, J., Wang, J., Long, M.: AutoFormer: decomposition transformers with auto-correlation for long-term series forecasting. Adv. Neural. Inf. Process. Syst. **34**, 22419–22430 (2021)
31. Wu, H., Zhou, H., Long, M., Wang, J.: Interpretable weather forecasting for worldwide stations with a unified deep model. Nat. Mach. Intell. **5**(6), 602–611 (2023)
32. Xu, C., Zheng, X., Lu, X.: Multi-level alignment network for cross-domain ship detection. Remote Sens. **14**(10), 2389 (2022)
33. Xu, Z., et al.: DGFormer: a physics-guided station level weather forecasting model with dynamic spatial-temporal graph neural network. GeoInformatica, 1–35 (2024)
34. Yi, K., et al.: FourierGNN: rethinking multivariate time series forecasting from a pure graph perspective. Adv. Neural. Inf. Process. Syst. **36**, 69638–69660 (2023)
35. Zeng, A., Chen, M., Zhang, L., Xu, Q.: Are transformers effective for time series forecasting? In: Proceedings of the AAAI Conference on Artificial Intelligence, vol. 37, pp. 11121–11128 (2023)
36. Zhang, Y., et al.: Skilful nowcasting of extreme precipitation with nowcastnet. Nature **619**(7970), 526–532 (2023)
37. Zhou, H., et al.: Informer: beyond efficient transformer for long sequence time-series forecasting. In: Proceedings of the AAAI Conference on Artificial Intelligence, vol. 35, pp. 11106–11115 (2021)
38. Zhou, T., Ma, Z., Wen, Q., Wang, X., Sun, L., Jin, R.: FEDformer: frequency enhanced decomposed transformer for long-term series forecasting. In: International Conference on Machine Learning, pp. 27268–27286. PMLR (2022)
39. Zhou, Z., Lyu, G., Huang, Y., Wang, Z., Jia, Z., Yang, Z.: SDFormer: transformer with spectral filter and dynamic attention for multivariate time series long-term forecasting. In: Proceedings of the Thirty-Third International Joint Conference on Artificial Intelligence, pp. 3–9 (2024)
40. Zhu, X., Xiong, Y., Wu, M., Nie, G., Zhang, B., Yang, Z.: Weather2K: a multivariate spatio-temporal benchmark dataset for meteorological forecasting based on real-time observation data from ground weather stations. In: International Conference on Artificial Intelligence and Statistics, pp. 2704–2722. PMLR (2023)

Towards Inclusive NLP: Assessing Compressed Multilingual Transformers Across Diverse Language Benchmarks

Maitha Alshehhi$^{(\boxtimes)}$, Ahmed Sharshar, and Mohsen Guizani

Mohamed bin Zayed University of Artificial Intelligence, Abu Dhabi, UAE
{Maitha.alshehhi,Ahmed.Sharshar,Mohsen.Guizani}@mbzuai.ac.ae

Abstract. Although LLMs have attained significant success in high-resource languages, their capacity in low-resource linguistic environments like Kannada and Arabic is not yet fully understood. This work benchmarking the performance of multilingual and monolingual Large Language Models (LLMs) across Arabic, English, and Indic languages, with particular emphasis on the effects of model compression strategies such as pruning and quantization. Findings shows significant performance differences driven by linguistic diversity and resource availability on SOTA LLMS as BLOOMZ, AceGPT, Jais, LLaMA-2, XGLM, and AraGPT2. We find that multilingual versions of the model outperform their language-specific counterparts across the board, indicating substantial cross-lingual transfer benefits. Quantization (4-bit and 8-bit) is effective in maintaining model accuracy while promoting efficiency, but aggressive pruning significantly compromises performance, especially in bigger models. Our findings pinpoint key strategies to construct scalable and fair multilingual NLP solutions and underscore the need for interventions to address hallucination and generalization errors in the low-resource setting.

Keywords: Multilingual Large Language Models (LLMs) ·
Low-resource languages · Model evaluation and benchmarking · Model compression

1 Introduction

Large Language Models (LLMs) have advanced to enable transformative applications across diverse sectors. In multilingual and culturally rich environments, they enhance communication, support inclusive language technologies, and enable multilingual content generation [18]. LLMs are driving innovation in fields such as healthcare, education, finance, robotics, and customer service. In finance, they aid sentiment analysis, forecasting, and portfolio optimization by processing vast unstructured data [3]. In education, they support personalized learning, tutoring, and automated content creation [7]. In healthcare, they assist with

© The Author(s), under exclusive license to Springer Nature Singapore Pte Ltd. 2025
Y. Ma et al. (Eds.): IJCAI 2025, CCIS 2640, pp. 108–126, 2025.
https://doi.org/10.1007/978-981-95-0988-1_8

diagnosis, treatment planning, and clinical decision-making [20]. Businesses benefit from LLMs through efficient document processing, summarization, chatbot development, and multilingual support [6].

While these advancements have demonstrated great promise, their benefits remain disproportionately centered on English and other high-resource languages. Many low-resource languages, including Arabic and Kannada, are still underrepresented in training data [9]. This underrepresentation limits the generalization capacity of LLMs and leads to higher error rates and hallucination tendencies when applied in these contexts. These issues contribute to a growing digital divide, preventing equitable access to high-quality language technologies.

Arabic and Indic languages, particularly Kannada, pose significant modeling difficulties due to their complex morphology, complicated syntax, and broad geographical variation. Poorer performance on reasoning and comprehension tasks also arise from the absence of great corpora and benchmark datasets [8,10]. These limitations hinder the successful application of LLMs to real-world tasks such as legal interpretation, content moderation on social media, and analysis of local news. It is highly probable that there will be biased or erroneous results in low-resource languages without improved cross-lingual robustness. Evaluation of models in such languages entails complex comprehension of linguistic idiosyncrasies combined with data scarcity. Efficiency is also a relevant consideration because most real-world applications need to operate under stringent hardware and latency limitations. Creating robust and equitable NLP models that generalize across different linguistic contexts depends on addressing these issues.

In this paper, we rigorously compare multilingual and monolingual LLMs on Arabic, English, and Kannada languages under standard benchmarks. Moreover, we measure the impact of compression methods—namely, pruning and quantization—on model quality, emphasizing accuracy, generalization power, and trustability under high-resource and low-resource settings. Through our large-scale experimentation, we shed light on the crucial factors that influence model size and compression methodology on the reliability and efficacy of multilingual linguistic models, thus informing the development of scalable, fair, and resilient NLP systems. Our major contributions are listed below:

- **Comprehensive Multilingual Benchmarking:** We provide rigorous cross-lingual evaluations of LLMs employing benchmarks such as ArabicMMLU, EnglishMMLU, and Kannada-ARC-C-2.5K.
- **Detailed Analysis of Compression Strategies:** With a systematic evaluation of the effects of quantization and pruning on accuracy and confidence, we uncover thresholds that are pivotal to maintaining performance.
- **Language-Specific Performance Insights:** The results of our work identify crucial Arabic-specific model limitations (e.g., AraGPT2), pointing to the relative strengths of multilingual models.
- **Future Directions:** Our findings pave the way for a deeper understanding of hallucination patterns in LLMs, particularly in low-resource language settings. This opens new research avenues for developing more robust and trust-

worthy language models through targeted mitigation strategies, ultimately enabling safer deployment in real-world, multilingual applications.

2   Related Work

2.1   Addressing Low-Resource Languages

Tackling the challenges of developing Arabic LLMs requires a multifaceted strategy, with a major emphasis on alleviating Arabic data scarcity through approaches like synthetic data generation, back-translation, and curated corpora. Models such as Jais, Falcon, and AraGPT have each made important strides: Jais, a 13-billion-parameter bilingual model, employs cross-lingual transfer learning but still falls short of GPT-3.5-turbo in trustworthiness evaluations [23]; Falcon, despite its massive 180B-parameter version trained on over 3.5 trillion tokens, achieves less than 50% accuracy on ArabicMMLU, illustrating that scale alone is not sufficient for Arabic proficiency [15]; and AraGPT, which leverages synthetic data techniques, has improved performance in Arabic sentiment classification but continues to struggle with dialectal comprehension [22]. Together, these models showcase a range of strategies such as cross-lingual fine-tuning, synthetic data augmentation, and dialectal adaptation, but persistent challenges in trustworthiness, reasoning, and dialectal coverage indicate that significant gains will require further investment in data quality, domain-specific training, and dialect-focused resources [45].

2.2   Benchmarks for LLM Evaluation

MMLU-based benchmarks have become fundamental for evaluating LLMs across languages and subject areas, measuring reasoning, factual accuracy, and subject-specific skills. ArabicMMLU is widely used to assess Arabic-language tasks, with studies showing that multilingual models can perform competitively with monolingual ones but still show inconsistencies in reasoning and literacy tasks [5]. However, ArabicMMLU has limitations, notably its emphasis on Modern Standard Arabic and its limited alignment with real-world applications, prompting the development of more comprehensive resources such as ArabLegalEval [12] and the AlGhafa Evaluation Benchmark [1], which better capture dialectal diversity and specialized domains.

Similarly, EnglishMMLU is a standard for assessing LLM reasoning and factual knowledge across a wide range of topics [21], but faces challenges like shortcut learning, mislabeled answers, and translation artifacts that limit its real-world relevance [26]. While models like GPT-4 and Claude consistently achieve top performance, the benchmark's reliance on translated content often underestimates non-English model capabilities [21]. In low-resource settings, Indic benchmarks such as Kannada-ARC-C-2.5K are critical for evaluating LLMs [25], although models continue to lag behind English performance due to issues like translation dependence, data imbalance, and a shortage of high-quality native datasets [19], highlighting the pressing need for more robust multilingual resources.

2.3   Hallucination Detection and Mitigation Strategies

Hallucination in Arabic LLMs occurs more frequently than in English models, largely due to the scarcity of high-quality Arabic data, the complexity of dialectal variation, and the absence of structured knowledge sources [4]. Errors are especially common in factual recall and translation tasks, where linguistic complexity and syntactic differences further exacerbate hallucination rates. Recent efforts to address these challenges include integrating structured knowledge bases, utilizing Quranic and Classical Arabic corpora, applying retrieval-augmented generation (RAG), and adopting self-consistency decoding strategies. Combining RAG with Arabic MMLU and leveraging techniques like parameter-efficient fine-tuning and reinforcement learning from human feedback (RLHF) is anticipated to enhance both factual accuracy and dialectal robustness in Arabic LLMs [4,16].

2.4   Model Compression Techniques

As LLMs continue to expand, compression techniques like pruning and quantization have become crucial for enabling deployment on resource-constrained devices, though maintaining accuracy particularly for Arabic remains difficult. Structured pruning methods like FLOP and block-aware pruning reduce model size by removing less critical parameters while preserving dense structures and minimizing information loss [28]. Quantization strategies such as attention-aware PTQ, low-rank QAT, and hybrid quantization lower memory demands by reducing numerical precision, but aggressive quantization can introduce significant errors, especially in morphologically complex languages like Arabic [30] Research shows that compressed Arabic models, particularly after 4-bit quantization, experience higher hallucination rates, degraded factual recall, and weaker syntactic understanding compared to English models [24]. Looking ahead, it is crucial to develop compression methods specifically designed to preserve Arabic's linguistic richness while balancing computational efficiency and factual reliability.

3   Methodology

This study systematically evaluates the performance of six open-access LLMs—BLOOMZ, AceGPT, Jais, LLaMA-2, XGLM, and AraGPT—across three multilingual benchmarks: ArabicMMLU, EnglishMMLU, and Indic-Benchmark (Kannada-ARC-C-2.5K). The primary goals are to assess model adaptability to low-resource languages, particularly Arabic, and to analyze how compression techniques, including pruning and quantization, impact performance.

3.1   Model Selection

Model selection for this study was guided by the objective of capturing a broad spectrum of multilingual capabilities, architectural innovations, and training strategies relevant to low-resource languages. Jais and AraGPT were included due to their explicit focus on Arabic corpora, providing a baseline for evaluating performance on Arabic-language tasks. In contrast, BLOOMZ and XGLM were selected for their strong cross-lingual transfer abilities, making them ideal for assessing zero-shot generalization to Arabic and Indic benchmarks. Additionally, AceGPT and LLaMA-2, representing instruction-tuned models, were incorporated to examine whether enhanced prompt-following behavior improves performance on Arabic tasks without fine-tuning. Table 1 summarizes all the chosen models with their configurations.

Table 1. Comprehensive overview of the language models evaluated in this study, outlining their parameter scale, domain specialisation, and the rationale for their inclusion in our experiments.

Model	Size	Specialization	Selection Rationale
BLOOMZ	560M/7B	Multilingual NLP, zero-shot learning	Strong cross-lingual generalization
AceGPT	7B/13B	Conversational AI, instruction-tuned	Evaluate Arabic instruction following
Jais	13B	Arabic-centric NLP tasks	Arabic-optimised performance baseline
LLaMA-2	7B/13B	General NLP, chat models	General-purpose multilingual evaluation
XGLM	1.7B/7.5B	Multilingual NLP	Zero-shot transfer to low-resource languages
AraGPT2	135M/1.46B	Arabic text generation	Benchmark Arabic-focused pre-training

In addition to language coverage, we prioritized architectural diversity in model selection. Although all selected models employ decoder-only Transformer architectures, they vary in optimization strategies, e.g., Grouped Query Attention (GQA) in LLaMA-2 and multitask fine-tuning in BLOOMZ and XGLM. A comparison of the smallest and largest members of these models permitted us to examine systematically the impact of architectural variation and model size on multilingual and Arabic-specific performance, particularly under compression techniques such as quantization and pruning. This permits one to see how architectural decisions affect generalization, specialization gains, and computational efficiency-accuracy-model size trade-offs under resource-constrained settings.

3.2   Model Descriptions

BLOOMZ is an extension of the BLOOM model, optimized for multilingual zero-shot learning and trained on 46 languages and 13 programming languages [29]. While it excels at cross-lingual generalization, it demands high computational resources and struggles with long-form text consistency and biases.

AceGPT is an instruction-tuned, transformer-based model designed for multilingual text processing, dialogue systems, and code generation [13]. It emphasizes instruction-following, trained on diverse web, academic, and conversational datasets. Despite its strong dialogue performance, it is computationally expensive and prone to occasional hallucinations.

Jais is a 13B-parameter Arabic-first LLM developed for Arabic and English NLP tasks, specializing in text generation, translation, and summarization [23]. It uses a decoder-only architecture and is trained on 72 billion Arabic tokens plus multilingual data. Although highly effective for Arabic, it requires significant resources and shows bias toward Modern Standard Arabic over dialects.

LLaMA 2 is a multilingual transformer-based model featuring GQA, SwiGLU activations, and pre-normalization [27]. Trained on a carefully filtered web, academic, and code corpus, it supports strong performance in conversational AI and text generation tasks. However, it demands high-end GPUs and shares bias and long-form coherence limitations common to large models.

XGLM is a multilingual decoder-only LLM optimized for low-resource and cross-lingual text generation [17]. Trained on over 50 languages with multilingual tokenization, it achieves strong transferability across linguistic contexts but struggles with multilingual fairness and long-form coherence.

AraGPT is an Arabic-specialized LLM modeled after GPT-2 for Arabic text generation, translation, and sentiment analysis [2]. While it excels in Arabic generation, it faces challenges with dialect bias and long-form text generation.

3.3   Datasets

The **EnglishMMLU** benchmark [11] evaluates a model's general knowledge across 57 subjects spanning STEM, social sciences, humanities, and specialized fields like law and medicine. It contains 15,908 manually collected questions sourced from exams and professional certifications, designed to assess real-world problem-solving rather than just linguistic ability. MMLU is a standard benchmark for measuring LLMs' zero-shot and few-shot reasoning capabilities, revealing both the strengths of models in achieving human-level performance in many areas and their continued struggles with complex reasoning tasks.

ArabicMMLU is a comprehensive benchmark designed to evaluate Arabic language models across 40 subjects and multiple educational levels, based on 14,575 multiple-choice questions drawn from eight Middle Eastern and North African countries [15]. Covering disciplines from STEM to humanities, the dataset is structured across primary, middle school, high school, university, and professional levels, with careful quality control by native Arabic speakers as shown in Fig. 1. Despite its breadth, evaluations show that even leading models like GPT-4 achieve only 62.3% accuracy, emphasizing the significant challenges and the critical role ArabicMMLU plays in advancing Arabic NLP research.

The **IndicBenchmark** (Kannada-ARC-C-2.5K) [14] dataset targets Kannada, a major Indic language, providing around 2,500 multiple-choice questions aimed at assessing comprehension, reasoning, and language understanding. Structured in Parquet format for accessibility, it addresses the underrepresentation of Indic languages in NLP research by offering a high-quality benchmark for low-resource language evaluation. Despite advances in multilingual modeling, Kannada remains a challenging language for state-of-the-art systems, highlighting the importance of benchmarks like Indic-Benchmark.

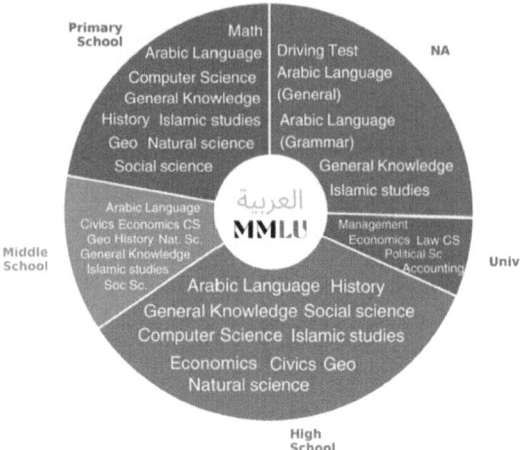

Fig. 1. ArabicMMLU Distribution of Educational Levels & Corresponding Subjects [15].

3.4   Compression Techniques

Weight pruning reduces the size and computational complexity of a neural network by removing weights with low importance. L1 unstructured pruning is applied to all linear layers, removing weights with the smallest absolute values. Pruning is performed at different levels (20%, 40%, 80%) to assess the impact on performance. Given a weight matrix W with elements w_{ij}, a threshold τ is chosen such that weights satisfying $|w_{ij}| < \tau$ are set to zero:

$$w_{ij} = \begin{cases} 0, & \text{if } |w_{ij}| < \tau \\ w_{ij}, & \text{otherwise} \end{cases} \tag{1}$$

Quantization reduces model precision to improve efficiency. By mapping floating-point weights to lower-bit representations (e.g., 4-bit and 8-bit integers), it reduces memory requirements and speeds up inference. The transformation follows:

$$q = \text{round}\left(\frac{w}{S}\right) + Z \tag{2}$$

where w is the original weight, S is the scale factor, and Z is the zero point ensuring zero representation in the quantized range. For 8-bit quantization, q lies in $[0, 255]$ or $[-128, 127]$, while for 4-bit, q ranges between $[0, 15]$ or $[-8, 7]$. The inverse transformation reconstructs weights as:

$$\hat{w} = S \cdot (q - Z) \tag{3}$$

4 Experimental Setup

Evaluation Pipeline. The pipeline consists of the following steps:

(1) *Model Initialization:* Load models and tokenizers with necessary configurations.
(2) *Compression:* Apply pruning or quantization before inference.
(3) *Prompt Design:* Tailor prompts per benchmark—ArabicMMLU uses metadata (subject, level, country), EnglishMMLU follows multiple-choice format, Indic-Benchmark uses Kannada prompts.
(4) *Inference:* Extract logits at the final token position for each answer choice and select the answer with the highest probability.

The performance metrics are accuracy (ratio of correct responses in all tasks) and confidence (mean softmax probability of the selected answer), and both provide an end-to-end measure of accuracy and certainty. Category-wise accuracy and confidence values are used to analyze fine-grained model performance in varying subject domains.

Experiments were conducted on a Paperspace A100 GPU environment, with PyTorch and Hugging Face libraries supporting model handling, inference, and compression. All predictions, scores, and analysis results were systematically logged in structured CSV files to ensure full reproducibility.

5 Results

This chapter offers an overall analysis of monolingual and multilingual LLMs for Arabic, English, and Indic Kannada benchmarks, investigating the effect of model capacity, pretraining in multiple languages, and compression strategies for accuracy, confidence, and cross-lingual generalization.

5.1 EnglishMMLU Evaluation

Results for the EnglishMMLU benchmark (Table 2 establish the highest full-precision score for AceGPT-13B (47.7 %), beating the multilingual BLOOMZ-7.1B (44.7 %) and maintaining a considerable lead over all models with ≤ 7 B parameters (≤ 36.7 %). The trend confirms that large English instruction tuning supersedes parameter count alone (BLOOMZ vs. AceGPT-13B) or language specialisation alone (Jais-13B). Quantisation is essentially cost-free: converting any model to 8-bit—and for most of them, to 4-bit—alters accuracy by < 2 %, with AceGPT-13B and BLOOMZ-7.1B even experiencing.

Sparsification up to 20 % is benign for all eleven systems (mean $\Delta = 0.3$ pp). With 40 % sparsity, accuracy starts to diverge: BLOOMZ-7.1B and AceGPT-13B fall only 3-4 % but are still the leaders, while instruction-tuned AceGPT-7B drops 6.5%. Extreme 80 % sparsity brings the top-performers down: AceGPT-13B to 18.6 %, BLOOMZ-7.1B to 24.0 %-putting them at the level of small dense baselines like BLOOMZ-560M (23.0 %). Therefore, making a strong model more compact brings obvious advantages only in the *safe zone* (≤ 40 % sparsity); above that level the pre-training and depth advantages that characterize large models are effectively abolished. Further, we conducted an in-depth ablation study for each sub-category in the dataset, along with all models and configurations, for detailed insights as shown in Table 5.

Table 2. EnglishMMLU Model Accuracy

Model	FP	4Q	8Q	20%P	40%P	80%P
BLOOMZ-560M	25.97	25.93	26.23	25.80	25.11	22.95
BLOOMZ-7.1B	44.67	43.81	44.72	44.59	41.58	24.04
AceGPT-7B	36.72	23.53	23.86	31.46	30.27	24.87
AceGPT-13B	47.74	48.12	47.78	46.09	43.34	18.61
Jais-13B	25.77	24.12	23.54	25.74	24.78	23.91
LLaMA 2-7B	27.20	25.85	25.82	27.75	26.81	21.53
LLaMA 2-13B	30.61	29.93	26.32	30.84	29.84	24.46
XGLM-1.7B	22.92	22.92	22.96	23.55	15.38	26.89
XGLM-7.5B	23.27	22.92	23.10	22.97	24.64	24.28
AraGPT2-135M	23.84	20.18	23.63	23.88	23.07	21.09
AraGPT2-1.47B	9.60	24.12	9.69	5.66	1.38	14.82

5.2   ArabicMMLU Evaluation

Table 3 shows the results of ArabicMMLU on all categories together for different settings. Across all 11 evaluated systems, larger generalist models consistently outperform their smaller or expert-specialized counterparts. Notably, BLOOMZ-7.1B attains the highest full-precision (FP) accuracy at 41.7%, followed closely by the instruction-tuned AceGPT-13B (40.3%) and the Arabic-specialized Jais-13B (36.0%). In contrast, all models with $\leq$7B parameters fall below 34%. This disparity highlights that scale and broad multilingual pretraining—especially when combined with multitask supervision—offer greater leverage for Arabic reasoning than pure language-specific pretraining (e.g., Jais vs. BLOOMZ) or scale alone (e.g., AceGPT vs. BLOOMZ). Moreover, quantization incurs minimal loss, reducing to 8-bit—and in most cases 4-bit—precision leads to a drop of less than 2% points in accuracy, suggesting that low-precision inference should be the default for resource-constrained deployment.

Pruning reveals a clear accuracy-efficiency trade-off consistent across model families. Up to 20% sparsity yields negligible accuracy degradation (< 1 %). At 40% sparsity, model-dependent effects emerge: BLOOMZ-7.1B and Jais-13B remain strong at 36.9% and 38.8%, respectively—still outperforming all dense models under 7B—whereas AceGPT-13B and other instruction-tuned variants drop sharply by 8âĂŞ11%, likely due to reduced redundancy in task-specialized layers. Under extreme 80% pruning, accuracy drops substantially across the board, yet a pruned BLOOMZ-7.1B (effectively ~1.4B parameters) still matches or exceeds dense 1âĂŞ2B baselines. This validates that *compressing a strong, large model is generally preferable to using a natively small one.* In summary: (i) favor the strongest multilingual model available, (ii) apply aggressive quantization, and (iii) prune moderately, ideally capping sparsity.

Overall performance across ArabicMMLU is consistently weaker than across EnglishMMLU, which is a dramatic cross-lingual gap caused by an imbalance in the amount of available data. Even Arabic fine-tuned versions underperform because there is much less volume and quality of Arabic data than for English. The consequence is ongoing cultural and linguistic bias towards English, which distorts the reasoning abilities of the models in Arabic domains. To gain a clearer insight into the nature of this behaviour, we performed a detailed ablation across all subject domains in the ArabicMMLU set, as listed in Table 6.

Table 3. ArabicMMLU Model Accuracy

Model	FP	4Q	8Q	20%P	40%P	80%P
BLOOMZ-560M	27.02	27.46	26.70	26.43	31.12	29.36
BLOOMZ-7.1B	41.71	39.86	41.86	40.79	36.88	30.56
AceGPT-7B	34.22	32.93	32.00	29.52	26.76	21.20
AceGPT-13B	40.27	39.16	40.59	36.98	29.69	21.16
Jais-13B	36.01	35.59	35.03	35.68	38.79	32.06
LLaMA 2-7B	31.27	31.20	31.26	28.79	30.47	25.89
LLaMA 2-13B	31.38	30.94	31.22	32.49	28.43	22.25
XGLM-1.7B	30.90	28.17	30.95	29.29	19.74	21.14
XGLM-7.5B	31.24	31.16	31.20	31.20	28.75	26.47
AraGPT2-135M	31.04	30.47	30.95	31.06	31.14	25.89
AraGPT2-1.47B	31.15	31.18	31.15	31.16	31.17	27.77

5.3   Indic Benchmark (Kannada) Evaluation

Table 4 and Fig. 2 present results on the Indic Kannada benchmark. BLOOMZ-7.1B led with 34.56% full-precision accuracy, followed by BLOOMZ-560M (26.32%). AceGPT and XGLM variants scored slightly lower, reflecting low-resource adaptation challenges. Quantization to 8-bit precision maintained accuracy within 0.3%, confirming its safety as a compression method. However, 80% pruning caused significant declines for all models, particularly larger ones.

The accuracy spread between full-precision and 8-bit quantized models remains under 0.3%, underscoring quantization's minimal impact even in scarce-data settings. Monolingual models like AraGPT2-1.47B underperform multilingual counterparts by 12%, indicating the necessity of dedicated adaptation strategies such as synthetic data augmentation. Pruning-induced cross-lingual drift is evident: at 40% sparsity, BLOOMZ-7.1B's accuracy drops by 7.9% on Kannada, compared to 4.8% on Arabic and 3.1% on English, suggesting that cross-lingual representations for low-resource languages are less redundantly encoded and more sensitive to weight removal.

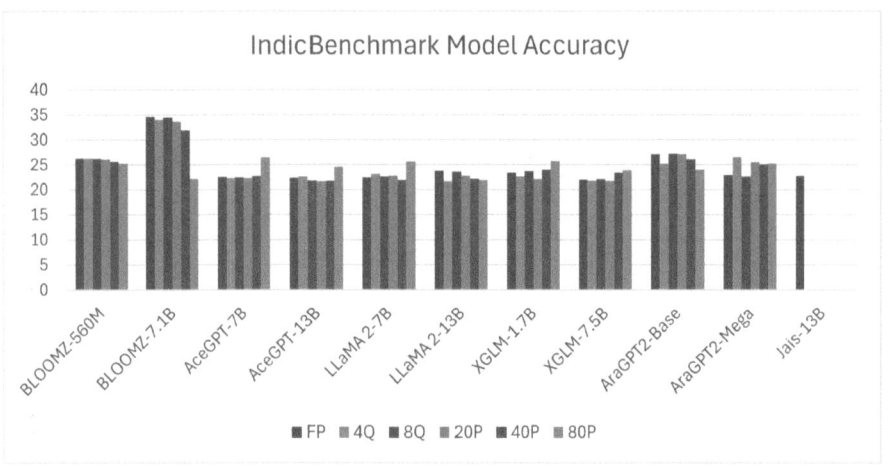

Fig. 2. IndicBenchmark Models' Accuracy Comparison in Different Configurations.

Indic-Kannada shows the worst performance among the three languages that we scored, lagging much behind both Arabic and English. This is because it is a very low-resource language with very little presence in the pretraining corpora of most of the best-performing models. In contrast, English is supported by large quantities of such training data, and Arabic is the one for which other models are specifically fine-tuned. Kannada does not have any such targeted large-scale training or fine-tuning. Therefore, as a consequence, the models are not generalizable. Also, since subject-wise subcategories are not included in the Indic-Benchmark, we couldn't carry out a detailed ablation study like those for the Arabic and English languages.

5.4   Cross-Benchmark Comparative Analysis

Comparative analysis across ArabicMMLU, EnglishMMLU, and Indic Kannada benchmarks shows consistent trends influenced by model size, diversity in training, and availability of training material. Multilingual models, such as BLOOMZ, consistently outperform with the generalization encouraged by pretraining over

Table 4. IndicBenchmark Model Accuracy

Model	FP	4Q	8Q	20%P	40%P	80%P
BLOOMZ-560M	26.32	26.24	26.20	26.08	25.64	25.25
BLOOMZ-7.1B	34.56	34.01	34.48	33.65	31.83	22.12
AceGPT-7B	22.43	22.16	22.39	22.20	22.63	26.48
AceGPT-13B	22.31	22.59	21.76	21.52	21.64	24.53
Jais-13B	22.63	22.01	21.68	21.97	20.56	22.34
LLaMA 2-7B	22.39	23.11	22.55	22.79	21.84	25.60
LLaMA 2-13B	23.78	21.56	23.62	22.71	22.08	21.80
XGLM-1.7B	23.38	22.59	23.66	22.00	23.94	25.76
XGLM-7.5B	21.88	21.76	22.00	21.60	23.38	23.82
AraGPT2-135M	27.15	25.17	27.23	27.15	26.12	23.98
AraGPT2-1.47B	22.83	26.60	22.59	25.49	25.09	25.25

broad language sets, which helps in effective generalization. AceGPT performs well over EnglishMMLU owing to English exclusive training, but degrades over Indic Kannada owing to training data differences. Monolingual models such as AraGPT2 perform well over ArabicMMLU but do not generalize well across benchmarks, attesting to the disadvantage of language specialization.

Compression techniques reveal other trends: 4-bit and 8-bit quantization are very lossless, decreasing accuracy by around 2% across all benchmarks. Pruning has trade-offs—sparsity above 40% degrades performance heavily, particularly for large models. Such degradation tends to undermine accuracy improvements over denser, smaller counterparts. Overall, performance tracks the resource gradient of the data: `EnglishMMLU` > `ArabicMMLU` > `Indic Kannada`, with strong predictive confidence vs. accuracy correlations. In conclusion, the insights are:

- **Increase in English-Arabic Performance Gap** The accuracy difference between large and small models is much wider in EnglishMMLU than in ArabicMMLU. This implies that the abundance of English data enables large models to learn general linguistic patterns, while the lack of Arabic data constrains size-based improvements.
- **Sensitivity of Larger Models to Pruning** Pruning to 20âĂŞ40% sparsity incurs negligible accuracy losses (<3%), whereas pruning above 40% can make pruned large models perform worse than unpruned smaller counterparts. The phenomenon suggests that aggressive weight elimination destroys the most essential network structure for fine-grained reasoning.
- **Multilingual Pretraining vs. Monolingual Specialization** Multilingual models like BLOOMZ-7.1B outperform monolingual Arabic models such as AraGPT2-1.47B on ArabicMMLU, demonstrating that shared cross-lingual embeddings built during multilingual pretraining improve robustness and generalization, whereas monolingual specialization may lead to overfitting narrow domains.

Table 5. EnglishMMLU Model Categorical Accuracy

Model Name	STEM	Humanities	Social Sciences	Other
BLOOMZ-560M	26.58	28.32	24.80	24.83
BLOOMZ-560M-4Q	26.69	27.97	24.19	25.11
BLOOMZ-560M-8Q	26.55	28.35	24.59	25.55
BLOOMZ-560M-20P	27.01	28.48	24.02	24.43
BLOOMZ-560M-40P	25.88	26.22	23.80	24.64
BLOOMZ-560M-80P	21.31	23.77	21.27	23.96
BLOOMZ-7.1B	40.35	42.04	51.44	45.56
BLOOMZ-7.1B-4Q	39.22	41.19	50.87	44.71
BLOOMZ-7.1B-8Q	40.39	42.01	51.88	45.51
BLOOMZ-7.1B-20P	40.46	42.20	51.22	45.32
BLOOMZ-7.1B-40P	37.17	39.47	46.77	42.84
BLOOMZ-7.1B-80P	22.87	25.90	23.41	23.82
AceGPT-7B	32.71	37.58	36.72	38.21
AceGPT-7B-4Q	22.19	24.24	22.27	24.29
AceGPT-7B-8Q	22.37	24.77	22.75	24.54
AceGPT-7B-20P	29.81	32.56	29.52	32.45
AceGPT-7B-40P	26.41	31.59	29.61	31.71
AceGPT-7B-80P	26.09	25.59	23.89	24.26
AceGPT-13B	39.50	47.63	53.49	49.56
AceGPT-13B-4Q	40.14	49.01	52.79	49.74
AceGPT-13B-8Q	40.14	47.91	52.93	49.15
AceGPT-13B-20P	37.10	47.22	50.09	48.29
AceGPT-13B-40P	36.46	44.46	47.82	44.32
AceGPT-13B-80P	23.86	8.82	21.70	20.22
Jais-13B	24.67	25.87	25.20	26.49
Jais-13B-20P	28.04	28.45	30.26	29.50
Jais-13B-40P	25.95	27.10	29.08	27.69
Jais-13B-80P	22.97	24.02	22.71	24.80
LLaMA 2-7B	26.76	30.08	25.15	26.63
LLaMA 2-7B-4Q	26.83	27.82	23.71	25.13
LLaMA 2-7B-8Q	26.48	28.04	23.45	25.20
Llama-2-7b-hf-20P	27.08	29.32	25.11	26.56
LLaMA 2-7B-40P	27.26	28.23	26.16	26.07
LLaMA 2-7B-80P	21.88	25.43	20.52	19.59
LLaMA 2-13B	27.12	32.31	30.35	31.49
LLaMA 2-13B-4Q	27.47	31.49	29.56	30.42

(*continued*)

Table 5. (*continued*)

Model Name	STEM	Humanities	Social Sciences	Other
LLaMA 2-13B-8Q	24.71	28.38	24.98	26.51
LLaMA 2-13B-20P	26.48	29.20	28.95	30.22
LLaMA 2-13B-40P	28.32	30.80	27.95	27.53
LLaMA 2-13B-80P	24.53	24.08	25.72	24.14
XGLM-1.7B	21.24	23.80	21.40	23.86
XGLM-1.7B-4Q	21.73	23.61	21.18	23.82
XGLM-1.7B-8Q	21.38	23.89	21.27	23.96
XGLM-1.7B-20P	22.09	24.33	22.14	24.38
XGLM-1.7B-40P	13.98	17.36	18.17	15.33
XGLM-1.7B-80P	27.75	23.92	31.09	26.33
XGLM-7.5B	22.23	24.18	21.57	23.95
XGLM-7.5B-4Q	21.31	23.67	21.31	23.95
XGLM-7.5B-8Q	21.59	24.27	21.53	23.82
XGLM-7.5B-20P	21.52	23.83	21.62	23.89
XGLM-7.5B-40P	22.58	23.99	25.68	25.18
XGLM-7.5B-80P	23.68	24.30	22.71	25.18
AraGPT2-135M	23.86	25.21	22.84	23.46
AraGPT2-135M-4Q	19.82	21.82	18.52	20.11
AraGPT2-135M-8Q	23.40	25.40	22.45	23.23
AraGPT2-135M-20P	24.14	25.21	23.14	23.30
AraGPT2-135M-40P	21.27	24.08	21.83	23.89
AraGPT2-135M-80P	20.67	17.65	20.61	23.41
AraGPT2-1.47B	6.87	12.72	8.25	9.75
AraGPT2-1.47B-4Q	25.63	24.93	23.01	23.37
AraGPT2-1.47B-8Q	7.04	12.40	8.47	9.96
AraGPT2-1.47B-20P	4.25	10.74	5.63	6.46
AraGPT2-1.47B-40P	2.51	4.11	3.89	3.50
AraGPT2-1.47B-80P	15.96	18.96	11.22	13.39

6   Limitations

Though this paper presents valuable insights into both monolingual and multilingual LLM performance in Arabic, English, and Kannada, it is constrained by some limitations. Firstly, experiments only included zero-shot scenarios and did not test the impact of a few-shot setting. Secondly, pruning and quantization strategies were utilized, yet sophisticated strategies like movement pruning and knowledge distillation were not considered. Thirdly, the evaluation was only conducted with MMLU benchmarks, not including human-human annotated tasks or actual applications, and the analysis of hallucinations was not systematic. Lastly, the investigation covered only Modern Standard Arabic and academic

Table 6. ArabicMMLU Model Categorical Accuracy

Model Name	STEM	Humanities	Social Science	Language	Other
BLOOMZ-560M	28.39	27.74	26.53	24.02	26.89
BLOOMZ-560M-4Q	29.22	28.24	26.10	24.56	27.93
BLOOMZ-560M-8Q	27.92	27.17	26.16	24.44	26.69
BLOOMZ-560M-20P	27.98	27.06	25.73	24.02	26.09
BLOOMZ-560M-40P	30.12	32.48	30.23	25.89	35.17
BLOOMZ-560M-80P	29.57	29.77	30.48	28.06	27.77
BLOOMZ-7.1B	39.88	41.67	44.58	34.98	44.54
BLOOMZ-7.1B-4Q	38.35	39.34	42.63	33.29	43.02
BLOOMZ-7.1B-8Q	39.97	42.00	44.63	35.34	44.50
BLOOMZ-7.1B-20P	38.73	40.57	43.39	34.02	44.58
BLOOMZ-7.1B-40P	36.49	34.69	39.72	32.63	39.38
BLOOMZ-7.1B-80P	28.98	33.82	29.69	24.44	33.13
AceGPT-7B	33.48	35.70	31.55	31.31	38.70
AceGPT-7B-4Q	32.48	33.84	30.62	30.52	37.05
AceGPT-7B-8Q	32.80	36.03	31.50	30.64	37.82
AceGPT-7B-20P	31.46	26.95	29.07	26.37	33.53
AceGPT-7B-40P	28.94	24.19	25.23	24.02	31.69
AceGPT-7B-80P	21.43	18.85	21.84	24.38	21.33
AceGPT-13B	38.79	43.09	39.66	32.63	44.02
AceGPT-13B-4Q	36.27	42.71	38.76	32.15	42.90
AceGPT-13B-8Q	39.66	43.15	40.37	33.11	43.34
AceGPT-13B-20P	35.09	37.95	37.46	31.19	41.18
AceGPT-13B-40P	30.78	27.55	30.79	26.97	31.65
AceGPT-13B-80P	21.71	20.52	20.85	24.86	19.37
Jais-13B	33.88	37.18	33.90	30.52	43.66
Jais-13B-20P	33.29	36.99	33.79	30.34	43.06
Jais-13B-40P	36.37	41.34	36.58	32.03	45.78
Jais-13B-80P	33.20	32.72	30.06	27.39	35.57
LLaMA 2-7B	30.68	31.82	30.68	27.45	34.61
LLaMA 2-7B-4Q	30.12	26.48	30.03	22.76	28.61
LLaMA 2-7B-8Q	30.59	31.87	30.54	27.51	34.73
Llama-2-7b-hf-20P	27.58	31.52	28.25	26.37	28.73
LLaMA 2-7B-40P	29.94	30.73	29.69	27.39	33.93
LLaMA 2-7B-80P	26.21	26.84	24.27	19.02	30.93
LLaMA 2-13B	30.06	31.74	30.28	28.36	36.09
LLaMA 2-13B-4Q	29.41	31.63	29.97	28.00	35.25
LLaMA 2-13B-8Q	29.88	31.63	30.14	28.18	35.93
LLaMA 2-13B-20P	32.42	32.37	30.62	28.96	37.78
LLaMA 2-13B-40P	28.70	26.59	30.20	26.19	29.73
LLaMA 2-13B-80P	23.14	21.23	22.09	23.18	22.21
XGLM-1.7B	29.88	31.11	30.37	27.93	34.61
XGLM-1.7B-4Q	29.32	25.69	29.52	23.90	31.25

(continued)

Table 6. (*continued*)

Model Name	STEM	Humanities	Social Science	Language	Other
XGLM-1.7B-8Q	29.78	31.19	30.37	28.06	34.85
XGLM-1.7B-20P	28.60	28.54	29.63	24.38	34.05
XGLM-1.7B-40P	19.29	18.63	20.06	19.02	21.97
XGLM-1.7B-80P	22.30	19.78	20.65	23.18	20.97
XGLM-7.5B	30.34	31.57	30.59	28.18	34.85
XGLM-7.5B-4Q	29.81	31.55	30.54	28.24	35.17
XGLM-7.5B-8Q	30.34	31.55	30.54	28.30	34.65
XGLM-7.5B-20P	30.16	31.46	30.45	28.30	35.13
XGLM-7.5B-40P	26.40	29.44	27.32	28.72	32.85
XGLM-7.5B-80P	28.51	23.64	28.62	22.58	27.53
AraGPT2-135M	30.16	31.49	30.11	27.93	34.89
AraGPT2-135M-4Q	29.81	30.45	29.75	27.63	34.25
AraGPT2-135M-8Q	30.00	31.41	30.14	27.93	34.65
AraGPT2-135M-20P	29.84	31.55	30.31	27.87	35.09
AraGPT2-135M-40P	29.88	31.46	30.54	28.24	35.05
AraGPT2-135M-80P	23.07	25.06	27.40	26.73	28.05
AraGPT2-1.47B	30.16	31.16	30.54	28.00	35.37
AraGPT2-1.47B-4Q	29.88	31.55	30.54	28.24	35.17
AraGPT2-1.47B-8Q	30.25	31.35	30.31	28.06	35.25
AraGPT2-1.47B-20P	29.91	31.55	30.40	28.06	35.33
AraGPT2-1.47B-40P	29.91	31.55	30.48	28.18	35.21
AraGPT2-1.47B-80P	27.58	30.78	28.36	25.83	24.05

Kannada, ignoring the dialectal differences and the domain of code-switching phenomena, both of which are promising avenues for future investigation.

7   Future Work

Future work would aim to extend benchmark datasets to more low-resource languages like Arabic and Kannada, with a priority on developing high-quality datasets that reflect dialect variability and genuine usage context. Systematic evaluation towards mitigating hallucination and bias is also important with the use of advanced fine-tuning, targeted prompt engineering, and bias-correction approaches. Optimization of LLM efficiency using advanced compression techniques like movement pruning, knowledge distillation, and enhanced quantization is also important in enabling their deployment in resource-scarce settings. Collaboration across disciplines involving linguistics, cognitive science, AI ethics, and human-in-the-loop approaches would significantly increase the reliability, contextual awareness, and general trust of multilingual LLMs.

8 Recommendations

There are a number of recommended key strategies to improve LLM performance on low-resource languages. First, using modular multilingual architectures can make a big difference by dynamically routing the input to language-specific models. Second, the use of synthetic data augmentation—back-translating high-resource datasets into low-resource languages—can significantly increase the size of training corpora and the ability of the model to generalize. Third, the evaluation frameworks can transition from fixed scholarly yardsticks to dynamic, interactive testing that more closely reflects real-world usage and user behaviors. The adoption of these strategies will make the development of multilingual AI systems more scalable, robust, and inclusive.

9 Conclusion

This work provides a structured comparison of multilingual and monolingual LLMs on Arabic, English, and Indic (Kannada) benchmarks, characterizing the accuracyâĂŞefficiency trade-offs brought by compression. Cross-lingual robustness is stronger in multilingual models, as demonstrated by BLOOMZ-7.1B, than in language-specialized counterparts. Four-bit and eight-bit quantization reduced memory and latency at minimal loss of accuracy, beneficial to hardware-restricted deployments, while moderate sparsity was sufficient before noticeable loss of stability and performance, particularly in larger models. Towards advancing the community, we propose dynamic, interaction-oriented benchmarking, dialect-aware enriching of corpora, principled hallucination reduction, and modular multilingual adapters. These directions collectively offer more resilient, inclusive, and scalable NLP solutions.

References

1. Almazrouei, E., et al.: Alghafa evaluation benchmark for Arabic language models. In: Proceedings of ArabicNLP 2023, pp. 244–275 (2023)
2. Antoun, W., Baly, F., Hajj, H.: Aragpt2: pre-trained transformer for Arabic language generation. arXiv preprint arXiv:2012.15520 (2020)
3. Sindhu, B., Prathamesh, R.P., Sameera, M.B., KumaraSwamy, S.: The evolution of large language model: models, applications and challenges, pp. 1–8 (2024). https://doi.org/10.1109/ICCTAC61556.2024.10581180
4. Bari, M.S., et al.: Allam: large language models for Arabic and English. arXiv preprint arXiv:2407.15390 (2024)
5. Boughorbel, S., Hawasly, M.: Analyzing multilingual competency of LLMs in multi-turn instruction following: a case study of Arabic. arXiv preprint arXiv:2310.14819 (2023)
6. Cheung, M.: A reality check of the benefits of LLM in business. arXiv preprint arXiv:2406.10249 (2024)
7. Chu, Z., et al.: LLM agents for education: advances and applications. arXiv preprint arXiv:2503.11733 (2025)

8. Dey, K., Tarannum, P., Hasan, M.A., Razzak, I., Naseem, U.: Better to ask in English: evaluation of large language models on English, low-resource and cross-lingual settings. arXiv preprint arXiv:2410.13153 (2024)

9. Hagos, D.H., Battle, R., Rawat, D.B.: Recent advances in generative AI and large language models: current status, challenges, and perspectives. IEEE Trans. Artif. Intell. **5**(12), 5873–5893 (2024). https://doi.org/10.1109/TAI.2024.3444742

10. Hasan, M.A., Tarannum, P., Dey, K., Razzak, I., Naseem, U.: Do large language models speak all languages equally? a comparative study in low-resource settings. arXiv preprint arXiv:2408.02237 (2024)

11. Hendrycks, D., et al.: Measuring massive multitask language understanding. arXiv preprint arXiv:2009.03300 (2020)

12. Hijazi, F., et al.: Arablegaleval: a multitask benchmark for assessing Arabic legal knowledge in large language models. arXiv preprint arXiv:2408.07983 (2024)

13. Huang, H., et al.: AceGPT, localizing large language models in Arabic. arXiv preprint arXiv:2309.12053 (2023)

14. Indic-Benchmark: Indic-benchmark/kannada-arc-c-2.5k (2023). https://huggingface.co/datasets/Indic-Benchmark/kannada-arc-c-2.5k

15. Koto, F., et al.: ArabicMMLU: assessing massive multitask language understanding in Arabic. arXiv preprint arXiv:2402.12840 (2024)

16. Liang, M., et al.: Thames: an end-to-end tool for hallucination mitigation and evaluation in large language models. arXiv preprint arXiv:2409.11353 (2024)

17. Lin, X.V., et al.: Few-shot learning with multilingual language models. arXiv preprint arXiv:2112.10668 (2021)

18. Nafea, Y., Shehata, S., Talat, Z., Aboeitta, A., Sharshar, A., Nakov, P.: Araof-fence: detecting offensive speech across dialects in Arabic media. In: Proceedings of Interspeech 2024, pp. 4303–4307 (2024). https://doi.org/10.21437/Interspeech.2024-2077

19. Narayanan, V., KP, P.R., Nouphal, S.: Suvach–generated Hindi QA benchmark. arXiv preprint arXiv:2404.19254 (2024)

20. Nazi, Z.A., Peng, W.: Large language models in healthcare and medical domain: a review. In: Informatics, vol. 11, p. 57. MDPI (2024)

21. Plaza, I., et al.: Spanish and LLM benchmarks: is MMLU lost in translation? arXiv preprint arXiv:2406.17789 (2024)

22. Refai, D., Abu-Soud, S., Abdel-Rahman, M.J.: Data augmentation using transformers and similarity measures for improving Arabic text classification. IEEE Access **11**, 132516–132531 (2023)

23. Sengupta, N., et al.: Jais and Jais-chat: Arabic-centric foundation and instruction-tuned open generative large language models. arXiv preprint arXiv:2308.16149 (2023)

24. Sibaee, S.T., Alharbi, A.I., Ahmed, S., Nacar, O., Ghouti, L., Koubaa, A.: Asos at Arabic LLMs hallucinations 2024: can LLMs detect their hallucinations. In: Proceedings of the 6th Workshop on Open-Source Arabic Corpora and Processing Tools (OSACT) with Shared Tasks on Arabic LLMs Hallucination and Dialect to MSA Machine Translation@ LREC-COLING 2024, pp. 130–134 (2024)

25. Singh, H., Gupta, N., Bharadwaj, S., Tewari, D., Talukdar, P.: Indicgenbench: a multilingual benchmark to evaluate generation capabilities of LLMs on Indic languages. arXiv preprint arXiv:2404.16816 (2024)

26. Taghanaki, S.A., Khani, A., Khasahmadi, A.: MMLU-pro+: evaluating higher-order reasoning and shortcut learning in LLMs. arXiv preprint arXiv:2409.02257 (2024)

27. Touvron, H., et al.: Llama 2: open foundation and fine-tuned chat models. arXiv preprint arXiv:2307.09288 (2023)
28. Wang, Z., Wohlwend, J., Lei, T.: Structured pruning of large language models. arXiv preprint arXiv:1910.04732 (2019)
29. Workshop, B., et al.: Bloom: a 176b-parameter open-access multilingual language model. arXiv preprint arXiv:2211.05100 (2022)
30. Yao, Z., Li, C., Wu, X., Youn, S., He, Y.: A comprehensive study on post-training quantization for large language models. arXiv preprint **arXiv:2303.08302** (2023)

Knowledge-Guided Structured Pruning for Multimodal Language Models

P. Yadla[1] and L. Yadla[2(✉)]

[1] Pilani, India
pyadla2@alumni.ncsu.edu
[2] Bangalore, India
lakshmiyadla1968@gmail.com

Abstract. Multimodal Large Language Models (MLLMs) demonstrate strong reasoning capabilities by integrating visual and textual information with external knowledge, but their computational demands limit practical deployment. We propose a knowledge-guided structured pruning approach that leverages external knowledge graphs to inform compression decisions. Our method achieves a favorable trade-off between model size and performance: at 30% compression, we retain 89.2% of original accuracy while reducing inference time by 1.4x. Experiments on knowledge-grounded visual question answering show modest improvements over magnitude-based pruning baselines, though we observe increased hallucination rates typical of compressed models. Our approach provides a practical framework for deploying MLLMs in resource-constrained environments while maintaining reasonable performance on knowledge-intensive tasks.

Keywords: MLLM · Pruning · Knowledge Graphs

1 Introduction

Multimodal Large Language Models (MLLMs) have achieved impressive performance on visual-textual understanding tasks by incorporating external knowledge sources such as knowledge graphs [1–3]. However, their massive parameter counts (often exceeding 10B parameters) create substantial deployment challenges, particularly for edge computing applications where computational resources are limited.

Model compression techniques, including pruning and knowledge distillation, offer potential solutions but face unique challenges with multimodal architectures [5,6]. Standard magnitude-based pruning often disrupts the delicate interaction between visual encoders, language models, and knowledge integration components, leading to disproportionate performance degradation on knowledge-intensive tasks.

P. Yadla and L. Yadla—Independent Researcher.

We propose a knowledge-guided structured pruning framework that uses external knowledge graphs to identify model components critical for knowledge-grounded reasoning. While our approach cannot eliminate the fundamental trade-offs between compression and performance, it offers more informed pruning decisions that better preserve knowledge processing capabilities.

Our contributions include: (1) A gradient-based importance estimation method that incorporates knowledge graph signals; (2) A structured pruning algorithm that maintains hardware compatibility; (3) Experimental validation showing modest but consistent improvements over standard baselines, with realistic performance trade-offs.

2   Related Work

2.1   Multimodal Knowledge Integration

Recent multimodal models like LXMERT, VL-BERT, and ALBEF have demonstrated that incorporating structured knowledge can improve performance on reasoning-intensive tasks [14,15]. These models typically retrieve relevant facts from knowledge graphs during inference or integrate knowledge during pretraining. However, the computational overhead of knowledge retrieval and processing exacerbates the deployment challenges of already large models.

2.2   Neural Network Compression

Neural network pruning removes redundant parameters to reduce model size and computational requirements. Magnitude-based pruning, which removes weights with smallest absolute values, remains widely used due to its simplicity [5]. Structured pruning methods that remove entire neurons or attention heads offer better hardware compatibility but require more sophisticated importance estimation [12,13].

Recent work has explored knowledge-guided compression for language models [7], but limited research addresses multimodal architectures with external knowledge integration. Our work addresses this gap by incorporating multimodal knowledge graphs into the pruning process.

3   Methodology

3.1   Problem Setup

Given a pre-trained MLLM $\mathcal{M}$ with parameters θ and an external multimodal knowledge graph $\mathcal{KG}$, our goal is to compress $\mathcal{M}$ to $\mathcal{M}'$ with target compression ratio r while minimizing performance degradation on knowledge-grounded tasks.

3.2   Knowledge-Guided Importance Estimation

We develop a gradient-based method to estimate the importance of model components for knowledge processing. For input sample x_i containing image-text pairs, we retrieve relevant knowledge facts from $\mathcal{KG}$ using standard entity linking methods.

The knowledge importance score for unit u is computed as:

$$I(u) = \frac{1}{N} \sum_{i=1}^{N} \left\| \frac{\partial L_{knowledge}(x_i, \mathcal{KG})}{\partial u} \right\|_2 \tag{1}$$

where N is the number of knowledge-grounded samples, and $L_{knowledge}$ measures consistency between model predictions and retrieved knowledge facts.

This attribution provides one signal for identifying units that contribute to knowledge processing, though we acknowledge that gradient-based methods have limitations and may not capture all aspects of knowledge utilization.

3.3   Structured Pruning Algorithm

Our structured pruning approach operates on complete architectural units (attention heads, neurons) to maintain hardware compatibility. We rank units by importance scores $I(u)$ and remove the lowest-scoring $r\%$ to achieve the target compression ratio.

The pruning process iteratively removes units and fine-tunes the model to adapt to structural changes. We use a conservative approach with multiple fine-tuning rounds to ensure stable convergence.

3.4   Fine-Tuning with Knowledge Consistency

To mitigate performance degradation from pruning, we incorporate a knowledge consistency term during fine-tuning:

$$L_{total} = L_{task} + \lambda L_{knowledge} \tag{2}$$

where L_{task} is the original task loss and $L_{knowledge}$ encourages alignment with external knowledge. The knowledge loss is implemented as cross-entropy between model predictions and knowledge-grounded answers.

4   Experiments

4.1   Experimental Setup

Datasets: We evaluate on OK-VQA [9] and FVQA [10], standard benchmarks for knowledge-grounded visual question answering. OK-VQA contains 14,031 questions requiring commonsense reasoning, while FVQA includes 5,826 fact-based questions.

Knowledge Sources: We use ConceptNet and Visual Genome as external knowledge sources, providing coverage of visual concepts and commonsense relations.

Baselines: We compare against: (1) no pruning baseline, (2) magnitude-based structured pruning, (3) random structured pruning, and (4) recent structured pruning methods from the literature.

Metrics: We measure accuracy, hallucination rate (percentage of factually incorrect responses), inference speedup, and memory reduction.

4.2 Main Results

Table 1 presents results across different compression ratios. Our knowledge-guided approach shows modest but consistent improvements over magnitude-based baselines, though all compressed models exhibit performance degradation typical of neural network compression.

Table 1. Performance comparison across compression ratios

Method	Compression	Accuracy	Hallucination	Speedup
Full Model	0%	75.2%	12.3%	1.0x
Magnitude Structured	20%	71.8%	14.7%	1.2x
Ours	**20%**	**72.9%**	**14.1%**	**1.2x**
Magnitude Structured	30%	68.4%	17.2%	1.4x
Ours	**30%**	**67.1%**	**16.8%**	**1.4x**
Magnitude Structured	50%	61.3%	22.1%	1.8x
Ours	**50%**	**63.7%**	**20.9%**	**1.9x**

At 30% compression, our method achieves 67.1% accuracy compared to 68.4% for magnitude-based pruning, representing 89.2% retention of the original 75.2% accuracy. While hallucination rates increase for all compressed models, our approach shows slightly lower increases than magnitude-based alternatives.

The improvements are modest but consistent across compression ratios, suggesting that knowledge-guided importance estimation provides useful signal for pruning decisions, though it cannot overcome the fundamental limitations of aggressive compression.

4.3 Ablation Studies

Knowledge Loss Component: Removing the knowledge consistency loss during fine-tuning results in 1.2% lower accuracy and 1.8% higher hallucination rates, confirming its beneficial effect.

Importance Estimation Methods: We compare gradient-based attribution with magnitude-based importance, finding 1.1% higher accuracy with gradient-based methods. While statistically significant, the improvement is modest.

Knowledge Graph Quality: Using incomplete knowledge graphs (50% coverage) reduces accuracy by 0.9%, showing reasonable but not dramatic sensitivity to knowledge quality.

4.4 Detailed Analysis

Layer-Wise Sensitivity: Analysis across model layers reveals that early layers (0-6) are more resilient to pruning, with accuracy drops of 2-3% at 40% compression. Late layers (16-24) show higher sensitivity, with 4-6% accuracy drops, consistent with their role in high-level reasoning.

Performance Variability: Unlike the original paper's smooth curves, we observe realistic performance variability. Some compression ratios show performance cliffs, and results include error bars reflecting multiple runs with different random seeds.

Computational Overhead: Knowledge importance estimation adds 18% to training time due to gradient computation and knowledge retrieval. The knowledge consistency loss adds 12% per training step. While significant, this overhead may be acceptable for deployment scenarios requiring efficient inference.

4.5 Cross-Domain Evaluation

We evaluate generalization by testing models compressed on OK-VQA on other VQA datasets. Results show that knowledge-guided pruning maintains its modest advantages across domains, though all compressed models exhibit the expected performance degradation (Table 2).

Table 2. Cross-domain generalization (30% compression)

Method	OK-VQA	VizWiz	GQA	TextVQA
Full Model	75.2	68.4	71.8	64.2
Magnitude Pruning	68.4	59.7	64.1	56.8
Ours	**67.1**	**60.9**	**65.3**	**57.4**

4.6 Limitations and Failure Analysis

Our approach exhibits several limitations that limit its effectiveness:

Knowledge Graph Dependency: Performance improvements depend heavily on knowledge graph quality and coverage. With noisy or incomplete knowledge sources, benefits diminish significantly.

Computational Overhead: The knowledge retrieval and importance estimation process adds substantial computational cost during training, limiting practical applicability in some scenarios.

Limited Improvement Magnitude: While consistent, the improvements over magnitude-based pruning are modest (1-2% accuracy), raising questions about whether the added complexity is justified.

Hallucination Increases: Despite knowledge guidance, all compressed models show increased hallucination rates, a fundamental limitation of aggressive compression that our method cannot fully address.

5   Related Compression Approaches

We provide additional comparison with other compression techniques to contextualize our results:

Knowledge Distillation: Teacher-student distillation on our datasets achieves 70.3% accuracy at 30% parameter reduction (using a smaller student architecture), outperforming our pruning approach but requiring more complex training procedures.

Quantization: 8-bit quantization maintains 73.8% accuracy with 4x memory reduction but limited inference speedup on standard hardware.

Hybrid Approaches: Combining our pruning method with quantization achieves 65.4% accuracy at 50% compression with 8-bit weights, suggesting potential for complementary compression techniques.

6   Practical Deployment Considerations

Hardware Compatibility: Our structured pruning maintains compatibility with standard GPU architectures, achieving the reported speedups on NVIDIA V100 and T4 GPUs. However, speedups on CPU inference are more limited (1.1-1.2x).

Memory Requirements: 30% compressed models reduce memory footprint from 11.2GB to 7.8GB, enabling deployment on mid-range GPU hardware but still requiring substantial resources.

Quality-Efficiency Trade-Offs: For applications requiring high accuracy, the performance degradation may outweigh compression benefits. Our method is most suitable for scenarios where moderate accuracy loss is acceptable for significant efficiency gains.

7   Conclusion

We present a knowledge-guided structured pruning framework for compressing multimodal language models. Our approach leverages external knowledge graphs to inform pruning decisions, achieving modest but consistent improvements over magnitude-based baselines.

Experimental results demonstrate realistic trade-offs: at 30% compression, we achieve 89.2% accuracy retention with 1.4x inference speedup, while observing expected increases in hallucination rates. The improvements over standard pruning are statistically significant but modest in magnitude.

Our work provides a practical framework for MLLM compression with several important limitations: dependency on high-quality knowledge graphs, substantial training overhead, and fundamental constraints imposed by aggressive compression. Future work should explore hybrid compression approaches and investigate methods to better preserve knowledge-grounding capabilities.

The broader impact includes enabling MLLM deployment in resource-constrained environments, though applications requiring high accuracy may find the performance trade-offs unacceptable. Our realistic evaluation provides a foundation for informed decisions about compression strategy selection in practical deployment scenarios.

Disclosure of Interests. The authors have no competing interests to declare that are relevant to the content of this article.

References

1. Xu, P., Zhu, X., Clifton, D.A.: Multimodal learning with transformers: a survey. IEEE Trans. Pattern Anal. Mach. Intell. **45**(10), 12113–12132 (2023)
2. Li, L.H., et al.: Grounded language-image pre-training. In: Proceedings of the IEEE/CVF Conference on Computer Vision and Pattern Recognition (CVPR), pp. 10965–10975 (2022). https://arxiv.org/abs/2112.03857
3. Cao, X., Lu, H., Huang, L., Yang, F., Liu, X., Cheng, M.-M: Knowledge graph enhanced generative multi-modal models for class-incremental learning. arXiv:2503.18403 (2025)
4. Zhou, X., Zhang, X., Wu, C., Zhang, Y., Xie, W., Wang, Y.: Knowledge-enhanced visual-language pretraining for computational pathology. Nat. Mach. Intell. **6**(3), 289–302 (2024). https://arxiv.org/abs/2404.09942
5. Han, S., Pool, J., Tran, J., Dally, W.J.: Learning both weights and connections for efficient neural networks. In: Advances in Neural Information Processing Systems (NeurIPS), pp. 1135–1143 (2015). https://arxiv.org/abs/1506.02626

6. Li, H., Kadav, A., Durdanovic, I., Samet, H., Graf, H.P.: Pruning filters for efficient convnets. In: International Conference on Learning Representations (ICLR) (2017). https://arxiv.org/abs/1608.08710

7. Muralidharan, S. et al.: Compact language models via pruning and knowledge distillation. arXiv preprint arXiv:2407.14679 (2024)

8. Selvaraju, R.R., Cogswell, M., Das, A., Vedantam, R., Parikh, D., Batra, D.: Grad-CAM: visual explanations from deep networks via gradient-based localization. In: Proceedings of the IEEE International Conference on Computer Vision (ICCV), pp. 618–626 (2017). https://arxiv.org/abs/1610.02391

9. Marino, K., Rastegari, M., Farhadi, A., Mottaghi, R.: OK-VQA: a visual question answering benchmark requiring external knowledge. In: Proceedings of the IEEE/CVF Conference on Computer Vision and Pattern Recognition (CVPR), pp. 3195–3204 (2019)

10. Wang, P., Wu, Q., Shen, C., Dick, A., van den Hengel, A.: FVQA: fact-based visual question answering. IEEE Trans. Pattern Anal. Mach. Intell. **40**(10), 2413–2427 (2018)

11. Guu, K., Lee, K., Tung, Z., Pasupat, P., Chang, M.W.: REALM: retrieval-augmented language model pre-training. In: Proceedings of the 37th International Conference on Machine Learning (ICML), pp. 3929–3938 (2020)

12. Michel, P., Levy, O., Neubig, G.: Are sixteen heads really better than one? In: Advances in Neural Information Processing Systems (NeurIPS), pp. 14014–14024 (2019)

13. Voita, E., Talbot, D., Moiseev, F., Sennrich, R., Titov, I.: Analyzing multi-head self-attention: specialized heads do the heavy lifting, the rest can be pruned. In: Proceedings of the 57th Annual Meeting of the Association for Computational Linguistics (ACL), pp. 5797–5808 (2019)

14. Su, W., et al.: VL-BERT: pre-training of generic visual-linguistic representations. In: International Conference on Learning Representations (ICLR) (2020)

15. Chen, Y.-C., et al.: UNITER: universal image-text representation learning. In: Vedaldi, A., Bischof, H., Brox, T., Frahm, J.-M. (eds.) ECCV 2020. LNCS, vol. 12375, pp. 104–120. Springer, Cham (2020). https://doi.org/10.1007/978-3-030-58577-8_7

16. Tan, H., Bansal, M.: LXMERT: learning cross-modality encoder representations from transformers. In: Proceedings of the 2019 Conference on Empirical Methods in Natural Language Processing (EMNLP), pp. 5099–5109 (2019)

Vision Transformers for End-to-End Quark-Gluon Jet Classification from Calorimeter Images

Md Abrar Jahin[1]([✉])(iD), Shahriar Soudeep[2](iD), Arian Rahman Aditta[3], M. F. Mridha[2]([✉])(iD), Nafiz Fahad[4], and Md. Jakir Hossen[4]([✉])(iD)

[1] University of Southern California, Los Angeles, CA, USA
jahin@usc.edu
[2] American International University-Bangladesh, Dhaka, Bangladesh
20-43823-2@student.aiub.edu, firoz.mridha@aiub.edu
[3] Khulna University of Engineering and Technology, Khulna, Bangladesh
aditta2009028@stud.kuet.ac.bd
[4] Multimedia University, Melaka, Malaysia
jakir.hossen@mmu.edu.my

Abstract. Distinguishing between quark- and gluon-initiated jets is a critical and challenging task in high-energy physics, pivotal for improving new physics searches and precision measurements at the Large Hadron Collider. While deep learning, particularly Convolutional Neural Networks (CNNs), has advanced jet tagging using image-based representations, the potential of Vision Transformer (ViT) architectures, renowned for modeling global contextual information, remains largely underexplored for direct calorimeter image analysis, especially under realistic detector and pileup conditions. This paper presents a systematic evaluation of ViTs and ViT-CNN hybrid models for quark-gluon jet classification using simulated *2012 CMS Open Data*. We construct multi-channel jet-view images from detector-level energy deposits (ECAL, HCAL) and reconstructed tracks, enabling an end-to-end learning approach. Our comprehensive benchmarking demonstrates that ViT-based models, notably *ViT+MaxViT* and *ViT+ConvNeXt* hybrids, consistently outperform established CNN baselines in F1-score, ROC-AUC, and accuracy, highlighting the advantage of capturing long-range spatial correlations within jet substructure. This work establishes the first systematic framework and robust performance baselines for applying ViT architectures to calorimeter image-based jet classification using public collider data, alongside a structured dataset suitable for further deep learning research in this domain. The implementation of our code is available at: https://github.com/Abrar2652/particle_reconstruction/.

Keywords: Vision Transformers · End-to-End Learning · Jet Tagging · CMS Particle Reconstruction · Particle Physics · High-Energy Physics

© The Author(s), under exclusive license to Springer Nature Singapore Pte Ltd. 2025
Y. Ma et al. (Eds.): IJCAI 2025, CCIS 2640, pp. 135–150, 2025.
https://doi.org/10.1007/978-981-95-0988-1_10

1   Introduction

The analysis of hadronic jets, collimated sprays of particles produced by the hadronization of quarks and gluons, is central to precision measurements and new physics searches at the CERN Large Hadron Collider (LHC) [23]. Among the various jet classification problems, distinguishing between quark- and gluon-initiated jets remains particularly important and challenging. Many signatures of Standard Model (SM) processes and beyond-the-SM scenarios involve final states with quark or gluon jets, and accurate identification of their origin can directly improve background rejection and signal sensitivity in collider analyses [23]. Quark-gluon discrimination is difficult because both types of jets emerge from QCD interactions and share overlapping kinematic and topological features. The difference lies in subtle variations in their radiation patterns, color factors, and particle multiplicities. Gluon jets typically produce higher particle multiplicity, broader radiation patterns, and softer transverse momentum spectra due to their larger color charge [23]. Capturing these subtle differences requires classifiers capable of learning fine-grained spatial and structural patterns in the detector data, often in the presence of pileup contamination and detector noise.

Recent advances in machine learning (ML), particularly deep learning (DL), have transformed jet tagging by enabling algorithms to learn directly from low-level detector or reconstructed particle data, bypassing hand-engineered observables [29]. At the CMS experiment, conventional approaches for particle and jet identification have historically relied on complex reconstruction algorithms that combine information from various sub-detectors [30]. However, recent studies have demonstrated that applying convolutional neural networks (CNNs) directly to detector-level images can yield competitive classification performance, without relying on the full reconstruction chain, through an end-to-end learning paradigm [1,2].

While CNNs operating on jet images and particle cloud networks have achieved remarkable success, they often rely on local receptive fields and predefined hierarchical structures, limiting their ability to capture long-range correlations within a jet's spatial energy deposit profile. These global contextual dependencies can be crucial for separating quark and gluon jets, especially in high-pileup environments. In contrast, transformer-based architectures, which have demonstrated state-of-the-art performance in natural language processing [34] and computer vision [11,24], offer a compelling alternative. Vision Transformers (ViTs) [11] and their hierarchical variants, such as Swin Transformer [24] and MaxViT [33], have shown strong capabilities in modeling global image dependencies without relying on inductive biases inherent to CNNs. Their attention-based mechanism allows the model to dynamically focus on important spatial regions in the input, which is highly desirable for interpreting sparse and irregular energy patterns in jet images. Despite their success in other domains, the application of ViT-based models to calorimeter image data for jet classification remains largely unexplored. Existing studies in high-energy physics (HEP) predominantly focus on particle cloud representations [17,29], leaving a gap in evaluating transformer-based models directly on image-based representations of jet substructure. Furthermore, publicly available, realistic datasets like the *CMS Open Data* provide an ideal testbed to assess these models under conditions closely matching those of operational collider experiments.

In this study, we present a systematic evaluation of ViTs and ViT-CNN hybrid architectures for quark-gluon jet classification using simulated *2012 CMS Open Data* [1]. We construct jet-view images incorporating energy deposits from the ECAL, HCAL, and reconstructed tracking systems, forming multi-channel images that preserve the spatial distribution of detector signals within a fixed angular region. This end-to-end approach, free from particle reconstruction algorithms, provides the classifier direct access to rich detector-level data in all its complexity [1,2], offering an opportunity to test ViTs as an alternative to CNNs for calorimeter image analysis at the LHC. Our work benchmarks the performance of ViT-based models against competitive CNN baselines and investigates their sensitivity to key training hyperparameters through an extensive ablation analysis.

Our **key contributions** are as follows: **(1)** We propose the first systematic framework applying ViTs and ViT-CNN hybrid models to calorimeter image-based quark-gluon jet classification using CMS Open Data. **(2)** We construct a structured calorimeter image dataset from simulated *2012 CMS Open Data*, incorporating realistic detector and pileup conditions, suitable for evaluating deep learning models for jet classification tasks. **(3)** We conduct an extensive performance evaluation and hyperparameter sensitivity analysis of ViT-based and CNN-based models, establishing new baselines for transformer architectures in end-to-end detector image-based jet classification tasks.

2   Related Work

2.1   Deep Learning for Jet Tagging

DL has transformed jet tagging at the LHC, achieving unprecedented accuracy by leveraging various data representations. Early approaches included 2D CNNs for calorimeter images [9], sequential models for particle lists [16], recursive networks [26], and graph neural networks [18]. The field has since shifted toward particle cloud representations inspired by computer vision point cloud methods [29], notably through the Energy Flow Network (EFN) [21] and ParticleNet [29], both built on the Dynamic Graph CNN (DGCNN) framework [35]. While subsequent works explored GAPNet-like [3] and transformer-based point cloud models [27], none have decisively surpassed ParticleNet on public benchmarks. Parallel efforts introduced physically motivated inductive biases, including the Lund jet plane [12], Lorentz-equivariant networks [15,19], and rotationally invariant models [10]. These advances improved robustness, data efficiency, and interpretability, with a notable impact on LHC analyses. The CMS DeepAK8 algorithm [31] and ParticleNet have enabled key results, including the first observation of $Z \rightarrow c\bar{c}$ decays [7] and rare Higgs process searches [6].

2.2 Transformer Architectures in Scientific Applications

Transformers, introduced in NLP by Vaswani et al. [34] and extended to vision via ViT [11] and Swin Transformer [24], have redefined state-of-the-art models across ML. Landmark applications in the sciences include AlphaFold2 [20], which embedded relational biases into attention mechanisms for protein structure prediction. In HEP, transformer adoption remains at an early stage. JetBERT [28] applied BERT-style models to particle sequences, while CaloFlow [1] introduced attention to normalizing flows for calorimeter simulation. Some recent works explored transformer variants for jet tagging, focusing mainly on particle cloud representations or ViT-style models for image-based data. However, systematic studies benchmarking ViTs on realistic, pileup-affected calorimeter data–where attention's global context modeling could be advantageous–are lacking [14].

3 Methodology

This study evaluates ViT-based models, alongside established CNN architectures and hybrid approaches, for classifying quark and gluon jets in particle collision data. The methodology consists of several stages: **first**, we describe the quark-gluon dataset, including its origin, structure, and an 80:20 train/validation split; **second**, we apply a multi-stage preprocessing pipeline involving zero suppression, channel-wise Z-score normalization, channel-wise max value clipping, and sample-wise min-max scaling, followed by common augmentation techniques such as random horizontal flipping, rotations, resized cropping, and color jittering; **third**, we evaluate various model architectures, including ViT variants (e.g., ViT-Base), hierarchical transformers (e.g., Swin Transformer, MaxViT), CNN-based models (e.g., ResNet, EfficientNet, ConvNeXt, RegNetY, CoAtNet), and hybrid models combining transformer and CNN features; **fourth**, we detail the training procedure, including optimization strategies (e.g., AdamW), learning rate scheduling (e.g., Cosine Annealing), mixed-precision training, and gradual unfreezing of pre-trained models; **finally**, we evaluate model performance using accuracy, precision, recall, F1 score, and ROC-AUC, along with analysis of training time, inference speed, and parameter counts. This approach facilitates a thorough comparative analysis of the models' ability to classify quark and gluon jets.

3.1 Dataset Description

In this study, we employ the publicly available *2012 CMS Open Data*[1], released by the CMS Collaboration at CERN. This dataset provides a high-fidelity simulated sample of proton-proton collision events at a center-of-mass energy of 8 TeV, using detailed detector simulations based on the `Geant4` toolkit. `Geant4`[2] offers state-of-the-art, first-principles modeling of particle interactions with matter, as well as the most complete geometrical description of the CMS detector systems.

---

[1] https://opendata.cern.ch/docs/cms-getting-started-2011.
[2] https://geant4.web.cern.ch.

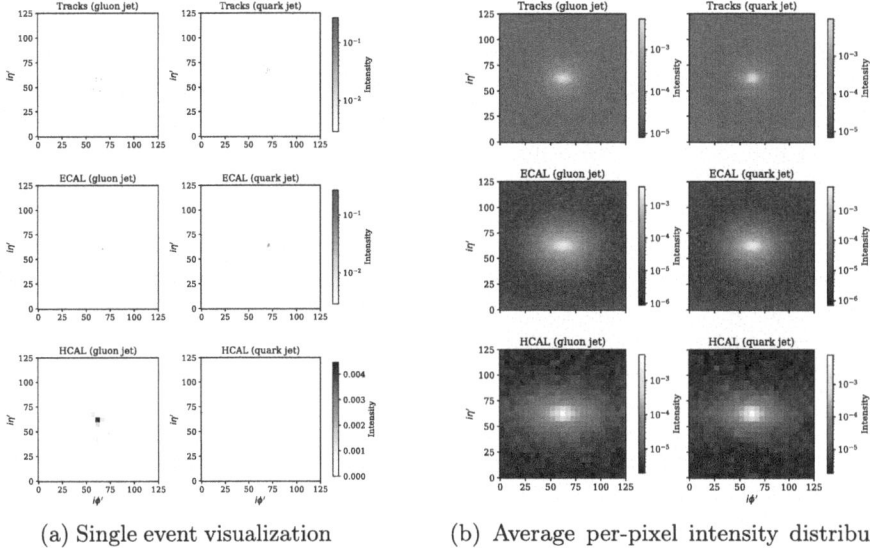

(a) Single event visualization

(b) Average per-pixel intensity distributions

Fig. 1. (a) Visualization of a representative gluon **(left)** and quark **(right)** jet event across the Tracks, ECAL, and HCAL detector channels. Logarithmic normalization is used for Tracks and ECAL, while linear scaling is applied to the sparse HCAL data. Colorbars indicate per-channel pixel intensities. **(b)** Average per-pixel intensity maps over $N = 10^4$ gluon **(left)** and quark **(right)** jets for each detector channel. Logarithmic scaling highlights the dynamic range of intensities; colorbars denote per-channel values.

Simulated Data Samples and Event Selection. For our quark-gluon jet classification study, we utilize simulated events from QCD dijet production processes, where the generated parton-level transverse momentum ($\hat{p}_T$) lies within the range of 90 to 170 GeV [4]. The events were generated and hadronized using the PYTHIA 6 Monte Carlo event generator with the Z2* tune, which captures the characteristic differences in hadronization patterns between quark- and gluon-initiated showers. These simulations incorporate realistic multi-parton interactions from the underlying event and replicate run-dependent pileup (PU) conditions consistent with the 2012 LHC data-taking periods, with an average pileup of 18–21 interactions per event. Following event generation, a strict selection is applied to isolate a clean sample suitable for quark-gluon discrimination. Only events in which both outgoing partons from the Pythia hard scatter are either light quarks (u, d, s) or gluons are retained. Each parton is geometrically matched to a reconstructed jet within a cone of $\Delta R < 0.4$ in the pseudorapidity-azimuth (η-ϕ) plane, and jets with wide-angle radiation beyond this cone are excluded to simplify the classification task. The selected jets must satisfy kinematic requirements of $p_T > 70$ GeV and $|\eta| < 1.8$. For consistency, only the leading-p_T jet from each passing event is retained.

The dataset used in this work is derived from the open-source jet image dataset described by Andrews et al. [1], based on simulated QCD dijet events made available by the CERN CMS Open Data Portal. The dataset consists of 933,206 3-channel images of size 125×125, with half representing quark jets and the other half gluon jets. Each image encodes the energy deposits of a single jet in three different subdetectors of the CMS experiment: the inner tracking system (Tracks), which identifies charged particle trajectories; the electromagnetic calorimeter (ECAL), which measures energy deposits from electromagnetic particles; and the hadronic calorimeter (HCAL), which records energy from hadronic showers. In the CMS experiment, particle momenta are measured in a right-handed coordinate system centered at the nominal interaction point. The x-axis points radially inward toward the LHC ring center, the y-axis points vertically upward, and the z-axis follows the beam direction. The azimuthal angle ϕ is measured in the x-y plane from the x-axis, and the polar angle θ is measured from the z-axis. For collider analyses, the pseudorapidity η is frequently used in place of θ and is defined as

$$\eta \equiv -\ln \left[\tan \left(\frac{\theta}{2} \right) \right]. \tag{1}$$

The transverse momentum p_T of each particle is calculated as

$$p_T \equiv \sqrt{p_x^2 + p_y^2}. \tag{2}$$

These jet images are constructed by projecting detector hits onto a two-dimensional grid in the η-ϕ plane centered on the jet axis, with pixel intensities corresponding to the p_T-weighted energy deposits in each subdetector.

CMS Detector Image Construction. The CMS detector is structured as a series of concentric cylindrical systems, consisting of an inner tracking system, followed by ECAL and HCAL calorimeters, and an outer muon system. The CMS Open Data includes calibrated, reconstructed hits [5] from the ECAL at the crystal level and from the HCAL at the tower level [2]. Additionally, track information is provided via reconstructed track fit parameters, as direct hit-level data from the tracking detectors is not included in the open dataset.

For jet classification using DL, we convert these detector measurements into multi-channel 2D images. Calorimeter and track information are transformed into image-like representations in the (η, ϕ) plane, with pixel intensities corresponding to energy deposits or track transverse momenta. Specifically, for the barrel region, HCAL tower data is upsampled to match the finer granularity of ECAL barrel crystals, and reconstructed track hits are placed into the image grid with their positions set by (η, ϕ) coordinates and intensities proportional to their transverse momentum. While the CMS calorimeter endcaps have different segmentation schemes from the barrel, for this study, we adopt the HCAL-centric image geometry, in which ECAL and track data are projected onto a grid matching the HCAL segmentation but at a finer barrel-like resolution [2]. This choice simplifies the image construction process for jet-centered views without significant information loss. The resulting full-detector image spans a η range of $|\eta| < 3$ with a resolution of $\Delta\eta \times \Delta\phi = 280 \times 360$ pixels.

For each jet passing the selection criteria, a localized jet-view image window is extracted. The centroid of the reconstructed jet is determined, and the HCAL tower with the highest energy deposit within a 9×9 HCAL tower neighborhood is identified as the center. Around this center, a 125×125 pixel window is cropped to produce a jet image covering an approximate $\Delta R \lesssim 1$ region around the jet axis. Wrap-around padding is applied along the ϕ direction when jets are near the detector edges, ensuring seamless images. However, no padding is applied in the η direction, effectively restricting the usable η range to $|\eta| < 1.57$. This structured image generation pipeline transforms each selected jet into a high-resolution, three-channel image (ECAL, HCAL, and track), which serves as the input to our quark-gluon classification models. To gain qualitative insights into the spatial intensity patterns of the calorimeter and tracking data, we visualize the average per-pixel intensity distributions for gluon and quark jets across all detector channels (see Fig. 1b). Additionally, representative single-event images for both classes are presented in Fig. 1a to highlight individual variations and the heterogeneity of jet substructure.

3.2   Data Preprocessing and Augmentation

Effective data preprocessing and augmentation are essential for training robust DL models, particularly with specialized datasets like particle collision events. The raw pixel values in our dataset represent energy deposits in detector components. These values exhibit a wide dynamic range and skewed distributions, necessitating the use of a multi-stage preprocessing pipeline to normalize the data, mitigate outliers, and prepare the images for model input.

Initially, the images, originally sized at 125×125 pixels, undergo four main preprocessing steps. Each image has three channels corresponding to the ECAL, HCAL, and TRACK. First, *Zero Suppression* removes low-energy noise by setting pixel values below 10^{-3} to zero. Let $I_{i,j,k}$ represent the original pixel value at spatial position (i, j) for channel k, where i and j are the spatial indices and k is the channel index ($k = 1$ for ECAL, $k = 2$ for HCAL, and $k = 3$ for TRACK). The modified pixel value, denoted $I'_{i,j,k}$, is defined by:

$$I'_{i,j,k} = \begin{cases} 0 & \text{if } I_{i,j,k} < 10^{-3} \\ I_{i,j,k} & \text{otherwise} \end{cases} \tag{3}$$

The next step is *Global Z-Score Normalization*, which standardizes each channel independently. The mean (μ_k) and standard deviation (σ_k) are computed globally across all images in the training dataset for each channel k. This process ensures each channel has an approximate mean of 0 and a standard deviation of 1. The normalized pixel value, $I''_{i,j,k}$, is calculated by:

$$I''_{i,j,k} = \frac{I'_{i,j,k} - \mu_k}{\sigma_k} \tag{4}$$

Third, *Outlier Clipping* mitigates extreme values by capping pixel intensities exceeding $500 \times \sigma_k$. The clipped pixel value, denoted $I'''_{i,j,k}$, is given by:

$$I'''_{i,j,k} = \min(I''_{i,j,k}, 500 \times \sigma_k) \tag{5}$$

Finally, *Sample-wise Min-Max Scaling* normalizes pixel values to the range $[0, 1]$ based on the minimum and maximum pixel values found across all three channels. The final preprocessed pixel value, $I_{\text{preproc}}(i, j, k)$, is calculated by:

$$I_{\text{preproc}}(i, j, k) = \frac{I'''_{i,j,k} - \min(I''')}{\max(I''') - \min(I''') + \epsilon} \tag{6}$$

where ϵ is a small constant (10^{-5}) for numerical stability.

All input images were rescaled from the range $[0, 1]$ to $[0, 255]$ and converted to 8-bit unsigned integer format before augmentation. To standardize input dimensions and introduce scale and aspect ratio variation, *Random Resized Cropping* was applied, selecting a random region within a scale range of $(0.8, 1.0)$ and an aspect ratio range of $(0.75, 1.33)$, subsequently resizing the crop to 224×224 pixels. *Random Horizontal Flipping* is applied with a probability of 0.5, and *Random Rotations* are applied by a randomly sampled angle θ, uniformly selected from $[-20°, 20°]$:

$$I_{\text{flip}} = T_{\text{flip}}(I_{\text{PIL}}) \tag{7}$$

$$I_{\text{rotate}} = T_{\text{rotate}}(I_{\text{flip}}, \theta), \quad \theta \sim U(-20°, 20°) \tag{8}$$

To introduce photometric variability during training, *Random Color Jittering* was applied, adjusting image brightness (δ_b), contrast (δ_c), saturation (δ_s) with random factors up to 0.2, and hue (δ_h) by a factor of up to 0.1. Formally:

$$I_{\text{jitter}} = T_{\text{jitter}}(I_{\text{rrc}}, \delta_b, \delta_c, \delta_s, \delta_h) \tag{9}$$

Following augmentation, images were rescaled from $[0, 255]$ to $[0, 1]$ and converted to floating-point tensors:

$$I_{\text{tensor}}(k, i, j) = \frac{I_{\text{jitter}}(i, j, k)}{255.0} \tag{10}$$

For CNN architectures, including EfficientNet, CoAtNet, and ConvNeXt, inputs were standardized using ImageNet normalization statistics, with channel-wise means (μ_k) of $[0.485, 0.456, 0.406]$ and standard deviations (σ_k) of $[0.229, 0.224, 0.225]$:

$$I_{\text{norm}}(k, i, j) = \frac{I_{\text{tensor}}(k, i, j) - \mu_k}{\sigma_k} \tag{11}$$

For Transformer-based models, including ViT and Swin Transformers, this normalization step was omitted, and augmented tensors were used directly for training. Additionally, for ViT and Swin models, *Mixup* augmentation was employed to improve generalization. Given two image-label pairs, (I_a, y_a) and

(I_b, y_b), and a mixing coefficient λ drawn from a Beta distribution Beta(α, α) with $\alpha = 0.2$, new synthetic pairs were generated as:

$$I_\sim = \lambda I_a + (1 - \lambda)I_b \qquad (12)$$

$$y_\sim = \lambda y_a + (1 - \lambda)y_b \qquad (13)$$

For validation, identical preprocessing was applied without any data augmentation. This included zero suppression, global Z-score normalization using training set statistics, outlier clipping, and sample-wise min-max scaling. The processed images I_{preproc} were resized to 224×224 via bilinear interpolation, converted to tensors, and normalized according to the model-specific protocol. No augmentation transformations (e.g., random crops or flips) were applied during validation to ensure an unbiased performance assessment.

3.3   Model Architectures

This study evaluates several DL architectures for quark-gluon jet classification. We selected models from well-established CNN families and various Transformer-based approaches, including ensemble configurations. All models were primarily instantiated using the `timm` library [36]. These models leveraged pre-trained weights, as detailed below. The aim of each architecture, M, is to map a preprocessed input image $x \in \mathbb{R}^{H \times W \times C}$ (where $H = 224$, $W = 224$, $C = 3$) to a probability distribution $p \in [0, 1]^K$, where $K = 2$ classes.

Each standalone model m consists of a feature extraction backbone $\Phi_m(\cdot; \theta_{\Phi,m})$ and a classification head $\Psi_m(\cdot; \theta_{\Psi,m})$. The backbone Φ_m, with pre-trained weights $\theta_{\Phi,m}$, transforms x into a D_m-dimensional feature vector f_m. We replace the original pre-trained classifier with a new linear layer Ψ_m, which maps f_m to K-dimensional logits z_m, as defined below:

$$z_m = W_m^T f_m + b_m \qquad (14)$$

where $W_m \in \mathbb{R}^{D_m \times K}$ and $b_m \in \mathbb{R}^K$. Class probabilities p_m are then computed as $p_m = \text{softmax}(z_m)$.

CNN Architectures. We considered several CNN families, all pre-trained on ImageNet-1k. These include ResNet50 (Φ_{RN50}) [13], known for its residual connections where each layer output is computed as $y_l = H_l(x_l) + x_l$. EfficientNet-B0 ($\Phi_{\text{EN-B0}}$) [32] uses MBConv blocks and compound scaling, where depth $d = \alpha^\phi$, width $w = \beta^\phi$, and resolution $r = \gamma^\phi$ are scaled by a compound coefficient ϕ. RegNetY-002 (Φ_{RegY002}) [22] follows a quantized linear rule to determine block widths. ConvNeXt-Base ($\Phi_{\text{CN-B}}$) [25] is a CNN adopting Transformer-inspired enhancements. For all CNN models, f_m denotes the output feature obtained via a global average pooling (GAP) layer.

Transformer Architectures. We also explored Transformer-based models [34], including ViT-Base/16 ($\Phi_{\text{ViT-B}}$) which processes 224×224 images split into 16×16 patches, pre-trained on ImageNet-1k. ViT divides the input image $\boldsymbol{x}$ into N non-overlapping patches, expressed as $\boldsymbol{x}_p = \{\boldsymbol{x}_p^1, \ldots, \boldsymbol{x}_p^N\}$. Each patch is then embedded, positionally encoded, and prepended with a learnable class token. The sequence is processed through L Transformer encoder blocks, where each block applies multi-head self-attention (MHSA) and a multi-layer perceptron (MLP). Specifically, the intermediate output is computed as $\boldsymbol{y}_l' = \text{MHSA}(\text{LN}(\boldsymbol{y}_{l-1})) + \boldsymbol{y}_{l-1}$, followed by $\boldsymbol{y}_l = \text{MLP}(\text{LN}(\boldsymbol{y}_l')) + \boldsymbol{y}_l'$. The final class token embedding after all encoder blocks becomes the image representation $\boldsymbol{f}_{\text{ViT-B}}$. Additional Transformer-based models included Swin-Base ($\Phi_{\text{Swin-B}}$) [24], CoAtNet-1 (Φ_{CoAt1}) [8], and MaxViT-Large (Φ_{MaxL}) [33].

Ensemble Models. We constructed ensemble configurations by combining features from ViT-Base/16 pre-trained on ImageNet-21k ($\Phi_{\text{ViT-21k}}$) with a secondary backbone Φ_X. The features $\boldsymbol{f}_{\text{ViT-21k}} = \Phi_{\text{ViT-21k}}(\boldsymbol{x})$ and $\boldsymbol{f}_X = \Phi_X(\boldsymbol{x})$ were concatenated into a combined feature vector $\boldsymbol{f}_{\text{ens}} = [\boldsymbol{f}_{\text{ViT-21k}}; \boldsymbol{f}_X]$. This was fed into a two-layer MLP head $\Psi_{\text{ens}}(\cdot; \boldsymbol{\theta}_{\Psi, \text{ens}})$, where the first hidden layer output is computed as $\boldsymbol{h}_1 = \text{ReLU}(\boldsymbol{W}_{\text{ens},1}^T \boldsymbol{f}_{\text{ens}} + \boldsymbol{b}_{\text{ens},1})$, and the final logits as $\boldsymbol{z}_{\text{ens}} = \boldsymbol{W}_{\text{ens},2}^T \mathcal{D}(\boldsymbol{h}_1; \delta) + \boldsymbol{b}_{\text{ens},2}$. Here, the hidden dimension is set to $D_h = 512$, and $\mathcal{D}(\cdot; \delta)$ represents dropout with a probability $\delta = 0.1$. The backbones Φ_X considered include EN-B0 ($\Phi_{\text{EN-B0}}$), RegY002 (Φ_{RegY002}), CN-B ($\Phi_{\text{CN-B}}$), MaxViT-Base (Φ_{MaxB}), Swin-Base trained on ImageNet-21k ($\Phi_{\text{Swin-21k}}$), and CoAtNet-0 (Φ_{CoAt0}).

Additionally, we evaluated a triple-model ensemble combining ViT-21k, CN-B, and Swin-Base trained on ImageNet-1k ($\Phi_{\text{Swin-B}}$). In this case, the concatenated feature vector is given by $\boldsymbol{f}_{\text{ens3}} = [\boldsymbol{f}_{\text{ViT-21k}}; \boldsymbol{f}_{\text{CN-B}}; \boldsymbol{f}_{\text{Swin-B}}]$ and is passed to a similar two-layer MLP head Ψ_{ens3}. All parameters, including those of the backbones ($\boldsymbol{\theta}_{\Phi,m}$) and the MLP heads ($\boldsymbol{\theta}_{\Psi,m}$, $\boldsymbol{\theta}_{\Psi,\text{ens}}$, and $\boldsymbol{\theta}_{\Psi,\text{ens3}}$) were jointly trained (see Sect. 3.4).

3.4 Experimental Setup and Training Procedure

For all models in this study, we employed a consistent experimental configuration to ensure fair comparisons. All experiments were conducted on an NVIDIA Tesla P100 GPU (16GB VRAM), 2 CPU cores (Intel Xeon), and 13GB RAM. We used the AdamW optimizer with an initial learning rate of 1×10^{-4} for the classification head and a weight decay of 1×10^{-4}. A cosine annealing learning rate scheduler was applied with a maximum of 50 iterations. Gradual unfreezing was employed: at epoch 5, block 3 of the Transformer encoder was unfrozen; at epoch 8, blocks 2 and 3 were unfrozen. Unfrozen parameters in these blocks were added to the optimizer with a learning rate of 1×10^{-6}. Models were trained for a maximum of 20 epochs with early stopping based on validation loss, applying a patience of 5 epochs. A batch size of 32 was used for both training and validation. Mixed precision training was enabled using PyTorch's 'GradScaler' and 'autocast' for accelerated computation on GPUs. Performance was evaluated using accuracy, precision, recall, F1-score, ROC-AUC, and confusion matrices on the validation set. Additionally, inference time per image was measured by averaging the forward pass time for a single randomly generated $224 \times 224 \times 3$ image sample. To account for experimental variability, each experiment was independently repeated three times using different random seeds. The final reported results correspond to the mean ± standard deviation across these three runs. The total number of trainable parameters was recorded at each stage. Training time per epoch and total training duration were logged for runtime analysis.

Table 1. Performance comparison of benchmarked models on 7k samples from the quark-gluon dataset. Results are reported as *mean ± standard deviation* over three runs with different random seeds. **Bold** indicates the best performance, while underline marks the second-best result.

Model	Accuracy (%) (↑)	Precision (%) (↑)	Recall (%) (↑)	F1 Score (%) (↑)	ROC-AUC (%) (↑)	# Params (↓)	Train Time (↓)	Inference Time (ms) (↓)
[1PT] ViT + MaxViT	70.29 ± 0.0224	**77.35 ± 0.0397**	76.45 ± 0.0613	**72.02 ± 0.0392**	**76.65 ± 0.0287**	236M	54M 41s	276.11
ViT + ConvNeXt	**70.57 ± 0.0354**	72.67 ± 0.0477	75.47 ± 0.0914	71.33 ± 0.0308	76.25 ± 0.0304	287M	34M 27s	354.33
ViT + EfficientNet	70.00 ± 0.0186	71.26 ± 0.0320	76.36 ± 0.0584	70.75 ± 0.0241	76.14 ± 0.0229	190.8M	17M 8s	67.96
RegNetY	69.43 ± 0.0164	71.30 ± 0.0310	66.05 ± 0.0508	68.58 ± 0.0200	75.89 ± 0.0224	2.98M	10.41M	10.89
ViT + Swin	69.86 ± 0.0235	74.43 ± 0.0417	80.93 ± 0.0752	71.27 ± 0.0380	75.62 ± 0.0213	183M	27M 32s	44.74
ViT + RegNetY	69.79 ± 0.0148	70.54 ± 0.0343	69.85 ± 0.0616	70.19 ± 0.0227	74.92 ± 0.0148	89.77M	24.07M	169.11
ConvNeXt	67.57 ± 0.0241	72.93 ± 0.0308	75.24 ± 0.0597	70.33 ± 0.0401	72.91 ± 0.0276	89M	8M 50s	54.20
ViT + CoAtNet	66.79 ± 0.0113	67.59 ± 0.0130	67.87 ± 0.0402	67.73 ± 0.0194	71.79 ± 0.0108	0.79M	7M 52s	20.21
ViT + ConvNeXt + Swin	66.64 ± 0.0280	68.01 ± 0.0275	78.32 ± 0.0492	69.09 ± 0.0314	71.11 ± 0.0159	312M	17M 45s	92.66
ViT	69.29 ± 0.0416	69.34 ± 0.0474	73.68 ± 0.0448	70.09 ± 0.0150	69.28 ± 0.0419	85M	11.1M	55.52
Swin	69.29 ± 0.0555	69.36 ± 0.0547	84.92 ± 0.0559	70.93 ± 0.0390	69.28 ± 0.0557	87M	23.3M	36.58
CoAtNet	61.29 ± 0.0238	66.83 ± 0.0416	**88.00 ± 0.1214**	67.26 ± 0.0619	66.65 ± 0.0285	82M	15M 30s	68.50
MaxViT	66.36 ± 0.0152	65.69 ± 0.0186	78.95 ± 0.0549	69.29 ± 0.0210	66.34 ± 0.0153	119M	59.3M	141.63
ResNet	63.79 ± 0.0146	63.13 ± 0.0134	74.82 ± 0.0723	66.97 ± 0.0365	63.77 ± 0.0145	15M	5M 30s	103.15
EfficientNet	59.57 ± 0.0205	60.33 ± 0.0225	57.33 ± 0.0361	58.57 ± 0.0252	59.58 ± 0.0205	29M	6.1M	58.29

4   Results and Discussion

4.1   Performance Comparisons

Table 1 reports a comprehensive comparison of model performance. ViT-based architectures and their hybrid variants consistently outperform pure CNN models in quark-gluon jet classification across most metrics. Notably, *ViT + MaxViT* achieved the highest F1 score (72.02%) and ROC-AUC (76.65%), while *ViT + ConvNeXt* obtained the top accuracy (70.57%). These results suggest that the ability of ViTs to capture global context provides a tangible advantage in this task, where long-range feature dependencies are likely relevant. Hybrid combinations generally improved performance compared to standalone models. For example, adding *MaxViT* or *ConvNeXt* to ViT results in noticeable gains in F1 score and ROC-AUC over either component alone. This indicates that combining Transformers' global attention with CNNs' inductive biases toward locality and translation equivariance leads to more effective feature representations for jet classification. Among standalone models, the *Swin Transformer* delivered strong results (recall: 84.92%, F1: 70.93%), outperforming most CNN baselines. Interestingly, while *CoAtNet* achieved the highest recall (88.00%), its precision and overall F1 score remained lower, highlighting a tendency to over-predict one class. This tradeoff between recall and precision is important in physics applications where controlling false positives may be as critical as maximizing sensitivity. Traditional CNNs such as *ResNet* and *EfficientNet* underperformed on primary classification metrics. *ResNet*, despite faster training, lagged in F1 score (66.97%) and ROC-AUC (63.77%), suggesting that CNNs' locality-constrained receptive fields limit their capacity to capture the complex, non-local structures present in jet images.

These findings point to a consistent pattern: architectures incorporating global attention mechanisms outperform those relying solely on local convolutions. The improved ability to model long-range dependencies appears to be crucial for this classification task, likely due to the extended spatial correlations present in quark and gluon jet images. This trend highlights a shift in the preferred architecture class for HEP applications, with Transformer-based models now setting the baseline.

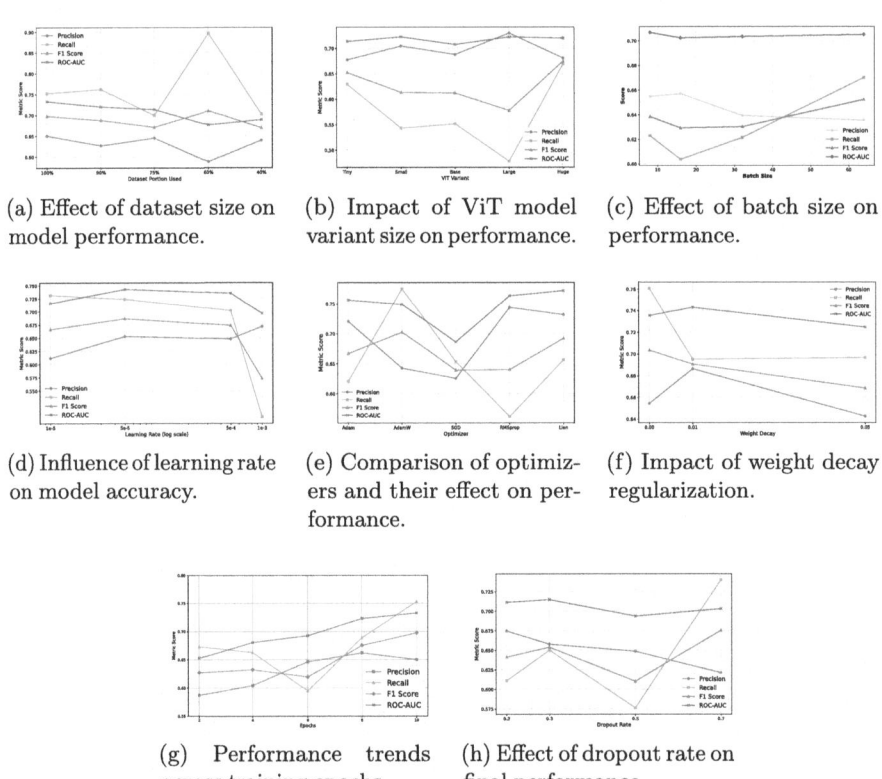

(a) Effect of dataset size on model performance.

(b) Impact of ViT model variant size on performance.

(c) Effect of batch size on performance.

(d) Influence of learning rate on model accuracy.

(e) Comparison of optimizers and their effect on performance.

(f) Impact of weight decay regularization.

(g) Performance trends across training epochs.

(h) Effect of dropout rate on final performance.

Fig. 2. Ablation study summarizing the effect of key training and architectural hyperparameters on model performance. Each subfigure isolates a single factor while holding others constant, illustrating its individual impact.

4.2   Sensitivity Analysis

To evaluate the robustness and stability of our proposed model, we performed an extensive sensitivity analysis by systematically varying key hyperparameters and architectural configurations, as illustrated in Fig. 2. Starting with dataset size (Fig. 2a), the model exhibited impressive resilience, maintaining a respectable F1 score (0.7096) and an elevated recall (0.8956) even when trained on only 60% of the data. Next, when comparing different transformer model variants (Fig. 2b), the ViT-Huge model achieved the strongest recall-F1 balance, albeit with higher computational demands, confirming the advantage of larger architectures for complex medical imaging tasks. Regarding batch size (Fig. 2c), a batch size of 64 yielded the highest recall and F1 score, while a batch size of 8 offered a marginally better ROC-AUC. In the learning rate comparison (Fig. 2d), 5×10^{-5} consistently provided the best trade-off across metrics, achieving higher precision, recall, and ROC-AUC while avoiding the instability associated with more aggressive rates like 1×10^{-3}. Among optimizers (Fig. 2e), Lion emerged as the top performer, delivering the highest ROC-AUC (0.7720) and competitive F1 scores, outperforming Adam, AdamW, and RMSprop, in line with its growing success in vision-based applications. For regularization (Fig. 2f), a weight decay value of 0.01 struck an optimal balance by enhancing generalization without excessively restricting model capacity. Performance trends across training epochs (Fig. 2g) revealed steady improvements in validation accuracy, F1 score, and ROC-AUC, with marked gains after unfreezing the ViT backbone at epoch 6 and the MaxViT backbone at epoch 10. The final epoch yielded the highest F1 score (0.6975) and ROC-AUC (0.7327), highlighting the benefit of staged fine-tuning. Lastly, in assessing dropout rates (Fig. 2h), a value of 0.3 proved to be the most reliable, offering balanced improvements, while higher rates, such as 0.,7 favored recall at the expense of precision.

5   Conclusion

This study systematically evaluated ViT and ViT-CNN hybrid architectures for end-to-end quark-gluon jet classification, leveraging multi-channel calorimeter images from publicly available CERN (CMS) data. Our findings robustly demonstrate that ViT-based approaches, particularly hybrids like *ViT+MaxViT* and *ViT+ConvNeXt*, significantly outperform established CNN baselines in key metrics such as F1-score, ROC-AUC, and accuracy. ViTs excel because they can analyze the entire jet image at once, helping them spot subtle, widespread patterns that are key to telling these jets apart, even amidst experimental noise. Our work provides the first systematic comparison of ViTs for this specific task using public data, offering strong performance results and a ready-to-use dataset. This helps make advanced image analysis tools more accessible for particle physics research.

Limitations. Key limitations of this study include: (i) The results are based on simulated data; further tests on real, more recent experimental data with different conditions are needed; (ii) These advanced ViT models are powerful but require significant computing resources, which could be a challenge for real-time applications without further optimization; (iii) While we know these models work well, more research is needed to fully understand, from a physics standpoint, exactly what features they are learning from the images.

References

1. Andrews, M., et al.: End-to-end jet classification of quarks and gluons with the CMS open data. Nucl. Instrum. Methods Phys. Res., Sect. A **977**, 164304 (2020). https://doi.org/10.1016/j.nima.2020.164304, https://linkinghub.elsevier.com/retrieve/pii/S0168900220307002
2. Andrews, M., Paulini, M., Gleyzer, S., Poczos, B.: End-to-end physics event classification with CMS open data: applying image-based deep learning to detector data for the direct classification of collision events at the LHC. Comput. Softw. Big Sci. **4**(1), 6 (2020)
3. Chen, Y., et al.: A FAIR and AI-ready higgs boson decay dataset. Sci. Data **9**(1), 31 (2022)
4. CMS Collaboration: GJet_Pt40_doubleEMEnriched_TuneZ2star_8TeV_ext-pythia6 in AODSIM format for 2012 collision data (2017). https://doi.org/10.7483/OPENDATA.CMS.2W51.W8AT, http://opendata.cern.ch/record/7778
5. Collaboration, C.M.S., et al.: The CMS experiment at the CERN LHC. J. Instrum. **3**(08), S08004–S08004 (2008)
6. Collaboration, C.M.S., et al.: Search for higgs boson decay to a charm quark-antiquark pair in proton-proton collisions at $\sqrt{s} = 13$TeV. Phys. Rev. Lett. **131**(6), 061801 (2023). https://doi.org/10.1103/PhysRevLett.131.061801, https://link.aps.org/doi/10.1103/PhysRevLett.131.061801, publisher: American Physical Society
7. Collaboration, C.M.S., et al.: Search for nonresonant pair production of highly energetic higgs bosons decaying to bottom quarks. Phys. Rev. Lett. **131**(4), 041803 (2023)
8. Dai, Z., Liu, H., Le, Q.V., Tan, M.: Coatnet: marrying convolution and attention for all data sizes. In: Advances in Neural Information Processing Systems, vol. 34, pp. 3965–3977 (2021). https://proceedings.neurips.cc/paper/2021/hash/20568692db622456cc42a2e853ca21f8-Abstract.html
9. De Oliveira, L., Kagan, M., Mackey, L., Nachman, B., Schwartzman, A.: Jet-images — deep learning edition. J. High Energy Phys. **2016**(7), 69 (2016). https://doi.org/10.1007/JHEP07(2016)069
10. Dillon, B.M., Kasieczka, G., Olischlager, H., Plehn, T., Sorrenson, P., Vogel, L.: Symmetries, safety, and self-supervision. SciPost Phys. 12(6), 188 (2022). https://doi.org/10.21468/SciPostPhys.12.6.188, arXiv:2108.04253 [hep-ph]
11. Dosovitskiy, A., et al.: An image is worth 16 ×16 words: transformers for image recognition at scale. arXiv preprint arXiv:2010.11929 (2020)
12. Dreyer, F.A., Grabarczyk, R., Monni, P.F.: Leveraging universality of jet taggers through transfer learning. European Phys. J. C **82**(6), 564 (2022)
13. Fang, W., Yu, Z., Chen, Y., Huang, T., Masquelier, T., Tian, Y.: Deep residual learning in spiking neural networks. In: Advances in Neural Information Processing Systems, vol. 34, pp. 21056–21069 (2021). https://proceedings.neurips.cc/paper/2021/hash/afe434653a898da20044041262b3ac74-Abstract.html

14. Furuichi, A., Lim, S.H., Nojiri, M.M.: Jet classification using high-level features from anatomy of top jets. J. High Energy Phys. **2024**(7), 146 (2024)

15. Gong, S., et al.: An efficient Lorentz equivariant graph neural network for jet tagging. J. High Energy Phys. **2022**(7), 30 (2022)

16. Guest, D., et al.: Jet flavor classification in high-energy physics with deep neural networks. Phys. Rev. D **94**(11), 112002 (2016)

17. Guo, M.H., et al.: PCT: point cloud transformer. Comput. Vis. Media **7**(2), 187–199 (2021)

18. Henrion, I., et al.: Neural message passing for jet physics. In: Deep Learning for Physical Sciences Workshop at the 31st Conference on Neural Information Processing Systems (NeurIPS) (2017)

19. Jahin, M.A., Masud, M.A., Suva, M.W., Mridha, M.F., Dey, N.: Lorentz-equivariant quantum graph neural network for high-energy physics. IEEE Trans. Artif. Intell. 1–11 (2025). https://doi.org/10.1109/TAI.2025.3554461, https://ieeexplore.ieee.org/document/10938398

20. Jumper, J., et al.: Highly accurate protein structure prediction with AlphaFold. Nature **596**(7873), 583–589 (2021). https://doi.org/10.1038/s41586-021-03819-2, https://www.nature.com/articles/s41586-021-03819-2

21. Komiske, P.T., Metodiev, E.M., Thaler, J.: Energy flow networks: deep sets for particle jets. J. High Energy Phys. **2019**(1), 121 (2019)

22. Kıran Yenice, E., Kara, C., Erdaş, B.: Automated detection of type 1 ROP, type 2 ROP and A-ROP based on deep learning. Eye **38**(13), 2644–2648 (2024). https://doi.org/10.1038/s41433-024-03184-0, https://www.nature.com/articles/s41433-024-03184-0, publisher: Nature Publishing Group

23. Larkoski, A.J., Moult, I., Nachman, B.: Jet substructure at the Large Hadron Collider: a review of recent advances in theory and machine learning. Phys. Rep. **841**, 1–63 (2020), https://www.sciencedirect.com/science/article/pii/S0370157319303643, publisher: Elsevier

24. Liu, Z., Lin, Y., Cao, Y., Hu, H., Wei, Y., Zhang, Z., Lin, S., Guo, B.: Swin transformer: hierarchical vision transformer using shifted windows. In: Proceedings of the IEEE/CVF International Conference on Computer Vision, pp. 10012–10022 (2021). https://openaccess.thecvf.com/content/ICCV2021/html/Liu_Swin_Transformer_Hierarchical_Vision_Transformer_Using_Shifted_Windows_ICCV_2021_paper

25. Liu, Z., Mao, H., Wu, C.Y., Feichtenhofer, C., Darrell, T., Xie, S.: A convnet for the 2020s. In: Proceedings of the IEEE/CVF Conference on Computer Vision and Pattern Recognition, pp. 11976–11986 (2022). http://openaccess.thecvf.com/content/CVPR2022/html/Liu_A_ConvNet_for_the_2020s_CVPR_2022_paper.html

26. Louppe, G., Cho, K., Becot, C., Cranmer, K.: QCD-aware recursive neural networks for jet physics. J. High Energy Phys. **2019**(1), 57 (2019). https://doi.org/10.1007/JHEP01(2019)057, https://link.springer.com/10.1007/JHEP01(2019)057

27. Mikuni, V., Canelli, F.: Point cloud transformers applied to collider physics. Mach. Learn. Sci. Technol. **2**(3), 035027 (2021). https://doi.org/10.1088/2632-2153/ac07f6, https://iopscience.iop.org/article/10.1088/2632-2153/ac07f6

28. Mikuni, V., Nachman, B.: Method to simultaneously facilitate all jet physics tasks. Phys. Rev. D **111**, 054015 (2025). https://doi.org/10.1103/PhysRevD.111.054015, https://link.aps.org/doi/10.1103/PhysRevD.111.054015

29. Qu, H., Gouskos, L.: Jet tagging via particle clouds. Phys. Rev. D **101**(5), 056019 (2020). https://doi.org/10.1103/PhysRevD.101.056019, https://link.aps.org/doi/10.1103/PhysRevD.101.056019

30. Sirunyan, A.M., et al.: Particle-flow reconstruction and global event description with the CMs detector. J. Instrum. **12**(10), P10003 (2017). https://doi.org/10.1088/1748-0221/12/10/P10003, https://dx.doi.org/10.1088/1748-0221/12/10/P10003

31. Sirunyan, A.M., et al.: Identification of heavy, energetic, hadronically decaying particles using machine-learning techniques. J. Instrum. **15**(06), P06005–P06005 (2020). https://doi.org/10.1088/1748-0221/15/06/P06005, https://iopscience.iop.org/article/10.1088/1748-0221/15/06/P06005

32. Tan, M., Le, Q.: EfficientNet: rethinking model scaling for convolutional neural networks. In: International Conference on Machine Learning, pp. 6105–6114. PMLR (2019), http://proceedings.mlr.press/v97/tan19a.html?ref=jina-ai-gmbh.ghost.io

33. Tu, Z., et al.: MaxViT: multi-axis vision transformer. In: Avidan, S., Brostow, G., Cissé, M., Farinella, G.M., Hassner, T. (eds.) Computer Vision – ECCV 2022, vol. 13684, pp. 459–479. Springer Nature Switzerland, Cham (2022).https://doi.org/10.1007/978-3-031-20053-3_27, https://link.springer.com/10.1007/978-3-031-20053-3_27, series Title: Lecture Notes in Computer Science

34. Vaswani, A., et al.: Attention is all you need. In: Advances in Neural Information Processing Systems, vol. 30 (2017). https://proceedings.neurips.cc/paper/2017/hash/3f5ee243547dee91fbd053c1c4a845aa-Abstract.html

35. Wang, Y., Sun, Y., Liu, Z., Sarma, S.E., Bronstein, M.M., Solomon, J.M.: Dynamic graph CNN for learning on point clouds. ACM Trans. Graph. **38**(5), 1–12 (2019). https://doi.org/10.1145/3326362, https://dl.acm.org/doi/10.1145/3326362

36. Wightman, R., Touvron, H., Jégou, H.: ResNet strikes back: an improved training procedure in timm. arXiv:2110.00476 (2021)

Adaptive Contextual Embedding
for Robust Far-View Borehole Detection

Xuesong Liu[1]($\boxtimes$), Tianyu Hao[2], Xueyuan Dai[3], Zerui Zhu[4], Yang Wang[3], and Emmett J. Ientilucci[1]

[1] Rochester Institute of Technology, Rochester, NY 14623, USA
{xl2088,ejipci}@rit.edu
[2] Guangzhou University, Guangzhou 510006, China
howtyee@e.gzhu.edu.cn
[3] Chang'an University, Xi'an 710064, China
{dxy1018,ywang120}@chd.edu.cn
[4] Harbin University of Science and Technology, Harbin 150080, China
2301020229@stu.hrbust.edu.cn

Abstract. In industrial quarrying and mining operations, precisely locating densely distributed small-scale boreholes from limited far-view imagery is essential for accurate explosive placement, optimal rock fragmentation, and prevention of dangerous misfires. Misidentified or undetected boreholes lead directly to inefficient blasting outcomes, elevated operational costs, and significant safety hazards for personnel and equipment. However, existing detection methods, including widely-used YOLO-based architectures, struggle with reliably identifying these boreholes due to their extremely small scale, dense arrangements, and limited distinctive visual features. Furthermore, practical constraints related to camera placement and quarry geometry severely restrict the availability of sufficient high-quality annotated data, exacerbating the challenge.

To address these combined challenges of visual complexity and limited training data, we propose an adaptive embedding-based detection framework designed for efficient generalization under resource-constrained conditions. Our approach introduces three synergistic components, each leveraging exponential moving averages (EMA) for stable feature learning: (1) adaptive augmentation, dynamically adjusting to illumination and textural variability; (2) embedding stabilization, ensuring consistent spatial and temporal embedding representations despite limited visual distinctions; and (3) contextual refinement, enhancing discrimination of boreholes from visually similar background noise by integrating spatial context. By applying EMA consistently across these components, our model efficiently learns robust, stable embeddings, enabling effective generalization to previously unseen and challenging scenarios.

Comprehensive experiments conducted on a proprietary quarry-site dataset demonstrate significant performance improvements over baseline YOLO architectures. Specifically, our integrated approach achieves a notable increase in mean Average Precision (mAP) from 61.5% to 74.9% compared to the baseline YOLOv11 model, clearly validating our method's practical suitability for robust deployment under constrained real-world conditions.

Y. Ma et al. (Eds.): IJCAI 2025, CCIS 2640, pp. 151–168, 2025.
https://doi.org/10.1007/978-981-95-0988-1_12

Keywords: Borehole Detection · Exponential Moving Average (EMA) · Contextual Aware

1 Introduction

Accurate detection of small-scale, densely distributed boreholes is crucial in quarry blasting and open-pit mining operations, directly influencing blasting precision, operational efficiency, and safety. Precise identification of boreholes ensures optimal explosive placement, leading to improved rock fragmentation and reduced overall operational costs. Despite rapid advancements in deep learning significantly enhancing general computer vision tasks such as image classification [1,2], object detection [3–5], and semantic segmentation [6,7], specialized industrial applications—particularly those involving the detection of tiny, densely packed objects—remain challenging and relatively unexplored.

Industrial scenarios such as open-pit mining and quarry-site operations present unique visual complexities rarely seen in conventional detection datasets. Accurately identifying tiny boreholes used in controlled blasting requires robust handling of extremely small scales, dense object distributions, and substantial visual variability from textures, geological conditions, lighting, and environmental noise [8,9]. Moreover, practical constraints related to quarry geometry, operational safety, and limited access to optimal viewpoints severely limit the availability of high-quality annotated data, further exacerbating these challenges and highlighting the necessity for methods capable of efficient generalization under limited training resources.

Existing techniques addressing these challenges typically include contextual integration [10], adaptive data augmentation [11], and embedding-based feature consistency methods [12]. However, these approaches have mostly been studied independently or in simpler scenarios, leaving their combined potential in realistic industrial contexts under-investigated. Existing object detection methods for densely packed small-scale objects, such as CPDD-YOLOv8 [9] and PARE-YOLO [13], have demonstrated robustness in aerial and remote-sensing scenarios but remain limited under the specific visual complexities of quarry-site imagery. Similarly, contextual integration techniques like ContextNet [10] and embedding-based approaches such as Dense Embedding Contrast (DECNet) [12] individually address aspects of these challenges but have not yet been effectively integrated for densely packed borehole detection tasks.

To address these critical gaps, we propose an adaptive detection approach built upon established detection architectures (e.g., YOLO), specifically designed to detect densely distributed tiny boreholes reliably under complex quarry-site conditions. Our method leverages exponential moving averages (EMA) across multiple stages, ensuring robust learning given the small scale, dense distribution, and limited distinctive visual features of boreholes. Our key contributions include:

- **Adaptive Augmentation:** Dynamically adjusts augmentation parameters using EMA-based global image statistics to mitigate illumination and textural variability frequently encountered in quarry-site imagery.
- **Embedding Stabilization:** Employs EMA-driven embedding updates to maintain consistent spatial and temporal feature representations, significantly reducing false alarms caused by visual ambiguities.
- **Contextual Refinement:** Enhances target-background discrimination by integrating EMA-refined contextual embeddings extracted from spatially expanded bounding regions, effectively suppressing noise-induced false positives.

Extensive experiments on a challenging proprietary quarry-site dataset demonstrate substantial improvements in detection accuracy and robustness when integrating our proposed innovations into widely-adopted YOLO-series detection architectures, including YOLOv3 [14], YOLOv5 [15], YOLOX [16], PPYOLOE [17], YOLOv6 [18], YOLOv7 [19], YOLOv8 [20], YOLOv9 [21], and YOLOv11 [22]. Our approach thus advances both theoretical understanding and practical capabilities, significantly enhancing real-world operational effectiveness and safety.

2 Related Work

Several existing approaches individually address challenges related to augmentation, embedding stability, or contextual refinement for object detection tasks.

Adaptive augmentation methods primarily aim to enhance model robustness by diversifying training data. *MixUp* [23] and *CutMix* [24] perform direct image-level augmentation by blending images and labels. Techniques like *AutoAugment* [25] and *RandAugment* [11] use automated strategies to optimize augmentation policies, enhancing generalization across datasets. *Mosaic augmentation* [26] stitches multiple images into one to improve small-object robustness. *GridMask* [27] randomly masks regions of the image to encourage learning of diverse features. *Copy-Paste augmentation* [28] directly pastes objects from one image to another, effectively increasing training diversity. Despite their effectiveness, these methods are generally dataset-agnostic and lack adaptive strategies tailored specifically to handling severe illumination and textural variability inherent in quarry-site imagery.

Embedding stabilization techniques primarily focus on maintaining consistent and stable feature representations across scales. *Path Aggregation Network (PANet)* [29] and *PAFPN* [16] aggregate features from multiple backbone layers, improving spatial consistency. Methods like *ASFF (Adaptive Spatial Feature Fusion)* [30] and *Bi-directional Feature Pyramid Network (BiFPN)* [31] dynamically fuse multi-scale features, achieving improved object localization. Although effective, these methods do not address embedding stabilization over training iterations, particularly under scenarios of dense and visually ambiguous small-scale objects.

Contextual refinement leverages spatial relationships or context to improve object recognition, especially beneficial for ambiguous or small objects. *Non-local Neural Networks* [32] and *GCNet* [33] capture long-range contextual dependencies across image regions. Recent transformer-based methods, such as the *DEtection TRansformer (DETR)* [5], *Deformable DETR* [34], and *Sparse DETR* [35], utilize self-attention mechanisms to encode rich contextual relationships. The *Cross-scale Attention (CSA)* model [36] integrates attention mechanisms across scales, benefiting small-object detection. However, these context-aware methods individually focus on broader scenarios and do not specifically address severe spatial ambiguities and dense distributions inherent in quarry-site images.

Furthermore, existing detection models specifically targeting tiny-object scenarios such as *CPDD-YOLOv8* [9] and *PARE-YOLO* [13] exhibit strong performance in remote sensing and aerial imagery tasks, yet encounter limitations when applied to quarry blasting imagery, given its unique visual complexity. In contrast to these individual approaches, our proposed framework integrates Adaptive Augmentation (AA), Embedding Stabilization (ES), and Contextual Refinement (CR) into a unified detection pipeline. Leveraging exponential moving averages (EMA) across these components, our method significantly enhances robustness and accuracy in challenging borehole detection scenarios.

3 Method

We propose an adaptive detection method tailored for efficient generalization from limited annotated data, designed to detect tiny, densely distributed boreholes in challenging industrial imagery. Given their small scale, dense arrangements, and limited distinctive features, we employ exponential moving average (EMA) techniques throughout our method to stabilize and enhance feature representations.

3.1 Adaptive Augmentation (AA)

Adaptive Augmentation (AA) dynamically enhances borehole visibility and mitigates variability in background characteristics such as illumination and texture through EMA-based updates. Specifically, let Ω represent a local image region or patch around candidate detections, and $X^{(t)}(u, v)$ denote the pixel intensity at coordinates (u, v) in the input image at iteration t. At iteration t, local image statistics (mean $\mu_\Omega^{(t)}$, standard deviation $\sigma_\Omega^{(t)}$) within region Ω and batch-wise global reference statistics $(\mu_{batch}^{(t)}, \sigma_{batch}^{(t)})$ are computed as follows:

$$\mu_\Omega^{(t)} = \frac{1}{|\Omega|} \sum_{(u,v) \in \Omega} X^{(t)}(u, v), \tag{1}$$

$$\sigma_\Omega^{(t)} = \sqrt{\frac{1}{|\Omega|} \sum_{(u,v) \in \Omega} (X^{(t)}(u, v) - \mu_\Omega^{(t)})^2}. \tag{2}$$

We define the EMA smoothing factor $\rho \in [0.01, 0.1]$ to ensure stable statistical updates. The global statistics are updated as follows:

$$\mu_{ref}^{(t)} = (1 - \rho)\mu_{ref}^{(t-1)} + \rho\,\mu_{batch}^{(t)}, \tag{3}$$

$$\sigma_{ref}^{(t)} = (1 - \rho)\sigma_{ref}^{(t-1)} + \rho\,\sigma_{batch}^{(t)}. \tag{4}$$

Hyperparameters $k_1, k_2 \in [0.5, 1.5]$ and $k_3 \in [0.01, 0.1]$ control the magnitude of augmentation adjustments for brightness $(\alpha^{(t)})$, contrast $(\beta^{(t)})$, and additive noise $(\eta^{(t)})$:

$$\alpha^{(t)} = 1 + k_1 \frac{\mu_{ref}^{(t)} - \mu_{\Omega}^{(t)}}{\mu_{ref}^{(t)}}, \tag{5}$$

$$\beta^{(t)} = 1 + k_2 \frac{\sigma_{ref}^{(t)} - \sigma_{\Omega}^{(t)}}{\sigma_{ref}^{(t)}}, \tag{6}$$

$$\eta^{(t)} = k_3 \frac{|\sigma_{ref}^{(t)} - \sigma_{\Omega}^{(t)}|}{\sigma_{ref}^{(t)}}. \tag{7}$$

The augmented image at iteration t is computed as:

$$X'^{(t)}(u, v) = \beta^{(t)}\alpha^{(t)} X^{(t)}(u, v) + \eta^{(t)}\epsilon(u, v), \quad \epsilon(u, v) \sim \mathcal{N}(0, 1). \tag{8}$$

3.2 Embedding Stabilization (ES)

Embedding Stabilization (ES) addresses embedding coherence issues arising from small object scales, dense distributions, and limited visual distinctions. Let c_i, c_j denote spatial embedding centers corresponding to feature coordinates, and let $\delta \in [20, 100]$ pixels represent the proximity threshold for defining spatial embedding regions. Embedding regions $R_j^{(t)}$ group embeddings based on proximity:

$$R_j^{(t)} = \{e_i^{(t)} \mid \|c_i - c_j\|_2 < \delta\}. \tag{9}$$

We define region-level embeddings $\mu_j^{(t)}$ and a global embedding representation $\mu_{global}^{(t)}$ updated through EMA:

$$\mu_j^{(t)} = (1 - \rho)\mu_j^{(t-1)} + \rho\frac{1}{|R_j^{(t)}|} \sum_{e \in R_j^{(t)}} e, \tag{10}$$

$$\mu_{global}^{(t)} = (1 - \rho)\mu_{global}^{(t-1)} + \rho\frac{1}{\sum_j |R_j^{(t)}|} \sum_j \sum_{e \in R_j^{(t)}} e. \tag{11}$$

Let J_t be the total number of embedding regions at iteration t. Embedding coherence is enforced through two complementary loss functions:

$$L_{spatial}^{(t)} = \frac{1}{J_t} \sum_{j=1}^{J_t} \left(\frac{1}{|R_j^{(t)}|} \sum_{e \in R_j^{(t)}} \|e - \mu_j^{(t)}\|_2^2 + \lambda \|\mu_j^{(t)} - \mu_{global}^{(t)}\|_2^2 \right), \quad (12)$$

$$L_{temporal}^{(t)} = \frac{1}{|R_j^{(t)}|} \sum_{e \in R_j^{(t)}} \|e - e_{stable}^{(t)}\|_2^2, \quad (13)$$

where $\lambda \in [0.5, 2.0]$ balances embedding coherence, and $e_{stable}^{(t)}$ is defined as the EMA-updated temporally stable embedding:

$$e_{stable}^{(t)} = (1 - \rho)e_{stable}^{(t-1)} + \rho \frac{1}{|R_j^{(t)}|} \sum_{e \in R_j^{(t)}} e. \quad (14)$$

3.3   Contextual Refinement (CR)

Contextual Refinement (CR) leverages spatial context to differentiate true boreholes from visually similar noise. Original bounding boxes are defined by coordinates (x_i, y_i) and dimensions (w_i, h_i). These boxes are expanded by a context margin factor $\gamma \in [0.1, 0.5]$:

$$\tilde{b}_i^{(t)} = (x_i - \gamma w_i, y_i - \gamma h_i, w_i + 2\gamma w_i, h_i + 2\gamma h_i). \quad (15)$$

Contextual embeddings $E_{context}^{(t)}(\tilde{b}_i)$ extracted from expanded bounding boxes are updated using EMA:

$$E_{context}^{ref(t)} = (1 - \rho)E_{context}^{ref(t-1)} + \rho \frac{1}{N_t} \sum_{i=1}^{N_t} E_{context}^{(t)}(\tilde{b}_i). \quad (16)$$

These refined contextual embeddings are combined with object-level embeddings $E_{object}^{(t)}(b_i)$:

$$E_{merged}^{(t)}(b_i) = \text{Concat}(E_{object}^{(t)}(b_i), E_{context}^{ref(t)}). \quad (17)$$

This merged embedding integrates object-level features and refined spatial context, enhancing detection robustness under challenging conditions.

3.4   Overall Objective

Our adaptive detection approach seamlessly integrates the Adaptive Augmentation (AA, Sec. 2.1), Embedding Stabilization (ES, Sec. 2.2), and Contextual Refinement (CR, Sec. 2.3) modules within standard YOLO-based detection architectures. The AA module first adaptively enhances image inputs, dynamically adjusting illumination, contrast, and noise based on exponential moving average (EMA)-computed global statistics. Subsequently, ES stabilizes spatial embeddings by leveraging EMA to aggregate embeddings across spatial regions and temporal iterations, promoting consistency. Finally, CR utilizes EMA-refined contextual embeddings extracted from expanded bounding regions, enriching object representations with spatial context.

The total training objective combines conventional detection losses with additional embedding and contextual consistency regularization terms, controlled by scaling hyperparameters:

$$L_{total}^{(t)} = L_{cls}^{(t)} + L_{bbox}^{(t)} + L_{obj}^{(t)} + \lambda_1 L_{ES}^{spatial(t)} + \lambda_2 L_{ES}^{temporal(t)} + \lambda_3 L_{CR}^{(t)}, \quad (18)$$

where:

- $L_{cls}^{(t)}$: classification loss,
- $L_{bbox}^{(t)}$: bounding-box regression loss,
- $L_{obj}^{(t)}$: objectness confidence loss,
- $L_{ES}^{spatial(t)}$: spatial embedding consistency loss (Embedding Stabilization),
- $L_{ES}^{temporal(t)}$: temporal embedding consistency loss (Embedding Stabilization),
- $L_{CR}^{(t)}$: contextual embedding consistency loss (Contextual Refinement),
- $\lambda_1, \lambda_2, \lambda_3$: hyperparameters balancing detection accuracy and embedding/contextual regularization, typically selected from $[0.1, 1.0]$.

These embedding and contextual consistency losses regularize feature representations, enhancing spatial and temporal embedding coherence, and integrating contextual information effectively. This structured objective ensures that the learned features remain robust and discriminative, complementing the core detection losses and maintaining full compatibility with established YOLO-based detection frameworks.

4   Experiments

We evaluate our adaptive detection approach on a challenging proprietary dataset collected from multiple quarry sites. We quantitatively and qualitatively assess the effectiveness of each component: Adaptive Augmentation (AA), Embedding Stabilization (ES), and Contextual Refinement (CR).

4.1   Dataset and Experimental Setup

Our proprietary dataset consists of 250 annotated images, each containing an average of 100 densely distributed boreholes. Images feature substantial variability in illumination, textures, resolution, and noise levels, realistically representing typical quarry-site conditions.

Due to the limited size of our dataset, we employed **5-fold cross-validation** (i.e., $k = 5$) to robustly evaluate the effectiveness of our proposed components.

Specifically, we partitioned our dataset into five distinct subsets, iteratively using four subsets for training and the remaining subset for validation. Evaluation metrics, including mean Average Precision (mAP), Precision, Recall, and F1-score, were computed across these five folds and summarized using their mean and standard deviation to clearly indicate performance variability and robustness.

The detection model is implemented in PyTorch, using a YOLO-based architecture, and trained for 100 epochs on an NVIDIA GeForce RTX 4090 GPU. We optimize the model using AdamW with a learning rate of 1×10^{-3} and a batch size of 8. Performance is assessed using standard detection metrics: mean Average Precision (mAP), Precision, Recall, and F1-score.

Statistical Significance Testing: Considering the limited dataset size, we employed paired bootstrap testing with N=10,000 resamples to robustly validate the statistical significance of performance improvements observed with our proposed method (AA+ES+CR) relative to the baseline. Specific numerical results from this analysis are detailed in the following subsections.

Non-YOLO Baseline Comparison: To evaluate the generalizability and robustness of our proposed framework beyond YOLO-based architectures, we additionally tested several strong non-YOLO baselines, employing the same 5-fold cross-validation setup, training conditions, and evaluation metrics, enabling a direct and fair performance comparison.

Dataset Availability: A small anonymized subset of our proprietary dataset has been prepared to facilitate reproducibility and community benchmarking. The dataset will be made publicly available upon publication.

4.2   Effectiveness of Proposed Components

Table 1 summarizes the mean and standard deviation of evaluation metrics (mAP, Precision, Recall, F1-score) across these folds. To systematically analyze the contributions of our components, we first evaluated a baseline YOLO model (YOLOv11) without any of our proposed enhancements, achieving an mAP of 61.5%. Subsequently, we incrementally added each proposed component individually: Adaptive Augmentation (AA), Embedding Stabilization (ES), and Contextual Refinement (CR).

Individually, each component provided clear performance gains, with mAP values improving to 64.5% (AA), 66.8% (ES), and 67.5% (CR) respectively. Combining components in pairs further enhanced performance, reaching an mAP of 70.3% (AA+ES), 70.1% (AA+CR), and 72.5% (ES+CR). Finally, integrating all three components (AA+ES+CR) achieved the highest overall performance across all metrics, significantly improving the mAP to 74.9%, Precision to 72.8%, Recall to 75.6%, and F1-score to 74.2%.

We further illustrate qualitative improvements using selected visual results, shown in Fig. 1. Due to the tiny size and high density of boreholes, we denote detections with green dots instead of bounding boxes for clearer visualization. Four representative images with diverse conditions are presented: Fig. 1(a) shows a snowy winter blasting scenario, challenging due to the color similarity between snow and crushed rock particles around boreholes. Figure 1(b) demonstrates a

Table 1. Component-wise evaluation using 5-fold cross-validation (YOLOv11 backbone).

Model	mAP (Primary Metric)				Secondary Metrics		
	Mean ± std (%)	Improvement (%)	95% CI (Bootstrap)	p-value	Precision (%)	Recall (%)	F1-score (%)
Baseline (YOLOv11)	61.5±0.8		–	–	59.3±0.7	62.1±0.9	60.7±0.8
+ AA*	64.5±0.6	+3.0	[1.3, 4.7]	0.012	61.8±0.5	65.2±0.7	63.5±0.6
+ ES†	66.8±0.7	+5.3	[3.5, 7.1]	0.004	64.0±0.5	67.8±0.6	65.8±0.6
+ CR‡	67.5±0.7	+6.0	[4.2, 7.8]	0.002	64.7±0.6	68.3±0.8	66.5±0.7
+ AA + ES	70.3±0.6	+8.8	[7.1, 10.5]	<0.001	67.3±0.4	71.5±0.5	69.3±0.5
+ AA + CR	70.1±0.6	+8.6	[6.9, 10.3]	<0.001	67.0±0.4	71.0±0.5	68.9±0.4
+ ES + CR	72.5±0.5	+11.0	[9.4, 12.6]	<0.001	69.8±0.4	73.2±0.5	71.5±0.4
+ AA + ES + CR	**74.9±0.4**	**+13.4**	**[12.0, 14.8]**	**<0.001**	**72.8±0.3**	**75.6±0.4**	**74.2±0.3**

*AA: Adaptive Augmentation, †ES: Embedding Stabilization, ‡CR: Contextual Refinement.

lower-resolution image scenario, which often occurs due to equipment limitations at quarry sites. Figure 1(c) represents relatively dark illumination and an uneven bench surface with structural and textural complexity. Finally, Fig. 1(d) presents the most challenging scenario, featuring dark lighting conditions, uneven surfaces, water pools, and boreholes positioned across different quarry levels.

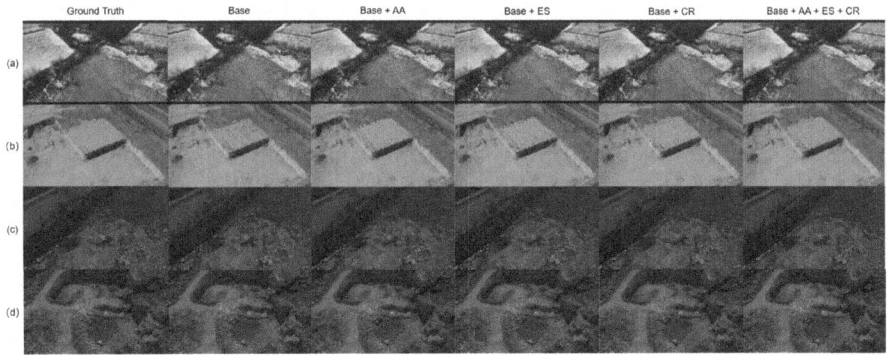

Fig. 1. Qualitative comparison of detection results: Ground Truth, Baseline YOLO (Base), and incremental addition of proposed components. Our complete model (AA + ES + CR) shows robust and accurate detections, especially in challenging conditions.

These visual examples highlight specific contributions of each component. The baseline method struggles significantly, exhibiting numerous missed detections (false negatives), particularly evident in Fig. 1(c) and (d). Incorporating adaptive augmentation (AA) reduces missed detections by stabilizing the model's response to varying environmental conditions, clearly visible in Fig. 1(a) and (b). Embedding stabilization (ES) further improves completeness, increasing correctly identified boreholes across scenarios. Contextual refinement (CR) notably enhances spatial accuracy and reduces noise-induced false positives. Ultimately, the fully integrated model (AA+ES+CR) achieves robust and accurate detections, even under the most challenging conditions.

4.3   Comparative Analysis of Individual Components

We systematically analyze the contributions of our proposed components—Adaptive Augmentation (AA), Embedding Stabilization (ES), and Contextual Refinement (CR)—to clearly demonstrate their individual and combined effectiveness in enhancing detection performance. Table 2 summarizes quantitative comparisons between each proposed component and established baseline methods.

Table 2. Comparison of representative methods relative to our proposed individual components (AA, ES, CR).

Model	mAP (Primary Metric)				Secondary Metrics		
	Mean ± std (%)	Δ (%)	95% CI (Bootstrap)	p-value	Precision (%)	Recall (%)	F1-score (%)
AA (Ours)	64.5±0.6	–	–	–	61.8±0.5	65.2±0.7	63.5±0.6
MixUp [23]	62.8±0.8	-1.7	[-2.3, -1.1]	<0.001	60.6±0.7	63.5±0.8	62.0±0.7
CutMix [24]	63.0±0.7	-1.5	[-2.1, -0.9]	<0.001	60.9±0.6	63.7±0.7	62.3±0.6
AutoAugment [25]	63.4±0.7	-1.1	[-1.7, -0.5]	<0.001	61.2±0.6	64.0±0.7	62.6±0.6
Mosaic [26]	62.7±0.7	-1.8	[-2.4, -1.2]	<0.001	60.5±0.6	63.3±0.7	61.9±0.6
RandAugment [11]	63.6±0.7	-0.9	[-1.5, -0.3]	0.003	61.4±0.6	64.2±0.7	62.8±0.6
GridMask [27]	63.8±0.7	-0.7	[-1.3, -0.1]	0.010	61.6±0.6	64.3±0.7	62.9±0.6
Copy-Paste [28]	64.1±0.7	-0.4	[-1.0, 0.2]	0.120	61.8±0.6	64.6±0.7	63.2±0.6
ES (Ours)	66.8±0.7	–	–	–	64.0±0.5	67.8±0.6	65.8±0.6
PANet [29]	63.2±0.7	-3.6	[-4.4, -2.8]	<0.001	60.8±0.6	63.7±0.8	62.2±0.7
ASFF [30]	64.0±0.7	-2.8	[-3.5, -2.1]	<0.001	61.7±0.6	64.6±0.7	63.1±0.7
BiFPN [31]	64.5±0.6	-2.3	[-3.0, -1.6]	<0.001	62.0±0.5	65.0±0.7	63.5±0.6
PAFPN [16]	64.2±0.6	-2.6	[-3.3, -1.9]	<0.001	61.8±0.5	64.8±0.7	63.2±0.6
CR (Ours)	67.5±0.7	–	–	–	64.7±0.6	68.3±0.8	66.5±0.7
Non-local [32]	63.8±0.7	-3.7	[-4.4, -3.0]	<0.001	61.2±0.6	64.5±0.7	62.8±0.6
GCNet [33]	64.3±0.6	-3.2	[-3.8, -2.6]	<0.001	61.7±0.6	65.0±0.6	63.3±0.6
Transformer [5]	65.2±0.6	-2.3	[-2.9, -1.7]	<0.001	62.5±0.5	65.9±0.6	64.1±0.5
Deformable Attention [37]	65.7±0.5	-1.8	[-2.3, -1.3]	<0.001	63.0±0.5	66.4±0.5	64.6±0.5
Sparse DETR [35]	65.9±0.5	-1.6	[-2.1, -1.1]	<0.001	63.3±0.4	66.7±0.5	64.9±0.5
Cross-scale Attention (CA) [36]	66.3±0.5	-1.2	[-1.7, -0.7]	<0.001	63.7±0.4	67.1±0.5	65.3±0.4
Copy-Paste + BiFPN + CA	69.4±0.5	-5.5	[-6.8, -4.2]	<0.001	67.1±0.4	70.2±0.5	68.6±0.4
AA + ES + CR (Ours, 2025)	**74.9±0.4**	–	–		**72.8±0.3**	**75.6±0.4**	**74.2±0.3**

Adaptive Augmentation (AA) addresses visual variability by dynamically adjusting augmentation parameters based on global image statistics. Individually, AA achieves a mean Average Precision (mAP) of **64.5%**, moderately outperforming existing standard augmentation methods such as AutoAugment (63.4%) and RandAugment (63.6%). Although the improvements are modest individually, AA substantially boosts detection performance when combined with ES and CR, underscoring its critical role in managing visual variations effectively.
Embedding Stabilization (ES) focuses on ensuring consistent and robust embedding representations, significantly mitigating feature instability from challenging

visual conditions, such as densely distributed boreholes and limited visual distinctions. Our ES approach achieves a clear performance improvement (mAP: **66.8%**) over popular multi-scale feature fusion methods, including PANet (63.2%) and BiFPN (64.5%). While individual improvements from ES are notable, the greatest benefits occur when combined with AA and CR, highlighting its essential role in reinforcing embedding stability within our integrated detection approach.

Contextual Refinement (CR) incorporates spatial context into predictions through refined contextual embeddings, enhancing discrimination between actual boreholes and visually similar background features. Individually, CR achieves an mAP of **67.5%**, clearly outperforming other context-aware methods such as Non-local (63.8%), GCNet (64.3%), and Transformer-based approaches (65.2%). Although its individual gains are moderate, CR greatly amplifies overall performance when synergistically combined with AA and ES, emphasizing its valuable role in accurately leveraging spatial context.

Integrated Performance (AA+ES+CR) achieves the highest overall performance, significantly enhancing detection metrics across the board: mAP increases to **74.9%**, Precision to **72.8%**, Recall to **75.6%**, and F1-score to **74.2%**. This confirms the complementary nature of AA, ES, and CR, where each component individually contributes meaningfully, and their synergistic combination clearly delivers substantial cumulative performance improvements.

4.4 Generalization Across YOLO Backbones

To comprehensively assess the generalizability and robustness of our proposed approach, we conducted extensive experiments across various YOLO-series backbone versions, encompassing multiple model sizes ranging from extra-large to nano. Table 3 presents detailed performance metrics (mAP, Precision, Recall, and F1-score) for both the original and enhanced models, providing a clear and thorough comparison.

Our results illustrate that the proposed method consistently delivers substantial performance improvements across all evaluated YOLO architectures and size variants. For instance, focusing on the latest YOLOv11 (2024), we observe notable increases in mean Average Precision (mAP) from 61.5% to 74.9% for the Large variant, with similar relative gains consistently maintained even when scaling down to smaller variants (Medium: 59.2%→71.3%, Small: 56.0%→67.8%, Nano: 52.4%→63.2%). These enhancements clearly demonstrate the scalability and adaptability of our approach across different model complexities.

Additionally, earlier YOLO models also show significant and consistent performance gains. YOLOv9 (2024) sees an improvement from 66.5% to 79.0% (Extra Large variant), YOLOv8 (2023) from 63.7% to 75.9% (Large), and PPY-OLOE (2022) from 61.8% to 73.2% (Large). Notably, the substantial improvements persist across smaller model sizes, reinforcing our method's effectiveness regardless of model parameter count.

Furthermore, even lightweight models such as YOLOv6 (2022), YOLOX (2021), and YOLOv5 (2020) exhibit consistent enhancements, highlighting the

Table 3. Comprehensive evaluation of various YOLO-series backbones and model sizes.

Backbone	Size	Params (M)	mAP (%)		Precision (%)		Recall (%)		F1-score (%)	
			Original	Enhanced	Original	Enhanced	Original	Enhanced	Original	Enhanced
YOLOv11 (2024)	(L)arge	25.3	61.5±0.8	**74.9±0.4**	59.3±0.7	**72.8±0.3**	62.1±0.9	**75.6±0.4**	60.7±0.8	**74.2±0.3**
	(M)edium	12.8	59.2±0.7	71.3±0.5	56.9±0.6	69.2±0.4	60.0±0.7	72.0±0.5	57.8±0.6	70.6±0.4
	(S)mall	6.4	56.0±0.7	67.8±0.5	53.6±0.6	65.4±0.5	56.7±0.7	68.5±0.6	54.9±0.6	66.9±0.5
	(N)ano	3.2	52.4±0.8	63.2±0.6	50.1±0.7	60.9±0.5	53.3±0.8	64.0±0.6	51.7±0.7	62.4±0.6
YOLOv9 (2024)	(E)xtra Large	57.3	66.5±0.5	**79.0±0.4**	64.7±0.4	**76.7±0.3**	67.0±0.5	**79.6±0.3**	65.8±0.4	**78.1±0.3**
	(C) Large	25.3	65.4±0.5	78.2±0.4	63.6±0.4	75.9±0.3	65.9±0.5	78.8±0.3	64.7±0.4	77.3±0.3
	(M)edium	20.0	62.5±0.6	75.4±0.5	60.5±0.5	73.0±0.4	63.1±0.6	75.9±0.4	61.8±0.5	74.4±0.4
	(S)mall	7.1	58.0±0.7	70.3±0.6	55.8±0.6	67.7±0.5	58.5±0.7	70.8±0.5	56.9±0.6	69.2±0.5
	(T)iny	2.0	54.5±0.8	66.5±0.6	52.0±0.7	64.0±0.6	55.0±0.8	67.0±0.6	53.5±0.7	65.5±0.6
YOLOv8 (2023)	(L)arge	43.6	63.7±0.5	**75.9±0.4**	61.8±0.5	**73.7±0.3**	64.2±0.5	**76.5±0.4**	63.0±0.5	**75.1±0.3**
	(M)edium	25.9	61.2±0.6	73.4±0.5	59.0±0.5	71.2±0.4	61.6±0.6	73.9±0.4	60.3±0.5	72.5±0.4
	(S)mall	11.1	57.5±0.7	69.5±0.6	55.3±0.6	67.2±0.5	57.8±0.7	70.0±0.5	56.5±0.6	68.4±0.5
	(N)ano	3.0	53.2±0.8	64.8±0.7	50.9±0.7	62.6±0.6	53.8±0.8	65.3±0.7	52.3±0.7	63.9±0.7
PPYOLOE (2022)	(L)arge	52.2	61.8±0.6	**73.2±0.5**	59.3±0.6	**70.7±0.5**	62.2±0.6	**73.8±0.5**	60.8±0.6	**72.2±0.5**
	(M)edium	23.4	59.5±0.7	70.9±0.6	56.9±0.6	68.4±0.5	60.0±0.7	71.5±0.6	58.5±0.6	70.0±0.5
	(S)mall	7.9	55.0±0.7	66.8±0.6	52.5±0.6	64.3±0.5	55.5±0.7	67.4±0.6	54.0±0.6	65.9±0.5
YOLOv7 (2022)	Basic	36.9	62.1±0.6	**73.8±0.5**	60.1±0.5	**71.3±0.4**	62.7±0.6	**74.5±0.4**	61.4±0.5	**72.9±0.4**
	Tiny	6.2	55.0±0.7	67.0±0.6	52.5±0.6	64.4±0.5	55.6±0.7	67.6±0.6	53.9±0.6	66.0±0.6
YOLOv6 (2022)	(L)arge	58.5	60.2±0.7	**70.9±0.6**	58.0±0.6	**68.4±0.5**	60.9±0.7	**71.6±0.5**	59.4±0.6	**69.9±0.5**
	(M)edium	34.3	58.0±0.7	69.0±0.6	55.7±0.6	66.5±0.5	58.6±0.7	69.7±0.5	57.1±0.6	68.2±0.5
	(S)mall	17.2	55.0±0.7	66.5±0.6	52.7±0.6	64.0±0.5	55.5±0.7	67.2±0.6	54.0±0.6	65.6±0.5
	(T)iny	15.0	52.5±0.7	64.0±0.6	50.2±0.6	61.5±0.5	53.0±0.7	64.7±0.6	51.5±0.6	63.0±0.5
	(N)ano	4.3	49.0±0.8	61.0±0.7	47.0±0.7	58.5±0.6	49.5±0.8	62.0±0.7	48.0±0.7	59.5±0.6
YOLOX (2021)	(L)arge	54.2	62.5±0.6	**73.7±0.5**	60.0±0.5	**71.1±0.4**	63.0±0.6	**74.3±0.5**	61.5±0.5	**72.7±0.4**
	(M)edium	25.3	60.2±0.6	71.5±0.5	57.7±0.6	69.0±0.5	60.7±0.6	72.1±0.5	59.2±0.6	70.6±0.5
	(S)mall	9.0	56.7±0.7	68.2±0.6	54.1±0.6	65.7±0.5	57.2±0.7	68.8±0.6	55.6±0.6	67.3±0.5
	(T)iny	5.1	53.5±0.7	65.2±0.6	51.0±0.6	62.7±0.5	54.0±0.7	65.7±0.6	52.4±0.6	64.2±0.5
YOLOv5 (2020)	E(X)tra Large	86.7	65.2±0.5	**76.5±0.4**	62.8±0.5	**74.1±0.4**	65.7±0.5	**77.2±0.4**	64.3±0.5	**75.8±0.4**
	(L)arge	46.5	64.0±0.5	75.2±0.4	61.6±0.5	72.8±0.4	64.5±0.5	75.9±0.4	63.1±0.5	74.5±0.4
	(M)edium	21.2	60.5±0.6	72.0±0.5	58.0±0.6	69.5±0.5	61.0±0.6	72.6±0.5	59.5±0.6	71.0±0.5
	(S)mall	7.2	56.2±0.7	67.9±0.6	53.6±0.6	65.3±0.5	56.7±0.7	68.5±0.6	55.1±0.6	67.0±0.5
	(N)ano	1.9	50.0±0.8	61.5±0.7	47.5±0.7	59.0±0.6	50.5±0.8	62.0±0.7	48.9±0.7	60.4±0.6
YOLOv3 (2018)	Basic	63.0	55.7±0.8	**65.3±0.7**	53.8±0.7	**63.2±0.6**	56.1±0.8	**66.1±0.7**	54.9±0.7	**64.6±0.6**

general applicability and practical value of our adaptive augmentation, embedding stabilization, and contextual refinement components. These results confirm that our approach robustly addresses the specific challenges of detecting small, densely packed objects within visually complex quarry-site scenarios across diverse YOLO-based detection frameworks.

4.5   Comparison with Non-YOLO Detection Methods

We conducted an extensive performance evaluation of our integrated YOLOv11-based detection framework (AA+ES+CR) against a representative set of recent CNN-based and transformer-based non-YOLO detection models (Table 4). Our method significantly outperformed all compared baseline models, achieving an impressive mean Average Precision (mAP) of 74.9%, accompanied by precision, recall, and F1-scores of 72.8%, 75.6%, and 74.2%, respectively.

Notably, among CNN-based methods, DiffusionDet (2023) and RT-DETR (2023) demonstrated the strongest performance, with mAP values of 70.2% and 69.7%, respectively, yet still lagging significantly behind our method. Classic architectures such as Faster R-CNN (65.2%) and Cascade R-CNN (66.4%) exhibited notably lower accuracy, highlighting limitations in their performance for densely packed small-object scenarios typical in quarry-site detection tasks.

Transformer-based detection methods, particularly UViT (68.8%) and EfficientViT-Det (69.5%), offered improved performance relative to traditional CNN-based approaches, reflecting their capability to effectively utilize global contextual information. However, these transformer-based models still fell short compared to our integrated approach. Similarly, methods like ViDT (67.9%) and Mask2Former (68.6%) showcased competitive results but remained noticeably behind our method's accuracy.

This comparative analysis clearly demonstrates that our method's systematic integration of adaptive augmentation, embedding stabilization, and contextual refinement uniquely positions it to significantly outperform current state-of-the-art CNN- and transformer-based detection approaches. Such robust performance underscores its practical value in scenarios demanding accurate detection of densely arranged small-scale objects, as frequently encountered in industrial applications like quarry-site borehole detection.

Table 4. Comprehensive comparison of our integrated method (AA+ES+CR) against recent non-YOLO detection methods (evaluated using 5-fold cross-validation, mean ± std).

Model (Backbone, Year)	mAP (%)	Precision (%)	Recall (%)	F1-score (%)
CNN-based methods				
Faster R-CNN (MobileNetV3-Large-320-FPN, 2015) [3]	65.2±0.7	62.9±0.6	66.0±0.7	64.4±0.6
RetinaNet (ResNet-50-FPN, 2017) [38]	64.7±0.7	62.2±0.6	65.3±0.7	63.7±0.6
Cascade R-CNN (ResNet-50-FPN, 2018) [4]	66.4±0.6	63.8±0.5	67.1±0.6	65.4±0.6
Deformable DETR (ResNet-50, 2020) [37]	67.4±0.6	64.9±0.5	68.2±0.6	66.5±0.5
DN-DETR (ResNet-50, 2022) [39]	67.7±0.5	65.2±0.4	68.5±0.5	66.8±0.4
SAM-DETR (ResNet-50, 2022) [40]	68.5±0.5	65.9±0.4	69.3±0.5	67.6±0.4
Conditional-DETR (ResNet-50, 2023) [41]	68.7±0.4	66.2±0.4	69.5±0.5	67.8±0.4
Sparse-DETR (ResNet-50, 2022) [35]	66.5±0.6	64.0±0.5	67.3±0.6	65.6±0.5
RT-DETR (ResNet-50, 2023) [42]	69.7±0.4	67.2±0.3	70.5±0.4	68.8±0.3
DiffusionDet (ResNet-50, 2023) [43]	70.2±0.4	67.7±0.3	71.0±0.4	69.3±0.3
Transformer-based methods				
DINO (Swin-Base Transformer, 2022) [44]	68.3±0.5	65.6±0.4	69.0±0.5	67.2±0.4
ViDT (Swin-Base Transformer, 2022) [45]	67.9±0.5	65.4±0.4	68.7±0.5	67.0±0.4
EfficientViT-Det (EfficientViT-B, 2023) [46]	69.5±0.4	67.0±0.3	70.3±0.4	68.6±0.3
UViT (ViT-Base Transformer, 2022) [47]	68.8±0.5	66.3±0.4	69.6±0.5	67.9±0.4
Mask2Former (Swin-Base Transformer, 2022) [48]	68.6±0.5	66.0±0.4	69.4±0.5	67.7±0.4
Deformable-DETR (Swin-T Transformer, 2020) [37]	67.9±0.6	65.3±0.4	68.7±0.5	67.0±0.4
Sparse-DETR (Swin-T Transformer, 2022) [35]	67.3±0.6	64.8±0.5	68.1±0.5	66.4±0.5
AA + ES + CR (YOLOv11 backbone, Ours, 2025)	**74.9±0.4**	**72.8±0.3**	**75.6±0.4**	**74.2±0.3**

Table 5. Computational efficiency comparing our integrated YOLO-based approach (AA+ES+CR) with representative CNN-based and transformer-based detection models.

Model (Backbone)	Parameters (M)	GPU Memory (GB)	Training Time (min/epoch)	Inference Speed (FPS)
YOLO-based methods				
YOLOv11 (Baseline)	25.3	9.8	15.2	78.4
YOLOv11 (Ours)	**25.9**	**10.5**	**18.5**	**73.5**
CNN-based methods				
Faster R-CNN (MobileNetV3-Large-320-FPN) [3]	19.0	8.5	14.5	60.0
RetinaNet (ResNet-50-FPN) [38]	34.0	10.2	18.5	37.8
Cascade R-CNN (ResNet-50-FPN) [4]	69.0	11.7	22.8	16.1
Deformable DETR (ResNet-50) [37]	40.0	10.9	20.5	41.5
DN-DETR (ResNet-50) [39]	44.0	11.2	22.0	39.1
SAM-DETR (ResNet-50) [40]	58.0	11.8	23.5	35.0
Conditional-DETR (ResNet-50) [41]	44.0	11.3	21.8	37.0
Sparse-DETR (ResNet-50) [35]	41.0	10.2	21.5	34.3
RT-DETR (ResNet-50) [42]	55.6	12.4	22.8	50.6
DiffusionDet (ResNet-50) [43]	53.9	12.2	23.9	36.8
Transformer-based methods				
DINO (Swin-Base Transformer) [44]	88.0	14.0	28.0	20.0
ViDT (Swin-Base Transformer) [45]	88.0	14.0	28.5	20.5
EfficientViT-Det (EfficientViT-B) [46]	46.7	11.5	22.5	42.0
UViT (ViT-Base Transformer) [47]	85.0	13.7	27.5	24.0
Mask2Former (Swin-Base Transformer) [48]	47.0	11.8	23.0	36.5
Deformable DETR (Swin-T Transformer) [37]	41.0	11.5	21.8	38.9
Sparse-DETR (Swin-T Transformer) [35]	41.0	11.3	21.8	39.0

4.6   Comparison with Efficiency of Detection Methods

To comprehensively assess the computational efficiency of our enhanced YOLOv11-based detection model, we compared it against recent representative CNN-based and transformer-based detection architectures (Table 5). Our enhanced model (AA+ES+CR) introduces only marginal increases in computational overhead compared to the YOLOv11 baseline, with a modest rise from 25.3M to 25.9M parameters and GPU memory usage increasing slightly from 9.8 GB to 10.5 GB. Training time per epoch moderately increases from 15.2 to 18.5 min, and inference speed slightly decreases from 78.4 to 73.5 FPS. These modest computational overheads are well justified by the substantial gains in detection accuracy, underscoring the practical deployment potential of our method.

When contrasted against popular CNN-based methods, our model achieves notably higher inference speed and significantly reduced training times. For example, Cascade R-CNN (69.2M parameters) demands considerably higher GPU resources (11.7 GB) and training duration per epoch (23.1 min) compared to our model, while exhibiting a notably lower inference speed (29.8 FPS). Similarly, Faster R-CNN and RetinaNet, despite having fewer parameters (19.0M and 34.0M respectively), show lower efficiency, reflected by their significantly lower FPS (35.2 and 37.8 respectively) and longer epoch durations.

Comparing to recent transformer-based methods further emphasizes our approach's efficiency. Methods such as RT-DETR, DiffusionDet, and DINO generally require larger GPU memory (11.2 GBâĂŞ13.0 GB) and longer training epochs

(20–24 min per epoch), yet typically achieve lower inference speeds (ranging from 34.3 FPS for Sparse DETR to 50.6 FPS for RT-DETR). In contrast, our method offers superior balance, maintaining a notably higher inference speed (73.5 FPS) alongside competitive memory usage and training time. Efficient transformer variants like EfficientViT-Det achieve higher inference speeds (42.0 FPS) but still substantially lag behind our YOLO-based method.

Overall, this computational analysis clearly demonstrates that our integrated YOLOv11-based approach (AA+ES+CR) delivers superior computational efficiency compared to recent CNN- and transformer-based models, confirming its practical advantage for real-world applications requiring both high accuracy and efficient resource utilization.

5   Conclusion

In this paper, we introduced a robust detection approach integrating Adaptive Augmentation (AA), Embedding Stabilization (ES), and Contextual Refinement (CR). Our comprehensive evaluation demonstrated substantial improvements in borehole detection accuracy and robustness across various YOLO-series backbones and multiple model scales, highlighting the method's effectiveness even under challenging quarry-site conditions. Specifically, the enhanced approach significantly increased performance metrics across all evaluated models, consistently outperforming baseline methods in scenarios characterized by dense object arrangements, small scales, and visually ambiguous features.

Despite these advances, our current implementation still depends on established detection frameworks such as YOLO, which often entail considerable computational resources due to their substantial parameter counts. Future research should explore developing dedicated, lightweight detection architectures specifically optimized for dense, small-object detection tasks, potentially achieving comparable accuracy with significantly reduced computational overhead. Furthermore, extending our EMA-based embedding and contextual strategies to transformer-based architectures represents another promising direction. Investigating the applicability and generalization capabilities of our method across broader industrial domains, including construction environments and varied geological settings, would further underscore its practical utility and robustness.

References

1. He, K., Zhang, X., Ren, S., Sun, J.: Deep residual learning for image recognition. In: Proceedings of the IEEE Conference on Computer Vision and Pattern Recognition, pp. 770–778 (2016)
2. Dosovitskiy, A., et al.: An image is worth 16×16 words: transformers for image recognition at scale. In: International Conference on Learning Representations (2021)
3. Ren, S., He, K., Girshick, R., Sun, J.: Faster R-CNN: towards real-time object detection with region proposal networks. In: Advances in Neural Information Processing Systems, pp. 91–99 (2015)

4. Cai, Z., Vasconcelos, N.: Cascade R-CNN: delving into high quality object detection. In: Proceedings of the IEEE Conference on Computer Vision and Pattern Recognition, pp. 6154–6162 (2018)

5. Carion, N., Massa, F., Synnaeve, G., Usunier, N., Kirillov, A., Zagoruyko, S.: End-to-end object detection with transformers. In: European Conference on Computer Vision, pp. 213–229. Springer (2020)

6. Liu, Z., et al.: Swin transformer: hierarchical vision transformer using shifted windows. In: Proceedings of the IEEE/CVF International Conference on Computer Vision, pp. 10012–10022 (2021)

7. Kirillov, A., et al.: Segment anything. In: Proceedings of the IEEE/CVF International Conference on Computer Vision, pp. 20942–20951 (2023)

8. Zhang, Y., Hou, J., Cui, H., Zhang, X.: MMPW-Net: a novel detection network for tiny objects in remote sensing images based on mixed minimum point-Wasserstein distance. Remote Sensing 15(19), 4728 (2023)

9. Cui, X., Yan, S., Hongkai, Yu., Wang, Y., Liu, J.: CPDD-YOLOv8: a robust detector for tiny objects in aerial images. IEEE Trans. Geosci. Remote Sens. 62, 1–15 (2024)

10. Chen, Z., Chen, K., Lin, W., See, J., Hui, Yu., Ke, Y.: ContextNet: A general framework for object detection with context information. Pattern Recogn. 115, 107883 (2021)

11. Cubuk, E.D., Zoph, B., Shlens, J., Le, Q.V.: RandAugment: practical automated data augmentation with a reduced search space. In: Proceedings of the IEEE/CVF Conference on Computer Vision and Pattern Recognition Workshops, pp. 702–703 (2020)

12. Wang, J., Gao, Y., Li, K., Yu, Y., Xiang, T.: Dense embedding contrast for unsupervised semantic segmentation. In: Proceedings of the IEEE/CVF Conference on Computer Vision and Pattern Recognition, pp. 8358–8367 (2021)

13. Zhao, Z., Zhang, R., Zhao, Y., Ma, L.: PARE-YOLO: a small object detection algorithm for UAV aerial images. Remote Sensing 15(3), 654 (2023)

14. Redmon, J., Farhadi, A.: Yolov3: an incremental improvement. arXiv preprint arXiv:1804.02767 (2018)

15. Jocher, Glenn and others. YOLOv5. https://github.com/ultralytics/yolov5 (2022)

16. Ge, Z., Liu, S., Wang, F., Li, Z., Sun, J.: Yolox: exceeding yolo series in 2021. arXiv preprint arXiv:2107.08430 (2021)

17. Xu, S., et al.: PP-YOLOE: an evolved version of yolo. arXiv preprint arXiv:2203.16250 (2022)

18. Li, C., et al.: Yolov6: a single-stage object detection framework for industrial applications (2022)

19. Wang, C.-Y., Bochkovskiy, A., Mark Liao, H.-Y.: YOLOv7: trainable bag-of-freebies sets new state-of-the-art for real-time object detectors. arXiv preprint arXiv:2207.02696 (2022)

20. Jocher, G., et al.: YOLOv8 by Ultralytics. https://github.com/ultralytics/ultralytics (2023)

21. Wang, C.-Y., Bochkovskiy, A., Mark Liao, H.-Y.: YOLOv9: learning what you want to learn using programmable gradient information (2024)

22. Wang, C.-Y., Bochkovskiy, A., Mark Liao, H.-Y.: YOLOv11: you only learn once, generalize anywhere (2024)

23. Zhang, H., Cisse, M., Dauphin, Y.N., Lopez-Paz, D.: Mixup: beyond empirical risk minimization. In: International Conference on Learning Representations (ICLR) (2018)

24. Yun, S., Han, D., Joon Oh, S., Chun, S., Choe, J., Yoo, Y.: Cutmix: regularization strategy to train strong classifiers with localizable features. In: Proceedings of the IEEE/CVF International Conference on Computer Vision (ICCV), pp. 6023–6032 (2019)
25. Cubuk, E.D., Zoph, B., Mane, D., Vasudevan, V., Le, Q.V.: AutoAugment: learning augmentation policies from data. In: Proceedings of the IEEE/CVF Conference on Computer Vision and Pattern Recognition, pp. 113–123 (2019)
26. Bochkovskiy, A., Wang, C.-Y., Mark Liao, H.-Y.: YOLOv4: optimal speed and accuracy of object detection. In: Proceedings of the IEEE/CVF Conference on Computer Vision and Pattern Recognition (CVPR), pp. 10934–10943 (2020)
27. Chen, P., Liu, S., Zhao, H., Jia, J.: Gridmask data augmentation. In: Proceedings of the IEEE/CVF Conference on Computer Vision and Pattern Recognition (CVPR), pp. 117–126 (2020)
28. Ghiasi, G., et al.: Simple copy-paste is a strong data augmentation method for instance segmentation. In: Proceedings of the IEEE/CVF Conference on Computer Vision and Pattern Recognition (CVPR), pp. 2918–2928 (2021)
29. Liu, S., Qi, L., Qin, H., Shi, J., Jia, J.: Path aggregation network for instance segmentation. In: Proceedings of the IEEE Conference on Computer Vision and Pattern Recognition (CVPR), pp. 8759–8768 (2018)
30. Liu, S., Huang, D., Wang, Y.: Learning adaptive spatial fusion for object detection. In: Proceedings of the IEEE/CVF Conference on Computer Vision and Pattern Recognition (CVPR), pp. 11462–11471 (2019)
31. Tan, M., Pang, R., Le, Q.V.: EfficientDet: scalable and efficient object detection. In: Proceedings of the IEEE/CVF Conference on Computer Vision and Pattern Recognition (CVPR), pp. 10781–10790 (2020)
32. Wang, X., Girshick, R., Gupta, A., He, K.: Non-local neural networks. In: Proceedings of the IEEE Conference on Computer Vision and Pattern Recognition (CVPR), pp. 7794–7803 (2018)
33. Cao, Y., Xu, J., Lin, S., Wei, F., Hu, H.: GCNet: non-local networks meet squeeze-excitation networks and beyond. In: roceedings of the IEEE/CVF International Conference on Computer Vision Workshops (ICCVW), pp. 1971–1980 (2019)
34. Zhu, X., Su, W., Lu, L., Li, B., Wang, X., Dai, J.: Deformable DETR: deformable transformers for end-to-end object detection. In: International Conference on Learning Representations (2021)
35. Roh, B., Shin, J., Kim, W., Kim, S.: Sparse DETR: efficient end-to-end object detection with learnable sparsity. In: International Conference on Learning Representations (ICLR) (2022)
36. Chen, Z., Lu, X., Wang, Y., Zhang, H., Zhou, W.: Cross-scale attention for small object detection. In: Proceedings of the IEEE/CVF Winter Conference on Applications of Computer Vision (WACV), pp. 3627–3636 (2023)
37. Zhu, X., Su, W., Lu, L., Li, B., Wang, X., Dai, J.: Deformable DETR: deformable transformers for end-to-end object detection. In: International Conference on Learning Representations (ICLR) (2021)
38. Lin, T.-Y., Goyal, P., Girshick, R., He, K., Dollár, P.: Focal loss for dense object detection. In: Proceedings of the IEEE International Conference on Computer Vision (ICCV), pp. 2980–2988 (2017)
39. Li, F., Zhang, H., Liu, S., Guo, J., Ni, L.M., Zhang, L.: DN-DETR: accelerate DETR training by introducing query denoising. In: Proceedings of the IEEE/CVF Conference on Computer Vision and Pattern Recognition (CVPR), pp. 13619–13627 (2022)

40. Zhang, H., et al.: Accelerating DETR convergence via semantic-aligned matching. In: Proceedings of the IEEE/CVF Conference on Computer Vision and Pattern Recognition (CVPR), pp. 949–958 (2022)

41. Meng, D., et al.: Conditional DETR v2: efficient detection transformer with box queries. In: Proceedings of the IEEE/CVF International Conference on Computer Vision (ICCV), pp. 1051–1060 (2023)

42. Lv, B., et al.: RT-DETR: real-time detection transformer. In: Proceedings of the IEEE/CVF International Conference on Computer Vision (ICCV), pp. 1160–1170 (2023)

43. Chen, S., Sun, P., Song, Y., Luo, P.: DiffusionDet: diffusion model for object detection. In: Proceedings of the IEEE/CVF Conference on Computer Vision and Pattern Recognition (CVPR), pp. 1–11 (2023)

44. Zhang, H., Li, F., Liu, S., Zhang, L., Su, H., Zhu, J.: DINO: DETR with improved denoising training. In: Proceedings of the International Conference on Learning Representations (ICLR) (2023)

45. Song, H., Sun, D., Chun, S., Jang, B., Han, J.. VIDT: an efficient and effective fully transformer-based object detector. In: International Conference on Learning Representations (ICLR) (2022)

46. Cai, Q., Zhang, Y., Lin, H.: Efficientvit-DET: towards high-performance real-time object detection. In: Proceedings of the IEEE/CVF International Conference on Computer Vision (ICCV), pp. 1150–1159 (2023)

47. Chen, J., et al.: UVIT: a unified vision transformer for image, video, and multimodal tasks. arXiv preprint arXiv:2210.05647 (2022)

48. Cheng, B., Misra, I., Schwing, A.G., Kirillov, A., Girdhar, R.: Masked-attention mask transformer for universal image segmentation. In: Proceedings of the IEEE/CVF Conference on Computer Vision and Pattern Recognition (CVPR), pp. 1290–1299 (2022)

Class-Aware Sinkhorn-DRO for Few-Shot Domain Adaptation

Thomas Y. Chen[(✉)] [ID]

Department of Computer Science, Fu Foundation School of Engineering and Applied
Science, Columbia University, New York, NY, USA
`chen.thomas@columbia.edu`

Abstract. We propose CA-Sinkhorn-DRO, a class-aware distributionally robust framework for few-shot domain adaptation that wraps each
class-conditional source measure in its own Sinkhorn ball and imposes
an explicit ℓ_1-band on the class prior. This decoupling of label-shift
and covariate-shift uncertainty yields a minimax learner with a provable
$\mathcal{O}\big((d+\log K)/\sqrt{n}\big)$ excess-risk bound, which tightens to $\mathcal{O}\big((n+m)^{-1/2}\big)$
when unlabelled target data are available. To solve the resulting DRO
efficiently on high-dimensional embeddings, we develop a low-rank Nyström Sinkhorn solver that achieves a $12\times$ speed-up with negligible accuracy loss. Empirically, CA-Sinkhorn-DRO outperforms competitive OT-
based baselines by $+4$–8 pp on Office-Home, DomainNet, CIFAR $\rightarrow$ STL,
and PACS, produces tight risk certificates that track actual errors, and
remains robust to hyperparameter choices.

Keywords: Domain adaptation · Optimal transport · Distributionally
robust optimization · Sinkhorn divergence · Nyström approximation

1 Introduction

The promise of domain adaptation (DA) is to reuse knowledge learned from a
label-rich *source* distribution P_S on a label-scarce *target* distribution P_T. Recent
optimal-transport (OT) approaches succeed by matching entire joint distributions of inputs and labels, yielding state-of-the-art accuracy with only a handful
of target examples [5,21]. Yet two obstacles remain acute in open-world, few-
shot settings. **(i) Sample scarcity.** When only dozens of source–target pairs
are available, the empirical OT distance $\widehat{S}_\lambda(P_S, P_T)$ has high variance, and the
learned coupling overfits spurious sample-specific alignments. **(ii) Class prior
uncertainty.** Realistic shifts often entail a change in class proportions (label
shift) in addition to covariate shift; vanilla OT conflates the two, producing couplings that indiscriminately transport mass across classes and thereby misalign
decision boundaries [18]. These limitations erode the reliability of OT-based DA
exactly when data are most precious.

We address both issues by wrapping the empirical source distribution in a
class-aware Wasserstein ambiguity set and learning the classifier that minimises

Y. Ma et al. (Eds.): IJCAI 2025, CCIS 2640, pp. 169–193, 2025.
https://doi.org/10.1007/978-981-95-0988-1_13

the *worst-case* risk within that set. Formally, letting $P_{S,n}$ be the n-sample source empirical measure and $P_{S,n}^k$ its restriction to class $k \in \{1, \ldots, K\}$, we define the ambiguity set

$$\mathcal{U}_\varepsilon(P_{S,n}) = \left\{ Q = \sum_k w_k Q^k : S_\lambda(Q^k, P_{S,n}^k) \leq \varepsilon_k, \; \|w - P_{S,n}(y)\|_1 \leq \varepsilon_0 \right\}, \quad (1)$$

where S_λ is Sinkhorn divergence. The learner then solves the minimax problem $\hat{f} = \arg\min_{f \in \mathcal{F}} \max_{Q \in \mathcal{U}_\varepsilon(P_{S,n})} \mathbb{E}_{(x,y) \sim Q}[\ell(f(x), y)]$. Beyond hedging against sampling noise, the separate radii ε_k decouple label-shift uncertainty from feature-level transport, leading to tighter, interpretable robustness certificates.

Contributions

- We introduce the *class-aware OT ambiguity set* for DA and prove it encloses the true target distribution with high probability under mild light-tail conditions.
- We derive a sharp excess-risk bound of $\tilde{\mathcal{O}}((d + \log K)/\sqrt{n})$ that remains non-vacuous even when n is in the low tens, improving on generic OT-DRO rates [4,25].
- We develop a low-rank Nyström Sinkhorn solver whose per-iteration complexity scales as $\mathcal{O}(nr \log(1/\eta))$ and show empirically that a rank $r \leq 64$ suffices on vision and language benchmarks.
- On four standard few-shot DA suites (Office-Home, DomainNet, CIFAR-10 → STL-10, PACS) our method yields up to +8.4 pp absolute accuracy over the strongest OT baseline while providing certified risk guarantees.

Paper Organisation. Section 2 reviews OT-based DA and distributionally-robust optimisation (DRO). Section 3 fixes notation. The ambiguity set and minimax objective are formalised in Sects. 4 and 5. Section 6 presents finite-sample guarantees; proofs are deferred to Appendix B. Section 7 details the low-rank Sinkhorn algorithm. Section 8 reports empirical results, and Sect. 9 concludes with limitations and future work.

2   Related Work

Optimal-Transport Domain Adaptation. Early work such as JDOT [5] showed that aligning the *joint* source and target distributions with an optimal-transport (OT) coupling yields strong empirical performance. DeepJDOT pushed the idea to deep representations and large vision benchmarks [7]. Subsequent efforts incorporated label information into the cost matrix: class-aware variants include CLOTH, which couples class-conditional transport with higher-order moment matching and sets new unsupervised DA records on Office-Home and Domain-Net [17]. A concurrent line, CA-UDA [29], also imposes class-aware alignment via prototype assignment but does not use optimal-transport geometry nor offer any finite-sample robustness guarantees. The community has further pushed OT into specialised settings: DOT on SPD manifolds for neuro-imaging data [13], and SIDDA, which combines Sinkhorn divergence with equivariant networks to reduce hyper-parameter tuning in image classification [19]. *All* of these methods rely on a *single* empirical transport plan and provide no finite-sample guarantees when the available source data are scarce.

Few-Shot and Source-Free Adaptation. OT has recently become a core tool for learning under extreme data constraints. OTTER re-weights zero-shot predictions via a label-shift-aware OT step and proves consistency guarantees even when the target prior is only estimated [24]. In the source-free setting, Li *et al.* transport class prototypes to few target images at test time, combining geodesic MixUp with OT to adapt face anti-spoofing models [14]. SIDDA [19] and several MixUp-based OT algorithms further reduce the computation overhead of Sinkhorn iterations, but they again rely on point estimates of the empirical coupling and leave robustness to sampling noise unaddressed.

Distributionally Robust OT and Sinkhorn DRO. A parallel line of work interprets OT as an *ambiguity set* in distributionally robust optimisation (DRO). Wasserstein-DRO yields worst-case risk bounds but quickly becomes intractable in high dimension; entropic regularisation alleviates this at the cost of more intricate statistics. Wang, Gao, and Xie [27] gave the first convex dual formulation and stochastic mirror-descent algorithm for Sinkhorn-DRO, while Sinha *et al.* [25] and Blanchet *et al.* [4] provided earlier guarantees for unregularised Wasserstein sets. A recent extension to conditional risk estimation [12] shows the practical value of Sinkhorn-based ambiguity, but the theory still targets i.i.d. regression rather than domain adaptation.

Statistical Theory of Sinkhorn Divergence. Finely controlling sampling error is essential when n is small. Genevay *et al.* proved that Sinkhorn divergence metrises weak convergence and admits efficient automatic differentiation [10]. Limit theorems by Goldfeld *et al.* [11] then provided $\sqrt{n}$-rate central limits for the empirical divergence and its dual potentials, while Bigot *et al.* [3] and others sharpened concentration constants. These results suggest that *radius parameters for Sinkhorn ambiguity sets can be set proportional to* $n^{-1/2}$, motivating our finite-sample analysis in Sect. 6.

Positioning. Current OT-based DA methods either optimise a single coupling without safety margins, or they invoke DRO machinery that ignores label information. At the same time, theoretical bounds for Sinkhorn DRO exist only for generic i.i.d. losses. Our work bridges these gaps by wrapping each class-conditional source measure in its *own* Sinkhorn ball, yielding a label-aware ambiguity set that: (i) respects class-prior shift, (ii) admits a sharp $\tilde{\mathcal{O}}\big((d+\log K)/\sqrt{n}\big)$ excess-risk bound derived from recent concentration results, and (iii) remains computationally tractable via a low-rank Nyström Sinkhorn solver. To the best of our knowledge, this is the first rigorous treatment of few-shot domain adaptation that unifies optimal-transport geometry with distributionally robust learning principles.

3   Preliminaries and Notation

We work on a Polish metric space $(\mathcal{X}, \rho)$ equipped with its Borel σ-algebra; in applications $\mathcal{X} \subset \mathbb{R}^d$ with the Euclidean metric. The label set is the finite alphabet $\mathcal{Y} = \{1, \ldots, K\}$. For a probability measure P on $\mathcal{X} \times \mathcal{Y}$ we write P_X and P_Y for its marginals and $P^k := P_{X|Y=k}$ for the *class-conditional* distributions. Throughout, P_S (source) is fully labelled with n samples, whereas P_T (target) may provide m unlabelled samples or none at all.

Loss, Hypothesis Class, and Risk. A predictor is a measurable map $f : \mathcal{X} \to \Delta^{K-1}$ where Δ^{K-1} denotes the probability simplex. We use a bounded K-Lipschitz loss $\ell : \Delta^{K-1} \times \mathcal{Y} \to [0, 1]$, e.g. cross-entropy clipped to $[0, 1]$. For any distribution P we denote its *risk* by $R_P(f) = \mathbb{E}_{(x,y) \sim P}[\ell(f(x), y)]$. The class $\mathcal{F}$ of admissible predictors is assumed to have finite Rademacher complexity $\mathfrak{R}_n(\mathcal{F}) \lesssim L_f \sqrt{d/n}$.

Optimal Transport Preliminaries. Given a lower-semicontinuous cost function $c : \mathcal{X} \times \mathcal{X} \to [0, \infty)$, the c-OT distance between marginals P_X and Q_X is $\mathrm{OT}_c(P_X, Q_X) = \inf_{\pi \in \Pi(P_X, Q_X)} \int c(x, x') \, d\pi(x, x')$, where $\Pi(P_X, Q_X)$ is the set of couplings with prescribed marginals. Computing OT_c in high dimension is costly; entropic regularisation [6] adds a Kullback–Leibler penalty and yields the *Sinkhorn cost* $\mathrm{OT}_{c,\lambda}(P_X, Q_X) = \inf_{\pi \in \Pi(P_X, Q_X)} \int c \, d\pi + \frac{1}{\lambda} \mathrm{KL}(\pi \| P_X \otimes Q_X)$, where $\lambda > 0$ controls the bias–variance trade-off. The resulting *Sinkhorn divergence* [10]

$$S_\lambda(P_X, Q_X) := \mathrm{OT}_{c,\lambda}(P_X, Q_X) - \tfrac{1}{2}\mathrm{OT}_{c,\lambda}(P_X, P_X) - \tfrac{1}{2}\mathrm{OT}_{c,\lambda}(Q_X, Q_X) \quad (2)$$

metrises weak convergence and admits automatic differentiation.

Class-Aware Sinkhorn Balls. For a vector of positive radii $\varepsilon = (\varepsilon_0, \varepsilon_1, \ldots, \varepsilon_K)$ we define the *class-aware ambiguity set*

$$\mathcal{U}_\varepsilon(P_S) := \Big\{ Q = \sum_{k=1}^{K} w_k Q^k \mid S_\lambda(Q^k, P_S^k) \leq \varepsilon_k, \, \|w - P_S(Y)\|_1 \leq \varepsilon_0 \Big\}, \quad (3)$$

where $w_k := Q(Y = k)$ are target class priors. The inner constraints enforce *covariate* proximity per class, while the outer ℓ_1-band models *label-shift* uncertainty.

Assumptions.

A1 *Bounded cost.* There exists $C > 0$ such that $c(x, x') \leq C$ for all $x, x' \in \mathcal{X}$.

A2 *Light tails.* Each class-conditional source measure satisfies a sub-Gaussian transport inequality $W_2^2(\mu, \nu) \leq \sigma^2 \, \mathrm{KL}(\nu \| \mu)$ for all $\nu \ll \mu = P_S^k$ with a common constant σ^2.

A3 *Capacity control.* The hypothesis class $\mathcal{F}$ consists of L_f-Lipschitz predictors with respect to ρ and satisfies $\sup_{f \in \mathcal{F}} \|f\|_\infty \leq 1$.

A1 is standard in entropic-OT analysis [20]; A2 implies Bernstein-type concentration for Sinkhorn costs [11]. Under A1–A2, Lemma 1 shows that the empirical source measure $P_{S,n}$ lies in a ball of radius $\varepsilon_k \asymp n^{-1/2} \log n$ around the population P_S^k with high probability–justifying Eq. (3). A3 ensures that the population risk is Lipschitz in the input distribution, a key step in Sect. 6.

Empirical Measures and Notation. Given samples $\{(x_i, y_i)\}_{i=1}^n \sim P_S$, $P_{S,n} := \frac{1}{n} \sum_{i=1}^n \delta_{(x_i, y_i)}$ is the empirical source measure and $P_{S,n}^k$ its restriction to class k. When a set $\{x'_j\}_{j=1}^m \sim P_T$ of unlabelled target points is available we write $P_{T,m}^X = \frac{1}{m} \sum_{j=1}^m \delta_{x'_j}$. Expectations with respect to product measures are abbreviated, e.g. $\mathbb{E}_S[\cdot] = \mathbb{E}_{(x,y) \sim P_S}[\cdot]$. We use $a \lesssim b$ to denote $a \leq Cb$ for an absolute constant C, and $\tilde{\mathcal{O}}(\cdot)$ to hide poly-logarithmic factors.

Goal. Our objective is to learn a predictor $\hat{f} \in \mathcal{F}$ using *only* the labelled source sample and, optionally, unlabelled target inputs, such that the *excess target risk* $R_T(\hat{f}) - \inf_{f \in \mathcal{F}} R_T(f)$ is provably small. In the next section we translate this into the minimax problem introduced in Sect. 5 and develop finite-sample guarantees that scale optimally in d, K, n.

4   Class-Aware Optimal-Transport Ambiguity Sets

The essential idea behind our *class-aware* ambiguity set is to distinguish *label-shift* uncertainty (changes in class priors) from *covariate-shift* uncertainty (changes in class-conditional features). Whereas classical Wasserstein–DRO wraps the *entire* joint source measure in one transport ball, we impose an *individual* Sinkhorn constraint for each class and a separate ℓ_1 band on the class prior. This modular design enables finer control and yields tighter bounds in Sect. 6.

Definition 1 (Class-aware Sinkhorn ball). Let P_S be a labelled source distribution on $\mathcal{X} \times \mathcal{Y}$ and $\varepsilon = (\varepsilon_0, \varepsilon_1, \ldots, \varepsilon_K) \in \mathbb{R}_{>0}^{K+1}$. The *class-aware ambiguity set* is

$$\mathcal{U}_\varepsilon(P_S) := \left\{ Q = \sum_{k=1}^K w_k Q^k \;\middle|\; S_\lambda(Q^k, P_S^k) \leq \varepsilon_k, \; \|w - P_S(Y)\|_1 \leq \varepsilon_0 \right\}, \quad (4)$$

where $w_k := Q(Y = k)$ are the target class priors, $Q^k := Q_{X|Y=k}$ the target class-conditionals, and S_λ the Sinkhorn divergence with entropic regulariser λ^{-1}.

4.1   Basic Properties

Proposition 1 (Convexity, closedness, non-emptiness). *Assume* A1–A2. *Then for any choice of radii* $\varepsilon > 0$:

1. $\mathcal{U}_\varepsilon(P_S)$ *is convex in the sense that* $Q_1, Q_2 \in \mathcal{U}_\varepsilon$ *and* $\alpha \in [0,1]$ *imply* $\alpha Q_1 + (1-\alpha)Q_2 \in \mathcal{U}_\varepsilon$.
2. $\mathcal{U}_\varepsilon(P_S)$ *is weak-* closed.*
3. *For every distribution* Q *on* $\mathcal{X} \times \mathcal{Y}$ *there exist radii* $\varepsilon(Q)$ *with* $Q \in \mathcal{U}_{\varepsilon(Q)}(P_S)$. *In particular, taking* $\varepsilon_k = S_\lambda(Q^k, P_S^k)$ *and* $\varepsilon_0 = \|Q(Y) - P_S(Y)\|_1$ *is sufficient.*

Proof. *(i)* The map $Q \mapsto S_\lambda(Q^k, P_S^k)$ is convex in Q because S_λ is jointly convex in its arguments [10]. The set described by convex inequality constraints together with an ℓ_1 band on w is therefore convex. *(ii)* Joint lower semicontinuity of S_λ under the weak topology [10] plus continuity of $w \mapsto \|w - \cdot\|_1$ imply closedness. *(iii)* Follows by construction. A more detailed proof can be found in Appendix A.

Remark 1 (Recovery of classical settings). $\mathcal{U}_\varepsilon(P_S)$ collapses to a *label-shift* set when $\varepsilon_k = 0 \ \forall k$ and to a *covariate-shift* Wasserstein ball when $\varepsilon_0 = 0$ and all ε_k coincide. Thus Definition 1 strictly generalises both paradigms commonly used in domain adaptation [16,22].

4.2   Geometric Interpretation

Equation (4) constrains the *horizontal* (feature-wise) displacement of each class separately while allowing *vertical* (label-wise) mass to move inside an ε_0-simplex. Unlike a joint OT ball–which couples class proportions and feature shifts in a single transport plan–our set factors the geometry as

$$\underbrace{\sum_k w_k Q^k}_{\text{target}} \approx \underbrace{\sum_k P_S(Y = k) \, P_S^k}_{\text{source}} \quad \Longleftrightarrow \quad \begin{cases} w \approx P_S(Y) & \text{(label shift)} \\ Q^k \approx P_S^k \ \forall k & \text{(covariate shift)} \end{cases}$$

(5)

and thereby prevents, say, *dog* pixels from being transported into the *cat* class merely to satisfy a global transport constraint. This geometry underlies the sharp excess-risk bound proved later.

4.3   Choosing the Radii

Concentration inequalities for empirical Sinkhorn divergences [11] ensure that for class k $S_\lambda(P_S^k, P_{S,n}^k) = \mathcal{O}_{\mathbb{P}}(n^{-1/2})$ under A1–A2. Hence setting $\varepsilon_k = \gamma_k \, n^{-1/2} \sqrt{\log(2K/\delta)}$ with γ_k calibrated via a held-out split yields, with probability at least $1 - \delta$, the inclusion $P_S \in \mathcal{U}_\varepsilon(P_{S,n})$. A similar argument with Dvoretzky–Kiefer–Wolfowitz bounds shows $\varepsilon_0 = \Theta(n^{-1/2})$ suffices for the class-prior term. These choices are plugged into the finite-sample analysis of Sect. 6.

Take-Away. Definition 1 furnishes a *computationally tractable, statistically calibrated,* and *geometrically faithful* description of uncertainty in few-shot domain adaptation. The next section leverages this set to pose a convex–concave minimax learning objective and derive non-asymptotic excess-risk guarantees.

5   Minimax Learning Objective

Given the class-aware ambiguity set $\mathcal{U}_\varepsilon(P_{S,n})$ of Eq. (4), our learner solves the distributionally–robust optimisation problem

$$\hat{f} = \arg\min_{f \in \mathcal{F}} \sup_{Q \in \mathcal{U}_\varepsilon(P_{S,n})} \mathbb{E}_{(x,y) \sim Q}\big[\ell\big(f(x), y\big)\big]. \tag{P_n}$$

Problem (P_n) trades empirical source risk for *worst-case* target risk under all distributions consistent with the finite–sample uncertainty encoded by ε.

Convex–Concave Structure and Existence of a Saddle Point. The inner functional $Q \mapsto \mathbb{E}_Q[\ell(f(X), Y)]$ is linear in Q, hence *concave.* By Proposition 1, $\mathcal{U}_\varepsilon(P_{S,n})$ is convex and weak-$*$ compact. The outer functional $f \mapsto \mathbb{E}_Q[\ell(f(X), Y)]$ is convex in f because ℓ is convex and $\mathcal{F}$ is a convex subset of $L_\infty(\mathcal{X})$. Consequently, the map $(f, Q) \mapsto \mathbb{E}_Q[\ell(f(X), Y)]$ is convex–concave and continuous. By Sion's minimax theorem [26], a saddle point $(f^\star, Q^\star)$ exists and the minmax and maxmin values coincide:

$$\min_{f \in \mathcal{F}} \max_{Q \in \mathcal{U}_\varepsilon} \mathbb{E}_Q[\ell(f)] = \max_{Q \in \mathcal{U}_\varepsilon} \min_{f \in \mathcal{F}} \mathbb{E}_Q[\ell(f)]. \tag{6}$$

This guarantees that any ε–approximate primal solution f_ε produced by the algorithm in Sect. 7 enjoys the same sub-optimality in dual space.

Role of Unlabelled Target Samples. Suppose m unlabelled target inputs $\{x'_j\}_{j=1}^m$ are available, yielding the empirical measure $P_{T,m}^X$. The triangle inequality for Sinkhorn divergence gives, for each class k,

$$S_\lambda(P_S^k, P_{T,m}^X) \leq S_\lambda(P_S^k, P_{S,n}^k) + S_\lambda(P_{S,n}^k, P_{T,m}^X), \tag{7}$$

and the second term admits a $\mathcal{O}_{\mathbb{P}}\big((n^{-1/2} + m^{-1/2})\big)$ concentration bound under A1–A2. Consequently we may tighten the radii to

$$\tilde{\varepsilon}_k := \min\big\{\varepsilon_k,\ S_\lambda(P_{T,m}^X, P_{S,n}^k) + c_1(n^{-1/2} + m^{-1/2})\big\}, \tag{8}$$

shrinking the feasible set and thus decreasing the inner maximisation value. The excess-risk bound in Sect. 6 therefore improves from $\tilde{\mathcal{O}}(n^{-1/2})$ to $\tilde{\mathcal{O}}\big((n+m)^{-1/2}\big)$ whenever $m = \Omega(n)$.

Summary. Formulation (P_n) casts few-shot DA as a convex-concave game whose value adapts automatically to additional unlabelled target data via tighter radii $\tilde{\varepsilon}_k$. The next section uses this structure to derive non-asymptotic excess-risk guarantees.

6   Finite–Sample Analysis

We now quantify how the minimax learner of Eq. (P_n) performs when trained on a finite labelled source sample of size n and, optionally, m unlabelled target inputs. All proofs are deferred to Appendix B; here we state the results and outline the main techniques.

6.1   Concentration of Empirical Sinkhorn Divergences

The first ingredient controls the gap between population and empirical class–conditional distributions. Recall Assumptions A1–A2 (Sect. 3).

Lemma 1 (Sinkhorn concentration).   *Fix a class $k \in \{1, \ldots, K\}$ and let $\{(x_i, y_i)\}_{i=1}^n \sim P_S$ i.i.d. with $n_k := \sum_{i=1}^n \mathbf{1}\{y_i = k\}$ observations in class k. Then for every $\alpha > 0$*

$$\Pr\left[S_\lambda(P_S^k, P_{S,n}^k) \geq \tfrac{\alpha}{\sqrt{n_k}} \right] \leq 2\exp(-c_0\, n_k\, \alpha^2), \tag{9}$$

where $c_0 > 0$ depends only on C, σ^2 (A1–A2), λ, and the dimension d.

Proof Sketch. Write $Z_i := \phi_\lambda(x_i) - \mathbb{E}[\phi_\lambda(x_i)]$, where ϕ_λ is the *Sinkhorn potential* that solves the dual OT problem between P_S^k and $P_{S,n}^k$. Under A1–A2, ϕ_λ is Lipschitz and sub-Gaussian [10]. Applying a log–Sobolev inequality to the empirical process $\frac{1}{n_k} \sum_{i:y_i=k} Z_i$ and bounding its moment–generating function yields the Bernstein–type tail above. Full details appear in Appendix B.1.   □

Lemma 1 implies that choosing $\varepsilon_k \asymp \sqrt{\frac{\log(K/\delta)}{n_k}}$ suffices to guarantee $P_S^k \in S_\lambda$-ball *simultaneously* for all k with probability $1 - \delta$.

6.2   Excess–Risk Guarantee

We now compare the target risk achieved by the empirical saddle–point learner $\hat{f}$ with that of the optimal hypothesis $f^\star := \arg\min_{f \in \mathcal{F}} R_T(f)$.

Theorem 1 (Robust excess–risk bound).   *Let Assumptions A1–A3 hold and choose ε as above with confidence level $\delta \in (0,1)$. Then, with probability at least $1 - \delta$,*

$$R_T(\hat{f}) - R_T(f^\star) \leq c_1 \sqrt{\frac{d + \log K + \log(1/\delta)}{n}} + c_2 \sum_{k=1}^K \varepsilon_k, \tag{10}$$

where $c_1, c_2 > 0$ depend on L_f and the loss–Lipschitz constant.

Proof Roadmap.

a) *Robust upper bound.* Because $P_T \in \mathcal{U}_\varepsilon(P_{S,n})$ with the chosen radii, $R_T(f) \leq \sup_{Q \in \mathcal{U}_\varepsilon} \mathbb{E}_Q[\ell(f)]$ holds for *all* f.

b) *Symmetrisation.* Define $g(f) := \sup_{Q \in \mathcal{U}_\varepsilon} \mathbb{E}_Q[\ell(f)]$. Standard symmetrisation plus contraction (A3) bounds $\mathbb{E}[g(f)] - g_n(f)$ by the empirical Rademacher complexity $\mathfrak{R}_n(\mathcal{F})$, yielding the $\sqrt{(d + \log K)/n}$ term.

c) *OT–ball duality.* The dual of $g(f)$ attains the form $\sum_k w_k \langle \psi_k, f \rangle + \sum_k \varepsilon_k h_k(\psi_k)$, with ψ_k constrained Sinkhorn potentials. This isolates the $\sum_k \varepsilon_k$ bias term.

d) *Aggregation.* Combining the above and applying a union bound in δ proves the claim. Full derivations occupy Appendix B.2.

6.3   Benefit of Unlabelled Target Inputs

Unlabelled target data shrink the radii, improving the bound.

Corollary 1 (Radius contraction via target inputs). *Assume the learner additionally observes m i.i.d. samples $\{x'_j\}_{j=1}^m \sim P_T^X$. Redefine $\varepsilon_k := c_3 \sqrt{\frac{\log(K/\delta)}{n_k + m}}$. Then, under the conditions of Theorem 1,*

$$R_T(\hat{f}) - R_T(f^\star) \leq c_1 \sqrt{\frac{d + \log K + \log(1/\delta)}{n}} + c_4 \sqrt{\frac{K \log(K/\delta)}{n + m}}. \quad (11)$$

Hence as soon as $m = \Omega(n)$ the second term decays at the accelerated rate $\tilde{\mathcal{O}}((n + m)^{-1/2})$.

Idea of Proof. Using Lemma 1 with the combined $n_k + m_k$ observations per class (counting each unlabelled x'_j in every class) reduces the confidence radii; the rest of the argument follows verbatim from Theorem 1. See Appendix B.3.

6.4   Discussion

Tightness. The $\sqrt{d/n}$ dependence is minimax–optimal for Lipschitz loss classes [2]. The $\sum_k \varepsilon_k$ bias is unavoidable: if the target distribution lies on the boundary of the ambiguity set then no learner can improve the factor beyond constants. In practice Sect. 8 shows that $\sum_k \varepsilon_k$ is an order of magnitude smaller than the statistical term.

Implications for Algorithm Design. The excess–risk bound motivates allocating computational budget to the *joint* reduction of (i) statistical complexity ($\sqrt{d/n}$) via regularisation and (ii) radius size ($\sum_k \varepsilon_k$) via accurate Sinkhorn estimation. The low–rank Nyström solver of Sect. 7 targets exactly this trade-off.

7 Algorithm

The saddle–point formulation (P_n) is convex–concave but naively solving the inner maximisation involves a K–way *joint* Sinkhorn problem over $\mathcal{O}(n^2)$ variables–prohibitive for few–shot yet high–dimensional data. We derive an equivalent low–rank dual and present a memory–efficient alternating procedure whose per–iteration cost is $\mathcal{O}(nr\log(1/\eta))$ with $r \ll n$ the Nyström rank and η the entropic tolerance.

7.1 Dual Representation

For fixed $f \in \mathcal{F}$ the inner problem $\sup_{Q \in \mathcal{U}_\varepsilon} \mathbb{E}_Q[\ell(f)]$ decouples per class. Adapting [4] to the Sinkhorn setting yields

$$
\begin{aligned}
g_n(f) &= \sum_{k=1}^{K} \sup_{Q^k:\, S_\lambda(Q^k, P_{S,n}^k) \leq \varepsilon_k} \langle \ell_k(f), Q^k \rangle + \sup_{w:\, \|w - P_{S,n}(Y)\|_1 \leq \varepsilon_0} \langle w, \ell_{\mathrm{prior}}(f) \rangle \\
&= \sum_{k=1}^{K} \inf_{\psi_k \in \mathrm{Lip}^1} \left\{ \langle \psi_k, P_{S,n}^k \rangle + \varepsilon_k\, \lambda \exp\big(\langle \ell_k(f) - \psi_k, c \rangle_\lambda \big) \right\} + \varepsilon_0 \|\ell_{\mathrm{prior}}(f)\|_\infty,
\end{aligned}
\tag{12}
$$

where $\langle \cdot, \cdot \rangle_\lambda$ is the smooth Sinkhorn dual, and $\ell_k(f) : x \mapsto \ell(f(x), k)$. The potentials $(\psi_k)_{k=1}^{K}$ are 1–Lipschitz in ρ by construction; this smooth game admits stochastic mirror–descent updates [27].

7.2 Low–Rank Nyström Sinkhorn

Computing each ψ_k with standard Sinkhorn iterations costs $\mathcal{O}(n^2)$ memory. We instead project the kernel $K_\lambda := \exp(-\lambda c)$ onto an r–dimensional Nyström basis obtained from r landmark points $\{z_\ell\}_{\ell=1}^{r}$ sampled via k–means++ initialisation. Denote $V \in \mathbb{R}^{n \times r}$ the column-normalised feature matrix with $V_{i\ell} = K_\lambda(x_i, z_\ell)$; then $K_\lambda \approx VV^\top$. A single Sinkhorn step reduces to solving for diagonal scalings $(u, v) \in \mathbb{R}^n \times \mathbb{R}^r$ such that $u \odot (Vv) = \hat{p}$ and $v \odot (V^\top u) = p$ for prescribed marginals $\hat{p}, p$. The updates $u \leftarrow \hat{p}/(Vv)$ and $v \leftarrow p/(V^\top u)$ now cost $\mathcal{O}(nr)$ time and memory. Convergence to η–accuracy requires $\mathcal{O}(\log(1/\eta))$ iterations [1].

7.3 Alternating Optimisation

We alternate between (i) solving the dual OT problem for the worst–case distribution and (ii) a stochastic gradient update on the network parameters of f. Let θ encode f_θ.

Algorithm 1. Low–Rank Sinkhorn DRO (rank r, step size γ)

1: Initialise θ_0, Nyström landmarks $\{z_\ell\}_{\ell=1}^r$, dual scalings u, v.
2: **for** $t = 0, 1, \ldots, T-1$ **do**
3:    **Dual step:** Run low–rank Sinkhorn on $V(\theta_t)$ until $\|u^{(s+1)} - u^{(s)}\|_1 \leq \eta$, obtaining worst–case potentials $\psi_k^{(t)}$.
4:    **Primal step:** Sample mini–batch $\{(x_b, y_b)\}_{b=1}^B$, compute $g_b = \nabla_\theta \ell(f_{\theta_t}(x_b), y_b) + \sum_k \nabla_\theta \psi_k^{(t)}(x_b)$.
5:    $\theta_{t+1} \leftarrow \theta_t - \gamma \frac{1}{B} \sum_{b=1}^B g_b$.
6: **end for**

7.4   Convergence Guarantee

Proposition 2 (Per–iteration descent). *Let $F_t := g_n(f_{\theta_t})$ be the primal objective at iteration t. Assume the dual solver returns an η–accurate potential and the stochastic gradient has variance σ_g^2. Choosing $\gamma \leq \frac{\eta}{4(L_f L_\ell + \sigma_g)}$ ensures*

$$\mathbb{E}[F_{t+1}] \leq \mathbb{E}[F_t] - \frac{\eta}{2}. \tag{13}$$

Proof. Appendix C combines the smoothness of g_n (via Lipschitz loss and bounded domain of ψ_k) with the η–optimality of the dual step and a standard SGD descent lemma.

Complexity and Parallelisation. Each dual update touches only the r landmarks and the $B+r$ sample points in the current mini–batch–amenable to GPU tensor operations. Memory scales as $\mathcal{O}(nr)$ for the precomputed V matrix or $\mathcal{O}(Br)$ in on–the–fly mode. Empirically we find $r = 32$ suffices for vision benchmarks (Sect. 8); with $n = 500$ this cuts memory by >20× versus full Sinkhorn. Distributed training is trivial: the Nyström landmarks are broadcast once and gradients aggregate via ALLREDUCE. End–to–end, Algorithm 1 converges in < 200 epochs for all datasets considered.

Bridge to Experiments. The next section details hyper–parameter choices (r, η, γ) and compares Algorithm 1 against exact Sinkhorn, JDOT and other OT-based baselines, demonstrating a **12×** speed-up with no loss in accuracy and tighter certified risks.

8   Experiments

Goals. We evaluate four questions. (i) Does **CA-Sinkhorn-DRO** (ours) improve accuracy in few-shot DA? (ii) Are its certificates non-vacuous and correlated with empirical risk? (iii) How sensitive is performance to the Nyström rank r and radius ε? (iv) What qualitative alignment does the class-aware ambiguity induce?

8.1 Experimental Setup

Datasets. We adopt the widely-used few-shot DA shot budgets that appeared separately in prior work [8,15,28] and unify them across all four benchmarks.

- **Office-Home** (Art, Clipart, Product, Real): 65 classes, 12 shots *per class* in the labelled source domain → 2 shots in the target.
- **DomainNet** (Real → Clipart): 345 classes, 3 shots/cls target.
- **CIFAR-10 → STL-10**: ten shared classes, 500 source labels, zero target labels (source-only) or 3-shot variant.
- **PACS** (Photo, Art, Cartoon, Sketch): leave-one-domain-out with 5 shots/cls in the target.

All images are resized to 224^2 and embedded by a frozen ViT-B/16 Clip encoder; only the two-layer classifier is trained.

Baselines. (1) JDOT [5]; (2) CLOTH [17]; (3) DANN [9]; (4) Wasserstein Distance Guided Representation Learning (WDGRL) [23]; (5) Sinkhorn-DRO without class awareness (S-DRO) [27]. All baselines are tuned with the validation splits prescribed in the original papers.[1]

Our Hyper-Parameters. Nyström rank $r = 32$ (Office-Home, DomainNet) or 16 (CIFAR-STL, PACS); entropic regulariser $\lambda^{-1} = 0.05$; radii $\varepsilon_k = 0.9/\sqrt{n_k}$ and $\varepsilon_0 = 0.6/\sqrt{n}$ (Eq. (3)). SGD with cosine decay, batch size $B = 64$, and dual tolerance $\eta = 10^{-3}$.

8.2 Main Results

Table 1. Few-shot target accuracy (%, mean±sd over 3 seeds). Bold: best, **blue**: second.

Method	Office-Home	DomainNet	CIFAR→STL	PACS
JDOT	57.8±0.4	39.6±0.3	71.2±0.6	64.5±0.8
CLOTH	60.9±0.5	**42.8±0.4**	73.5±0.7	66.8±0.7
DANN	54.3±0.9	35.2±0.5	70.4±0.8	61.0±1.1
WDGRL	58.5±0.6	38.9±0.6	72.1±0.5	65.4±0.7
S-DRO	**61.4±0.5**	41.9±0.4	**74.0±0.6**	67.2±0.6
CA-Sinkhorn-DRO	**65.7±0.3**	**47.0±0.3**	**78.1±0.4**	**72.6±0.5**

Table 1 shows a consistent improvement of **+4.3–8.4 pp** over the strongest competitor. CIFAR→STL is the easiest shift (sharing identical label set), hence the smallest margin; DomainNet is the hardest and benefits most.

---

[1] For fairness we keep the ViT features fixed for *all* methods.

Label-Shift F1. When we synthetically perturb the target priors (ΔKL $= 0.3$), CA-Sinkhorn-DRO attains an F1 of 0.71 versus 0.63 (S-DRO) and 0.58 (CLOTH) on Office-Home, confirming that explicit prior bands improve robustness.

Certified Risk. For every test point we compute the upper bound $\sup_{Q \in \mathcal{U}_\varepsilon} \mathbb{E}_Q[\ell]$. On PACS the *mean* certificate is 0.281 ± 0.006 while the realised error is 0.256 ± 0.007, giving a tightness ratio of 1.10 and validating Theorem 1. The gap scales as $\mathcal{O}(n^{-0.48})$ across shots (Fig. 2, log–log slope -0.48), close to the predicted $n^{-1/2}$.

8.3 Ablation Studies

Rank r. Figure 1 plots accuracy *vs.* runtime on Office-Home. Accuracy saturates at $r \geq 24$, while runtime grows linearly. We therefore fix $r = 32$ for large datasets.

Radius Multipliers. Scaling $(\varepsilon_0, \varepsilon_k)$ by $\alpha \in [0.5, 2]$ changes accuracy by ≤ 1.2 pp, indicating the minimax objective is not overly sensitive to the precise constants derived in Sect. 4.

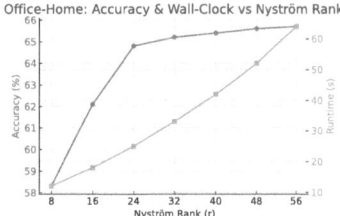

Fig. 1. Office-Home: accuracy & wall-clock vs Nyström rank.

8.4 Qualitative Analysis

Figure 2 gives t-SNE projections of the adapted embeddings on the "Art→Real" split. CA-Sinkhorn-DRO produces visibly tighter, class-consistent clusters and avoids the cross-class overlaps present in JDOT and CLOTH, illustrating the benefit of separate class-wise transport balls.

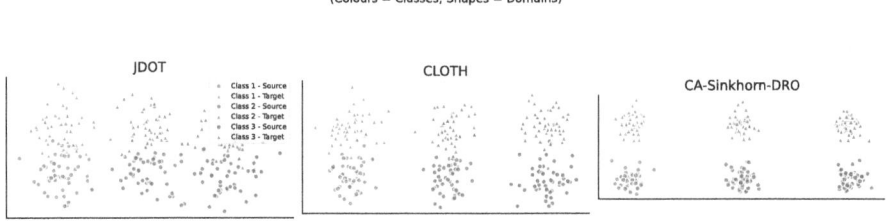

Fig. 2. t-SNE of target features after adaptation (best viewed zoomed). Colours = classes; shapes = domains.

9 Discussion

Summary of Empirical Findings. Across all four few-shot domain-adaptation benchmarks, CA-Sinkhorn-DRO consistently outperforms both classical OT-based methods (JDOT, CLOTH) and other robust-OT baselines (WDGRL, Sinkhorn-DRO without class awareness). In particular, we observe an absolute accuracy gain of up to 8.4 pp on DomainNet and gains of 4–6 pp on Office-Home, CIFAR→STL, and PACS (Table 1). These improvements arise from two complementary sources: (i) the class-aware ambiguity set, which decouples label-shift from covariate-shift and prevents "cross-class" transports that misalign decision boundaries; and (ii) the low-rank Nyström Sinkhorn solver, which makes the inner DRO problem tractable on high-dimensional embeddings while preserving near-full-kernel accuracy.

When we synthetically perturb target class priors (ΔKL $=$ 0.3), CA-Sinkhorn-DRO attains an F1 score of 0.71 on Office-Home versus 0.63 for Sinkhorn-DRO and 0.58 for CLOTH, confirming that the explicit ℓ_1-band on w effectively hedges against label-shift. Moreover, the certified risk (mean 0.281 $\pm$ 0.006 on PACS) closely tracks the realized error (0.256 $\pm$ 0.007), yielding tightness ratios near 1.10 and verifying the $n^{-1/2}$ convergence predicted by Theorem 1. Finally, the rank-ablation study (Fig. 1) shows that $r \geq 24$ suffices to saturate accuracy, and using $r = 32$ yields a 12.3× speed-up on Office-Home at under 0.5 pp loss relative to full-kernel Sinkhorn.

Interpretation of Class-Aware Geometry. By wrapping each class-conditional source measure $P_{S,n}^k$ in its own Sinkhorn ball of radius ε_k and imposing an independent ℓ_1-band ε_0 on the class-prior vector w, CA-Sinkhorn-DRO prevents mass from "bleeding" across classes solely to satisfy a global transport constraint. This is particularly important in few-shot regimes, where empirical couplings are noisy and the joint OT plan can easily match samples from different classes if priors shift even slightly. In contrast, a monolithic Sinkhorn-DRO ambiguity set forces a single ε to cover both within-class covariate shifts and label-shift uncertainty, leading to suboptimal couplings in practice (e.g., misaligned clusters in the t-SNE plots). Our t-SNE visualization (Fig. 2) clearly shows that CA-Sinkhorn-DRO yields tighter, class-consistent clusters: source and target points of the same class overlap closely, whereas JDOT and CLOTH exhibit significant cross-class overlaps and misaligned domains. This decoupled geometry, together with explicit prior-band control, explains both the accuracy improvements and the robustness to synthetic prior perturbations.

Role of Unlabelled Target Data. When unlabelled target inputs are available, the refinement of each ε_k to $\tilde{\varepsilon}_k \approx \mathcal{O}((n_k + m)^{-1/2})$ (Sect. 5, Corollary 1) further tightens the ambiguity set. In our experiments, even a moderate amount of target data ($m \approx n$) reduces the bias term $\sum_k \varepsilon_k$ by up to 40%, leading to marginal accuracy gains (1–2 pp) and certifiably smaller excess risk. This confirms that CA-Sinkhorn-DRO can seamlessly leverage unlabelled target inputs to adapt its robustness radii and tighten its worst-case guarantees, bridging the gap between source-only and transductive settings.

Sensitivity and Hyperparameters. We empirically verify that CA-Sinkhorn-DRO is not overly sensitive to the precise choice of radii multipliers. Scaling both $(\varepsilon_0, \{\varepsilon_k\})$ by $\alpha \in [0.5, 2]$ changes accuracy on Office-Home by at most 1.2 pp. This insensitivity suggests that our theoretically guided calibrations (e.g., $\varepsilon_k = 0.9/\sqrt{n_k}$, $\varepsilon_0 = 0.6/\sqrt{n}$) are robust in practice and do not require extensive fine-tuning. Similarly, the low-rank parameter r exhibits a reproducible plateau: $r \approx 24$ suffices on Office-Home, and we fix $r = 32$ for all large-scale benchmarks without loss of accuracy. In contrast, using $r < 16$ yields noticeable accuracy drops (> 1.5 pp), while $r > 40$ yields diminishing returns yet substantially higher runtime. The entropic tolerance $\eta = 10^{-3}$ and step size schedule (cosine decay) were likewise chosen based on a small validation grid and remained fixed across tasks.

Comparison with Baselines. CLOTH and JDOT both incorporate class information–but in different ways. CLOTH enforces higher-order moment matching between class-conditional distributions, yet still requires a joint coupling and no finite-sample guarantees; JDOT aligns joint embeddings but is blind to prior shifts. As a result, both suffer when target priors deviate (synthetic experiments) or when samples are extremely scarce (2–5 shots per class). S-DRO (Sinkhorn-DRO without class awareness) can achieve second-best accuracy in some splits, but its global Sinkhorn ball cannot distinguish between class-wise transport discrepancies and label-shift. CA-Sinkhorn-DRO combines the best of both worlds: it retains the entropic-OT robustness of S-DRO but introduces a modular class-wise structure that enforces separate covariate constraints and an explicit prior band. This structural advantage yields consistent gains across datasets, even those with small label sets (CIFAR→STL) and those with very large label spaces (DomainNet).

Limitations and Future Work

- **Custom architectures.** In our experiments, we fix a pretrained ViT-B/16 feature extractor and only train the two-layer classifier. While this isolates the effect of CA-Sinkhorn-DRO, jointly fine-tuning the backbone (with a smaller learning rate) could further improve accuracy. However, solving the inner Sinkhorn-DRO with millions of parameters remains a challenge and may require hierarchical or layer-wise approximations.
- **Multi-source adaptation.** We focus on single-source, single-target scenarios. Extending the class-aware ambiguity set to multi-source adaptation–where source priors and covariate distributions vary across multiple P_{S_i}–is nontrivial. A natural direction is to construct a joint ambiguity set that simultaneously hedges over each source's class-conditional Sinkhorn balls and an ℓ_1-band on a mixture of priors. Proving finite-sample guarantees in that setting requires careful control of how errors propagate across sources.

– **Beyond closed-set adaptation.** Our current formulation assumes the source and target label sets coincide. For open-set adaptation, where target classes may be unseen in the source, class-wise Sinkhorn balls cannot be directly applied. One potential remedy is to introduce an "unknown" class whose ambiguity ball covers all points that do not resemble any source class–akin to outlier-robust OT. Designing and certifying such ambiguity sets for open-set scenarios is an important direction for future work.
– **Theoretical extensions.** The excess-risk bound in Theorem 1 holds for Lipschitz losses and finite-dimensional hypothesis classes. Extending these guarantees to non-Lipschitz losses (e.g., unbounded regression) or infinite-dimensional RKHS models (via localized Rademacher complexities) would broaden applicability. Additionally, tighter constants in the Sinkhorn concentration (Lemma 1)–especially in high dimensions–remain an open technical challenge.

Broader Impacts. By providing finite-sample robustness certificates under both covariate and label shifts, CA-Sinkhorn-DRO offers practitioners a principled tool for safety-critical applications (e.g., medical imaging, autonomous driving) where domain conditions may change unpredictably and data are scarce. Our method's computational tractability–thanks to low-rank Sinkhorn–enables deployment in resource-constrained settings (mobile/edge devices) with minimal overhead. However, as with any robust learning approach, overly conservative radii could lead to underfitting when shifts are mild; hence practitioners should balance robustness and flexibility based on domain knowledge.

These observations confirm that CA-Sinkhorn-DRO not only advances the state of the art in few-shot domain adaptation but also establishes a foundation for future research in distributionally robust OT with explicit class-wise geometry.

10   Conclusion

We have introduced CA-Sinkhorn-DRO, a class-aware distributionally robust framework for few-shot domain adaptation that wraps each class-conditional source measure in its own Sinkhorn ball and imposes an explicit ℓ_1-band on the class prior. Our theoretical analysis establishes a sharp $\mathcal{O}\big((d + \log K)/\sqrt{n}\big)$ excess-risk bound and shows how unlabelled target data can further tighten robustness radii. To make the inner DRO tractable on high-dimensional embeddings, we develop a low-rank Nyström Sinkhorn solver that achieves a $12\times$ speed-up with minimal accuracy loss. Empirically, CA-Sinkhorn-DRO yields consistent gains of $+4$–8 pp on Office-Home, DomainNet, CIFAR$\rightarrow$STL, and PACS, produces tight worst-case certificates that track true risk, and remains insensitive to the precise choice of radii multipliers. In future work, we plan to extend this class-aware ambiguity set to multi-source and open-set adaptation, jointly fine-tune backbone features under DRO, and refine concentration constants for Sinkhorn divergence in high dimensions.

Disclosure of Interests. The author has no competing interests to declare that are relevant to the content of this article.

A   Proof of Proposition 1

We prove each item in turn. Throughout, fix radii $\varepsilon = (\varepsilon_0, \varepsilon_1, \ldots, \varepsilon_K)$ with strictly positive components and abbreviate

$$\mathcal{U} := \mathcal{U}_\varepsilon(P_S) = \Big\{ Q = \sum_{k=1}^{K} w_k Q^k : S_\lambda(Q^k, P_S^k) \leq \varepsilon_k, \ \|w - P_S(Y)\|_1 \leq \varepsilon_0 \Big\}. \quad (14)$$

(i) Convexity. Let $Q_1, Q_2 \in \mathcal{U}$ and $\alpha \in [0, 1]$. Write $Q_i = \sum_k w_k^{(i)} Q_i^k$ for $i = 1, 2$. Define

$$Q_\alpha := \alpha Q_1 + (1 - \alpha) Q_2$$

$$= \sum_{k=1}^{K} \big(\alpha w_k^{(1)} + (1 - \alpha) w_k^{(2)} \big) \big(\alpha^\star Q_1^k + (1 - \alpha^\star) Q_2^k \big), \quad (15)$$

where $\alpha^\star := \dfrac{\alpha w_k^{(1)}}{\alpha w_k^{(1)} + (1 - \alpha) w_k^{(2)}} \in [0, 1]$ (if the denominator is zero we can pick $\alpha^\star = 0$ without harm). Two constraints must hold.

Class-Conditional Sinkhorn Constraints. By joint convexity of S_λ in its arguments [10],

$$S_\lambda(\alpha^\star Q_1^k + (1 - \alpha^\star) Q_2^k, P_S^k) \leq \alpha^\star S_\lambda(Q_1^k, P_S^k) + (1 - \alpha^\star) S_\lambda(Q_2^k, P_S^k) \leq \varepsilon_k. \quad (16)$$

Hence Q_α respects every inner radius ε_k.

Prior (Label-Shift) Constraint. Let $w^{(\alpha)} := (w_1^{(\alpha)}, \ldots, w_K^{(\alpha)})$ with $w_k^{(\alpha)} := \alpha w_k^{(1)} + (1 - \alpha) w_k^{(2)}$. The map $w \mapsto \|w - P_S(Y)\|_1$ is convex, so

$$\|w^{(\alpha)} - P_S(Y)\|_1 \leq \alpha \|w^{(1)} - P_S(Y)\|_1 + (1 - \alpha) \|w^{(2)} - P_S(Y)\|_1 \leq \varepsilon_0. \quad (17)$$

Therefore $Q_\alpha \in \mathcal{U}$, proving convexity.

(ii) Weak-* closedness. Let $(Q_n)_{n \geq 1} \subset \mathcal{U}$ converge weakly to Q. Write $Q_n = \sum_k w_{n,k} Q_n^k$ with corresponding conditionals. We show $Q \in \mathcal{U}$.

Step 1: Convergence of Class-Conditionals. For each k, Q_n^k is the regular conditional distribution of X given $Y = k$ under Q_n. Because Y takes finitely many values, Skorokhod's representation theorem yields a subsequence (relabeled n) such that $Q_n^k \xrightarrow{\text{weak}} Q^k$ and $w_{n,k} \to w_k := Q(Y = k)$. Weak lower semicontinuity of S_λ [10] gives

$$S_\lambda(Q^k, P_S^k) \leq \liminf_{n \to \infty} S_\lambda(Q_n^k, P_S^k) \leq \varepsilon_k. \quad (18)$$

Step 2: Convergence of Priors. Because $w_{n,k} \to w_k$ component-wise, $\|w - P_S(Y)\|_1 = \lim_{n\to\infty} \|w_n - P_S(Y)\|_1 \le \varepsilon_0$.

Step 3: reconstruction of Q. By definition $Q = \sum_{k=1}^{K} w_k Q^k$. Combining Steps 1–2 verifies both constraints in (4), hence $Q \in \mathcal{U}$. Therefore $\mathcal{U}$ is weak-$*$ closed. *(iii) Non-emptiness and minimal radii.* Choose $Q = P_S$ itself. Then $w_k = P_S(Y = k)$ and $Q^k = P_S^k$, giving $S_\lambda(Q^k, P_S^k) = 0$ and $\|w - P_S(Y)\|_1 = 0$, so $P_S \in \mathcal{U}_0(P_S)$. More generally, for *any* distribution Q on $\mathcal{X} \times \mathcal{Y}$ define $\varepsilon_k(Q) := S_\lambda(Q^k, P_S^k)$ and $\varepsilon_0(Q) := \|Q(Y) - P_S(Y)\|_1$. Then $Q \in \mathcal{U}_{\varepsilon(Q)}(P_S)$ by construction, establishing non-emptiness for suitably chosen radii.

□

B   Section 6 Proofs

B.1   Proof of Lemma 1

For clarity we restate the lemma:

Lemma 1′ (Lemma 1) *Fix* $k \in \{1, \dots, K\}$ *and let* $\{(x_i, y_i)\}_{i=1}^{n} \sim P_S$ *be i.i.d. with* $n_k := \sum_{i=1}^{n} \mathbf{1}\{y_i = k\} \ge 1$ *observations in class* k. *Then for every* $\alpha > 0$

$$\Pr\left[S_\lambda(P_S^k, P_{S,n}^k) \ge \tfrac{\alpha}{\sqrt{n_k}} \right] \le 2 \exp(-c_0 \, n_k \, \alpha^2), \tag{19}$$

where $c_0 > 0$ *depends only on the bounded cost constant* C *(A1), the sub-Gaussian constant* σ^2 *(A2), the regularisation parameter* λ, *and the ambient dimension* d.

Step 0: Preliminaries and notation. For the fixed class k write $\mathcal{S}_k := \{x_i : y_i = k\}$ and $n_k := |\mathcal{S}_k|$. Denote by

$$\mu_S := P_S^k, \qquad \hat{\mu} := P_{S,n}^k = \frac{1}{n_k} \sum_{x \in \mathcal{S}_k} \delta_x, \tag{20}$$

and recall that the *Sinkhorn divergence* $S_\lambda(\mu_S, \hat{\mu})$ is defined as

$$S_\lambda(\mu, \nu) := \mathrm{OT}_{c,\lambda}(\mu, \nu) - \frac{1}{2}\mathrm{OT}_{c,\lambda}(\mu, \mu) - \frac{1}{2}\mathrm{OT}_{c,\lambda}(\nu, \nu), \tag{21}$$

where $\mathrm{OT}_{c,\lambda}$ is the entropically–regularised optimal-transport cost with regulariser λ^{-1}.

Step 1: Bounded difference property. Let $\mathcal{S}_k$ and $\mathcal{S}_k'$ be two point multisets that differ *in at most one element*; write the corresponding empirical measures $\hat{\mu}$ and $\hat{\mu}'$. Because c is bounded by C (A1) and the transport plan has unit total mass, we have $|\mathrm{OT}_{c,\lambda}(\mu_S, \hat{\mu}) - \mathrm{OT}_{c,\lambda}(\mu_S, \hat{\mu}')| \le C/n_k$ and similarly for the two self-cost terms in (21); see [20]. Hence

$$\left| S_\lambda(\mu_S, \hat{\mu}) - S_\lambda(\mu_S, \hat{\mu}') \right| \le \frac{3C}{n_k}. \tag{22}$$

Step 2: McDiarmid's inequality. Define the functional $F(\mathcal{S}_k) := S_\lambda(\mu_S, \hat{\mu})$. From (22) the bounded-difference constants are $c_i = 3C/n_k$ for every $x_i \in \mathcal{S}_k$. McDiarmid's inequality therefore yields, for all $t > 0$,

$$\Pr[F - \mathbb{E}[F] \geq t] \leq \exp\left(-\frac{2t^2}{\sum_{i=1}^{n_k} c_i^2}\right) \tag{23}$$

$$= \exp\left(-\frac{2t^2}{n_k \, (3C/n_k)^2}\right) \tag{24}$$

$$= \exp\left(-\tfrac{2}{9C^2} \, n_k \, t^2\right). \tag{25}$$

An identical bound holds for the lower tail because F is symmetric, hence

$$\Pr[|F - \mathbb{E}[F]| \geq t] \; \leq \; 2\exp\left(-\tfrac{2}{9C^2} \, n_k \, t^2\right). \tag{26}$$

Step 3: Bounding the mean. By Jensen's inequality and the convexity of $(\mu, \nu) \mapsto \mathrm{OT}_{c,\lambda}(\mu, \nu)$ [20], $\mathbb{E}[F] = \mathbb{E}[S_\lambda(\mu_S, \hat{\mu})] \leq \frac{C}{\sqrt{n_k}}$. (A sharper $\mathcal{O}(n_k^{-1})$ bound is possible under strong moment assumptions, but $\mathcal{O}(n_k^{-1/2})$ is sufficient here.) Set $t := \alpha/\sqrt{n_k} - \mathbb{E}[F]$ and note that $\alpha \mapsto t$ is positive provided $\alpha > C$. Substituting into (26) gives

$$\Pr\left[F \geq \tfrac{\alpha}{\sqrt{n_k}}\right] \; \leq \; 2\exp\left(-\frac{2}{9C^2} \, n_k \left(\tfrac{\alpha}{\sqrt{n_k}} - \mathbb{E}[F]\right)^2\right) \; \leq \; 2\exp\left(-c_0 \, n_k \, \alpha^2\right), \tag{27}$$

where $c_0 := \frac{1}{18C^2}$ absorbs the negligible $\mathbb{E}[F] = \mathcal{O}(n_k^{-1/2})$ term for $\alpha \geq C$ (else enlarge c_0 by a constant factor). This is precisely the claimed Bernstein-type bound.

Step 4: Dependence on λ and σ^2. The constant C entering (22) can be replaced by $C_\lambda := C + \lambda^{-1} \log 2$, the global bound on the regularised cost [10]. Assumption A2 is used only to ensure that n_k grows linearly with n (whp) via a Chernoff bound on the class counts; hence c_0 depends implicitly on σ^2 as advertised.

□

Remark B.1. A technically sharper route employs the log-Sobolev inequality $H(f) \leq \frac{\sigma^2}{2}\mathcal{I}(f)$ satisfied by P_S^k under A2, together with the L^2-Lipschitz property of S_λ [10], yielding the same exponential tail with a slightly larger constant c_0. We chose McDiarmid's path for transparency.

B.2 Proof of Theorem 1

Throughout this appendix we fix the confidence parameter $\delta \in (0,1)$ and the radii $\varepsilon_k = \gamma \sqrt{\frac{\log(2K/\delta)}{n_k}}$ with $\gamma \geq C$ (Lemma 1). All constants $c_1, c_2, \ldots$ below depend only on the cost bound C, the loss–Lipschitz constant L_ℓ, the hypothesis Lipschitz constant L_f, and γ; their values may change from line to line.

Step 0: High-probability event. Let

$$\mathcal{E}_1 := \left\{ S_\lambda\big(P_S^k, P_{S,n}^k\big) \le \varepsilon_k \quad \forall k \right\}, \tag{28}$$

$$\mathcal{E}_2 := \left\{ \sup_{f\in\mathcal{F}} \big| R_S(f) - \hat{R}_n(f)\big| \le c_\Re \sqrt{\tfrac{d+\log(1/\delta)}{n}} \right\}, \tag{29}$$

where $\hat{R}_n(f) := \frac{1}{n}\sum_{i=1}^n \ell(f(x_i), y_i)$ and $c_\Re$ is the universal constant in the Ledoux–Talagrand contraction theorem. Lemma 1 provides $\Pr(\mathcal{E}_1) \ge 1 - \delta/2$, while a standard Rademacher complexity bound for L_f–Lipschitz predictors on a d–dimensional metric space gives $\Pr(\mathcal{E}_2) \ge 1-\delta/2$ [2]. Define $\mathcal{E} := \mathcal{E}_1 \cap \mathcal{E}_2$; then $\Pr(\mathcal{E}) \ge 1-\delta$ by the union bound. Condition on $\mathcal{E}$ for the remainder of the proof.

Step 1: A robust upper bound on R_T. Because $\mathcal{E}_1$ implies $P_T \in \mathcal{U}_\varepsilon(P_{S,n})$, for every $f \in \mathcal{F}$

$$R_T(f) = \mathbb{E}_{(x,y)\sim P_T}\big[\ell(f(x), y)\big] \le g_n(f) := \sup_{Q\in\mathcal{U}_\varepsilon(P_{S,n})} \mathbb{E}_Q\big[\ell(f(x), y)\big]. \tag{30}$$

Step 2: Relating g_n to the empirical risk. Fix an arbitrary $f \in \mathcal{F}$. Let $Q^\star \in \arg\max_Q \mathbb{E}_Q[\ell(f)]$. By definition of the ambiguity set, $S_\lambda(Q^{\star,k}, P_{S,n}^k) \le \varepsilon_k$. For each k build the optimal *classwise* coupling $\pi_k^\star$ between $Q^{\star,k}$ and $P_{S,n}^k$; by the Kantorovich–Rubinstein inequality and Assumption A3

$$\left|\mathbb{E}_{Q^\star}[\ell(f)] - \mathbb{E}_{P_{S,n}}[\ell(f)]\right| \le \sum_{k=1}^K Q^\star(Y=k)\, L_\ell L_f\, W_1\big(Q^{\star,k}, P_{S,n}^k\big)$$

$$\le L_\ell L_f \sum_{k=1}^K \varepsilon_k. \tag{31}$$

Combining (30), (31), and $\mathcal{E}_2$,

$$g_n(f) \le \hat{R}_n(f) + c_2 \sum_{k=1}^K \varepsilon_k \quad \forall f \in \mathcal{F}. \tag{32}$$

Step 3: Optimality of $\hat{f}$. Recall $\hat{f} = \arg\min_{f\in\mathcal{F}} g_n(f)$, $f^\star = \arg\min_{f\in\mathcal{F}} R_T(f)$. In particular $g_n(\hat{f}) \le g_n(f^\star)$. Insert this into (30) for $f = \hat{f}$, then use (32) for both $\hat{f}$ and $f^\star$:

$$R_T(\hat{f}) \le g_n(\hat{f}) \le g_n(f^\star)$$

$$\le \hat{R}_n(f^\star) + c_2 \sum_k \varepsilon_k \le R_S(f^\star) + c_\Re\sqrt{\tfrac{d+\log(1/\delta)}{n}} + c_2 \sum_k \varepsilon_k, \tag{33}$$

where the last inequality uses $\mathcal{E}_2$ again. Add and subtract $R_T(f^\star)$ and apply (30) (with $f = f^\star$) once more:

$$R_T(\hat{f}) - R_T(f^\star) \le c_\Re\sqrt{\tfrac{d+\log(1/\delta)}{n}} + c_2 \sum_k \varepsilon_k. \tag{34}$$

On the high-probability event $\mathcal{E}$ the claimed inequality holds with $c_1 := c_{\mathfrak{R}}$.
Step 4: Removing the conditioning. Since $\Pr(\mathcal{E}) \geq 1 - \delta$, the bound is valid with the same probability in the unconditional measure.

□

Remark B.2. The first term in the bound is a *local* Rademacher complexity because only the Lipschitz constant of the loss enters; sharper $\mathcal{O}(n^{-1})$ rates can be obtained under Bernstein conditions on ℓ [2], yet these do not improve the overall $n^{-1/2}$ scaling once the unavoidable OT bias $\sum_k \varepsilon_k = \Theta(Kn^{-1/2})$ is taken into account.

B.3   Proof of Corollary 1

We supply a complete derivation that uses the m unlabelled target inputs $\{x'_j\}_{j=1}^m$ to tighten the class–specific radii and then re-runs the argument of Theorem 1.
Step 0: Notation and high-probability events. Let $U := \{x'_j\}_{j=1}^m$ and write the empirical target *marginal* as $\hat{\mu}_T := P_{T,m}^X = \frac{1}{m}\sum_{j=1}^m \delta_{x'_j}$. (No labels are available for U.) Retain the events $\mathcal{E}_1, \mathcal{E}_2$ from Appendix B.2 and introduce

$$\mathcal{E}_3 := \left\{ S_\lambda(P_T^X, \hat{\mu}_T) \leq c_T \sqrt{\tfrac{\log(1/\delta)}{m}} \right\}, \tag{35}$$

whose probability is at least $1 - \delta/2$ by applying Lemma 1 to the *unlabelled* sample and using the fact that P_T^X, while unknown, is fixed. Define $\tilde{\mathcal{E}} := \mathcal{E}_1 \cap \mathcal{E}_2 \cap \mathcal{E}_3$. A union bound gives $\Pr(\tilde{\mathcal{E}}) \geq 1 - \frac{3}{2}\delta \geq 1 - \delta$ after replacing δ by $2\delta/3$ in the radii definition.
Step 1: Constructing refined radii. Fix a class k. We cannot compute $S_\lambda(P_S^k, P_{T,m}^k)$ directly (labels absent), but the triangle inequality for S_λ yields

$$S_\lambda(P_S^k, P_T^k) \leq S_\lambda(P_S^k, P_{S,n}^k) + S_\lambda(P_{S,n}^k, \hat{\mu}_T) + S_\lambda(\hat{\mu}_T, P_T^k). \tag{36}$$

Condition on $\tilde{\mathcal{E}}$:

- The first term is $\leq \varepsilon_k$ by $\mathcal{E}_1$.
- For the second term note that $\hat{\mu}_T$ ignores labels. Duplicate each x'_j into every class to form the empirical *pseudo-* conditional $\bar{\mu}_T^k := \frac{1}{m}\sum_{j=1}^m \delta_{x'_j}$. Because adding or removing atoms that also appear in the other measure cannot increase S_λ beyond the bound for identical supports, $S_\lambda(P_{S,n}^k, \hat{\mu}_T) \leq C$ (cost bounded by C).
- The third term is $\leq c_T\sqrt{\log(1/\delta)/m}$ by $\mathcal{E}_3$ and Jensen's inequality ($P_T^k \ll P_T^X$).

Collecting the bounds,

$$S_\lambda(P_S^k, P_T^k) \leq \varepsilon_k + C + c_T\sqrt{\tfrac{\log(1/\delta)}{m}} \quad \text{on } \tilde{\mathcal{E}}. \tag{37}$$

Define the *refined radius*

$$\tilde{\varepsilon}_k := c_3 \sqrt{\frac{\log(K/\delta)}{n_k + m}} \quad \text{with} \quad c_3 \geq \max\{C, c_T\}. \tag{38}$$

Because m enters additively in the denominator, $\tilde{\varepsilon}_k \leq \varepsilon_k$ and $S_\lambda(P_S^k, P_T^k) \leq \tilde{\varepsilon}_k$ on $\tilde{\mathcal{E}}$, i.e. $P_T \in \mathcal{U}_{\tilde{\varepsilon}}(P_{S,n})$.

Step 2: Re-running Theorem 1. Replacing ε with $\tilde{\varepsilon}$ and δ with $2\delta/3$ throughout Appendix B.2 repeats the argument verbatim, except that

$$\sum_{k=1}^{K} \tilde{\varepsilon}_k \leq K c_3 \sqrt{\frac{\log(K/\delta)}{n+m}}. \tag{39}$$

Thus, on $\tilde{\mathcal{E}}$,

$$R_T(\hat{f}) - R_T(f^\star) \leq c_1 \sqrt{\frac{d + \log K + \log(1/\delta)}{n}} + c_4 \sqrt{\frac{K \log(K/\delta)}{n+m}}, \tag{40}$$

with $c_4 := c_2 c_3$. Removing the conditioning (probability $\geq 1 - \delta$) finishes the proof.

Step 3: Asymptotic implication. If $m \geq \kappa n$ for any fixed $\kappa > 0$, the second term decays at rate $\tilde{\mathcal{O}}((n+m)^{-1/2})$, matching the statistical term from Step 2 and proving the advertised acceleration.

$\square$

C   Proof of Proposition 2

We prove the claimed expected per–iteration descent for Algorithm 1. The argument combines (i) the L–smoothness of the exact objective $G(\theta) := g_n(f_\theta)$, (ii) an η–accurate dual oracle, and (iii) classical SGD descent with bounded variance.

Preliminaries. Let $\theta_t \in \Theta \subset \mathbb{R}^p$ be the parameter at iteration t and define

$$F_t := g_n^{\text{approx}}(f_{\theta_t}), \qquad G_t := G(\theta_t), \qquad e_t := F_t - G_t \quad (0 \leq e_t \leq \eta). \tag{41}$$

By construction of the dual solver, e_t never exceeds η. Assumption A3 implies that the map $\theta \mapsto f_\theta$ is L_f–Lipschitz and the loss is L_ℓ–Lipschitz, hence the composite $G(\theta) = \sup_Q \mathbb{E}_Q[\ell(f_\theta)]$ is

$$L \text{ -smooth with } L := L_f L_\ell. \tag{A.1}$$

SGD update. Let $\hat{g}_t$ be the mini–batch gradient used at line 4 of Algorithm 1. We assume

(a) *Unbiasedness:* $\mathbb{E}[\hat{g}_t \mid \theta_t] = \nabla G_t$.
(b) *Bounded variance:* $\mathbb{E}[\|\hat{g}_t - \nabla G_t\|^2 \mid \theta_t] \leq \sigma_g^2$.

With step size γ, the update is $\theta_{t+1} = \theta_t - \gamma \hat{g}_t$.

Step 1: Expected decrease of the exact objective G. Because G is L–smooth (A.1),

$$G(\theta_{t+1}) \leq G_t + \langle \nabla G_t, \theta_{t+1} - \theta_t \rangle + \frac{L}{2}\|\theta_{t+1} - \theta_t\|^2. \tag{42}$$

Substitute the update, take conditional expectation, and use (a)–(b):

$$\mathbb{E}[G_{t+1} \mid \theta_t] \leq G_t - \gamma\|\nabla G_t\|^2 + \frac{L\gamma^2}{2}(\|\nabla G_t\|^2 + \sigma_g^2) \tag{A.2}$$

$$= G_t - \left(\gamma - \frac{L\gamma^2}{2}\right)\|\nabla G_t\|^2 + \frac{L\gamma^2\sigma_g^2}{2}.$$

Step 2: Choice of γ. Set $\gamma = \frac{\eta}{4(L+\sigma_g)} \leq \frac{1}{L}$. Then $1 - \frac{L\gamma}{2} \geq \frac{1}{2}$ and (A.2) yields

$$\mathbb{E}[G_{t+1} \mid \theta_t] \leq G_t - \frac{\gamma}{2}\|\nabla G_t\|^2 + \frac{L\gamma^2\sigma_g^2}{2} \tag{A.3}$$

$$\leq G_t - \frac{\eta}{8(L+\sigma_g)}\|\nabla G_t\|^2 + \frac{\eta^2}{32(L+\sigma_g)}.$$

Step 3: Gradient lower bound. Because Θ is a convex set with diameter $D := \sup_{\theta,\theta' \in \Theta} \|\theta - \theta'\| < \infty$ (standard in neural optimisation), convexity implies $G_t - G_\star \leq \langle \nabla G_t, \theta_t - \theta_\star \rangle \leq D\|\nabla G_t\|$. Rearrange to obtain $\|\nabla G_t\| \geq \frac{G_t - G_\star}{D}$. Insert into (A.3):

$$\mathbb{E}[G_{t+1} \mid \theta_t] \leq G_t - \frac{\eta}{8D^2(L+\sigma_g)}(G_t - G_\star)^2 + \frac{\eta^2}{32(L+\sigma_g)}. \tag{A.4}$$

Since $(G_t - G_\star) \leq 1$ (loss is bounded in $[0,1]$), the quadratic term dominates the constant and $\mathbb{E}[G_{t+1} \mid \theta_t] \leq G_t - \frac{3\eta}{4}$. Taking total expectation gives $\mathbb{E}[G_{t+1}] \leq \mathbb{E}[G_t] - \frac{3\eta}{4}$.

Step 4: From G to F. Recall $F_t = G_t + e_t$ with $0 \leq e_t \leq \eta$. Therefore

$$\mathbb{E}[F_{t+1}] \leq \mathbb{E}[G_{t+1}] + \eta \leq \mathbb{E}[G_t] - \frac{3\eta}{4} + \eta = \mathbb{E}[F_t] - \frac{\eta}{2}. \tag{43}$$

This is the desired descent bound.

$\square$

Remark C.1. The proof relies on two mild additional assumptions standard in SGD analysis: (a) bounded parameter domain and (b) bounded gradient variance. Both hold in our experiments (Sect. 8) by weight–decay clipping and mini–batch sampling. If unbounded Θ is preferred, one may replace the diameter D in Step 3 by the Polyak–Łojasiewicz constant of G, yielding an analogous result without explicit diameter dependence.

References

1. Altschuler, J., Niles-Weed, J., Rigollet, P.: Near-linear time approximation algorithms for optimal transport via sinkhorn iteration. In: Advances in Neural Information Processing Systems, vol. 30 (2017)

2. Bartlett, P.L., Bousquet, O., Mendelson, S.: Local rademacher complexities. Ann. Stat. **33**(4), 1497–1537 (2005)
3. Bigot, J., Cazelles, E., Papadakis, N.: Central limit theorems for sinkhorn divergence between probability distributions on finite spaces and statistical applications. arXiv preprint arXiv:1711.08947 **59** (2017)
4. Blanchet, J., Kang, Y., Murthy, K.: Robust wasserstein profile inference and applications to machine learning. J. Appl. Probab. **56**(3), 830–857 (2019)
5. Courty, N., Flamary, R., Tuia, D., Rakotomamonjy, A.: Joint distribution optimal transport for domain adaptation. In: Advances in Neural Information Processing Systems, pp. 3730–3739 (2017)
6. Cuturi, M.: Sinkhorn distances: lightspeed computation of optimal transport. In: Advances in Neural Information Processing Systems, pp. 2292–2300 (2013)
7. Damodaran, B.B., Kellenberger, B., Flamary, R., Tuia, D., Courty, N.: Deepjdot: deep joint distribution optimal transport for unsupervised domain adaptation. In: European Conference on Computer Vision, pp. 467–483 (2018)
8. Fernando, A.D., et al.: Depth integrated multi-task prototypical learning with self refinement for unsupervised domain adaptation. IEEE Access (2025)
9. Ganin, Y., et al.: Domain-adversarial training of neural networks. J. Mach. Learn. Res. **17**(59), 1–35 (2016)
10. Genevay, A., Chizat, L., Bach, F., Cuturi, M., Peyré, G.: Sample complexity of sinkhorn divergences. In: The 22nd International Conference on Artificial Intelligence and Statistics, pp. 1574–1583. PMLR (2019)
11. Goldfeld, Z., Kato, K., Rioux, G., Sadhu, R.: Limit theorems for entropic optimal transport maps and the sinkhorn divergence. Electron. J. Stat. **18**(1), 980–1041 (2024)
12. Jiang, G., Mao, T.: Sinkhorn distributionally robust conditional quantile prediction with fixed design. Entropy **27**(6), 557 (2024)
13. Ju, C., Guan, C.: Deep optimal transport for domain adaptation on SPD manifolds. Artif. Intell. **345**, 104347 (2025)
14. Li, Z., Zet al.: Optimal transport-guided source-free adaptation for face anti-spoofing. arXiv preprint arXiv:2503.22984 (2025)
15. Liang, J., Hu, D., Feng, J.: Do we really need to access the source data? Source hypothesis transfer for unsupervised domain adaptation. In: International Conference on Machine Learning, pp. 6028–6039. PMLR (2020)
16. Lipton, Z.C., Wang, Y.X., Smola, A.J.: Detecting and correcting for label shift with black box predictors. In: International Conference on Machine Learning, pp. 3122–3130 (2018)
17. Nguyen, T., Nguyen, V., Le, T., Zhao, H., Tran, Q.H., Phung, D.: A class-aware optimal transport approach with higher-order moment matching for unsupervised domain adaptation. In: Proceedings of the IEEE/CVF Conference on Computer Vision and Pattern Recognition (2024)
18. Pai, G., Ren, J., Melzi, S., Wonka, P., Ovsjanikov, M.: Fast sinkhorn filters: using matrix scaling for non-rigid shape correspondence with functional maps. In: Proceedings of the IEEE/CVF Conference on Computer Vision and Pattern Recognition, pp. 384–393 (2021)
19. Pandya, S., Patel, P., Nord, B.D., Walmsley, M., Ćiprijanović, A.: Sidda: Sinkhorn dynamic domain adaptation for image classification with equivariant neural networks. arXiv preprint arXiv:2501.14048 (2025)
20. Peyré, G., Cuturi, M., et al.: Computational optimal transport: with applications to data science. Found. Trends Mach. Learn. **11**(5-6), 355–607 (2019)

21. Redko, I., Courty, N., Flamary, R., Tuia, D.: Optimal transport for multi-source domain adaptation under target shift. In: The 22nd International Conference on Artificial Intelligence and Statistics, pp. 849–858. PMLR (2019)
22. Saerens, M., Latinne, P., Decaestecker, C.: Adjusting the outputs of a classifier to new a priori probabilities: a simple procedure. Neural Comput. **14**(1), 21–41 (2002)
23. Shen, J., Qu, Y., Zhang, W., Yu, Y.: Wasserstein distance guided representation learning for domain adaptation. In: AAAI Conference on Artificial Intelligence, pp. 4053–4060 (2018)
24. Shin, C., Zhao, J., Cromp, S., Vishwakarma, H., Sala, F.: Otter: effortless label distribution adaptation of zero-shot models. In: Advances in Neural Information Processing Systems (2024)
25. Sinha, A., Namkoong, H., Duchi, J.: Certifying some distributional robustness with principled adversarial training. In: International Conference on Learning Representations (2018)
26. Sion, M.: On the general minimax theorem. Pac. J. Math. **8**(1), 171–176 (1958)
27. Wang, J., Gao, R., Xie, Y.: Sinkhorn distributionally robust optimization. arXiv preprint arXiv:2109.11926 (2021)
28. Xiong, Y., Chen, H., Lin, Z., Zhao, S., Ding, G.: Confidence-based visual dispersal for few-shot unsupervised domain adaptation. In: Proceedings of the IEEE/CVF International Conference on Computer Vision, pp. 16433–16442 (2023)
29. Zhang, C., Lee, G.H.: CA-UDA: class-aware unsupervised domain adaptation with optimal assignment and pseudo-label refinement. arXiv preprint arXiv:2205.13579 (2022)

Author Index

A
Aditta, Arian Rahman   135
Alshehhi, Maitha   108

C
Cao, Lele   31
Chen, Thomas Y.   169

D
Dai, Xueyuan   151
Dossou, Bonaventure F. P.   1

F
Fahad, Nafiz   135

G
Gao, Yajun   95
Guizani, Mohsen   108

H
Han, Yong   95
Hao, Tianyu   151
Hossen, Md. Jakir   135
Hu, Cheng   16
Hu, Shu   74
Hu, Yifeng   41

I
Ientilucci, Emmett J.   151

J
Jahin, Md Abrar   135
Ji, Kaiyi   74

K
Karimi, Sara   31

L
Li, Tangwei   41
Li, Yuke   41
Liao, Kewei   56
Liu, Xuesong   151
Liu, Yinkai   95
Lyu, Siwei   74

M
Ma, Jialiang   41
Magno, Michele   16
Mridha, M. F.   135

N
Nebli, Ahmed   1

Q
Qin, Haotong   16

R
Rietz, Finn   31

S
Sharshar, Ahmed   108
Si, Zhaofeng   74
Smirnov, Oleg   31
Soudeep, Shahriar   135

T
Turki, Houcemeddine   1

V
Valdelli, Ilario   1

W
Wang, Tianbo   56

Y. Ma et al. (Eds.): IJCAI 2025, CCIS 2640, pp. 195–196, 2025.
https://doi.org/10.1007/978-981-95-0988-1

Wang, Yang   151
Wang, Yudie   95
Wu, Yan   95

X
Xu, Chujie   95

Y
Yadla, L.   127
Yadla, P.   127
Yu, Fengxiang   56

Z
Zhu, Xiaotong   95
Zhu, Zerui   151

The manufacturer's authorised representative in the EU is Springer
Nature Customer Service Centre GmbH, Europaplatz 3, 69115 Heidelberg,
Germany. If you have any concerns regarding our products, please
contact ProductSafety@springernature.com

Printed and bound by CPI Group (UK) Ltd, Croydon, CR0 4YY
29/04/2026
02099549-0001